THE HISTORY
OF THE SOUL

FALLEN ANGELS, FORGOTTEN
ANCESTORS AND KARMIC
CATASTROPHES

IAN LAWTON

RATIONAL SPIRITUALITY PRESS

First published in 2010 by Rational Spirituality Press.

All enquiries to be directed to www.rspress.org.

A previous version of this book was published in 2003 under the title *Genesis Unveiled*.

A CIP catalogue record for this title is available from the British Library.

ISBN 978-0-9549176-4-7

Cover design by Ian Lawton.
Cover image by Jason Waskey (www.jasonwaskey.com).
Author photograph by Gaia Giakali.

To the perceptive eye the depth of their degeneration was clear enough, but to those whose judgment of true happiness is defective they seemed, in their pursuit of unbridled ambition and power, to be at the height of their fame and fortune.

from Plato's *Critias*, on the fall of the divine Atlanteans

CONTENTS

10. GEOLOGY   147

Ice ages; questionable evidence of destruction (mass extinctions, Siberian mammoths, Alaskan muck, anomalous animal remains); extraterrestrial bodies (the Carolina bays, the Younger-Dryas event); pole shifts and reversals (axis shifts versus crustal displacement, magnetic pole reversals and solar flares); memories; likely locales; conclusion.

11. LOST CONTINENTS   170

Plato's Atlantis; founding fathers; HPB; theosophical evolution; the colonel; the arcane tradition; the automatic author; the sleeping prophet; conclusion.

12. LET'S GET REAL   190

Technological non-mysteries (ancient weapons and aircraft, the Dogon, computers, batteries and spark plugs, maps and portolans); dating and other non-mysteries (no overnight development, the age of the Giza monuments, pyramid and temple construction, common origins, other pyramids, underwater structures); realistic skills (astronomy and navigation, crystal and magnification technology); conclusion.

EPILOGUE: IMPLICATIONS FOR TODAY   209

The 26,000 year energy cycle; the last three shifts (75,000 years ago, 50,000 years ago, 25,000 years ago); the history of the soul; the future of the soul.

LIST OF PLATES

These are located at the end of the book.

1 Burial in Qafzeh cave
2 Ochre block from Blombos cave
3 The Quneitra artifact
4 A variety of Venus figurines
5 The Venus of Brassempouy
6 One of the Sungir skeletons
7 Decorated spear thrower
8 Bison painting
9–12 The settlement of Jerf el-Ahmar
13–14 Etched plaquettes from Jerf el-Ahmar
15 Sumerian pictographic script
16 Hand-held model of the Celtic cross
17 Full-sized model of the Celtic cross
18 The crystal skull known as Max
19 The crystal skull known as Sha Na Ra
20 The Mitchell-Hedges crystal skull

LIST OF FIGURES

ACKNOWLEDGMENTS

Much of the material in this work comes from the original manuscript of *Genesis Unveiled*. Therefore it continues to owe a great deal to the assistance of those close friends and colleagues mentioned first time round: Flavio Barbiero, Nigel Blair, Michael Brass, Michael Carmichael, Simon Cox, David Elkington, Garret Fagan, Mark Foster, Nigel Foster, Adrian Gilbert, Paul Heinrich, Robin Crookshank Hilton, Edmund Marriage, Crichton Miller, Chris Ogilvie-Herald, Lynn Picknett, Clive Prince, Colin Reader, Nigel Skinner-Simpson, Danielle Stordeur, Greg Taylor, Marcus Williamson and all the staff at the British Library.

In addition for this new edition I am particularly indebted to my old friend Andrew Collins, with whom I discussed a number of my more recent ideas, and who apprised me of various new research in the area of catastrophes in particular. Even more so this work owes its existence to two friends without whose help during a difficult time I would have struggled to survive at all: Andy Tomlinson and Ken Huggins, to me you are the best friends any man could have.

PREFACE

In the predominantly Christianized Western world we are all familiar with the book of Genesis from the Old Testament: how God created the world in six days, and rested on the seventh; how he created the first man, Adam, and then his companion Eve; how Adam's descendants acted as patriarchs, overseeing human affairs up to the time of the great flood, which God sent to destroy humankind; and how Noah was spared in the ark and went on to father the new human race.

Over the last 150 years, spurred on by Darwin and the breakthroughs of scientists in all fields who have followed in his footsteps, we have increasingly been told to reject all of this as myth – a simple story constructed to bolster a religious outlook in simple people. Of course any Christian fundamentalist who still insists the world was created in 4004 BCE receives extremely short shrift. But many *postflood* biblical traditions that were originally dismissed as myth were validated when, in the late nineteenth century, multiple sites mentioned in the Old Testament were unearthed in Mesopotamia. At around the same time the discoveries of Troy by Heinrich Schliemann, and of the Minoan civilization of Knossos on Crete by Sir Arthur Evans, proved that settlements had existed at both sites since about 3000 BCE, forcing a similar revision of orthodox thinking about certain Greek traditions. These wonderful breakthroughs came from the dedication and bloody-mindedness of pioneers who refused to accept the conventional wisdom.

It has also become increasingly clear that a catastrophe tradition persists on a global scale, possibly backed up by geological evidence, and more recently this has received widespread publicity and a fair degree of acceptance.[1] So for many years I have been fascinated by the possibility that the sparse and enigmatic record of a *preflood* civilization in the early chapters of Genesis might also contain some elements of truth. My first surprise came when I investigated the older Mesopotamian texts on which many of the biblical traditions were based. A number of intriguing themes emerged, including some detailed accounts not only of the flood but also of life *before* it. Although a close examination of these original source texts led me to reject certain authors' interpretations that humankind was genetically created by visitors from another planet, I nevertheless felt there was something in this mass of material that deserved further investigation;

that it was wrong to write off the whole lot as superstitious fiction. Ultimately I decided to unearth as many of the ancient texts and indigenous traditions from around the world as I could, to find out what the rest of our ancestors had to say about the prehistory of humankind on earth.

It soon became clear that the people who compiled these texts and traditions were anything but intellectual dwarfs trying to concoct a simplistic philosophical framework with which to make sense of the world around them, as some would have us believe. It became equally clear, however, that those who attempt to take everything within them as literal truth are also misguided. One of the most respected scholars of comparative mythology, Joseph Campbell, reflects this view in his four-volume masterwork *The Masks of God,* published between 1959 and 1968:[2]

> It must be conceded, as a basic principle of our natural history of the gods and heroes, that whenever a myth has been taken literally its sense has been perverted; but also, reciprocally, that whenever it has been dismissed as a mere priestly fraud or sign of inferior intelligence, truth has slipped out the other door.

To a degree Campbell developed the work of his equally eminent predecessor Carl Gustav Jung, who prefaced the English version of his *Psychology and Alchemy,* first published in 1953, with the following overview:[3]

> Some thirty-five years ago I noticed to my amazement that European and American men and women coming to me for psychological advice were producing in their dreams and fantasies symbols similar to, and often identical with, the symbols found in the mystery religions of antiquity, in mythology, folklore, fairytales, and the apparently meaningless formulations of such esoteric cults as alchemy... From long and careful comparison and analysis of these products of the unconscious I was led to postulate a 'collective unconscious', a source of energy and insight in the depth of the human psyche which has operated in and through man from the earliest periods of which we have records.

There can be little doubt that Jung's symbols, or archetypes, are the key to unlocking the hidden meaning of much of the body of myth from around the world that our ancestors have left as their legacy. This is one of the main reasons why the most sacred texts and traditions of all ancient cultures can appear so enigmatic and obscure to the uninitiated – because to a large extent the archetypes, whether in picture or textual form, are not designed to speak to the logical left brain, but rather to the intuitive right brain that is the link to both the personal and the collective unconscious. Nowhere is this more clearly demonstrated than in the written texts of the ancient Egyptians that were recorded using hieroglyphs, pictographic symbols that often had multiple and subtly different meanings appreciated only by those fully initiated into their mystery. These were often accompanied by symbolic drawings of their gods, usually represented as part-animal, part-human beings, who in turn represented various *neters* or divine principles that could vary according to the context.[4]

It is also the case that the most important texts and traditions of our ancient cultures tended to be handed down orally, even after they had been recorded in writing. Indeed we often find important philosophical concepts embedded into a story format, yet not only so they could be more easily memorized and would be entertaining to relate, but also so that they might better penetrate the non-logical, subconscious mind. This allowed them to survive over centuries or millennia, even if the real understanding of their symbolic message was lost on most of the audience. In addition, of course, couching such traditions in symbolism and archetype was particularly useful when, as has happened throughout history, esoteric sects were trying to maintain them under threat from the dominant religious orthodoxy.

We must also recognize that many of the messages found in the ancient texts and traditions are explainable in sociological terms – for example, acting to reinforce the rule of the prevailing politico-religious hierarchy. Moreover it is clear that many of the versions that have survived have been repeatedly edited with similar motives in mind, making it much harder to see through the fog and establish the nature of the original underlying message, if any indeed existed.

The foregoing analysis is fine as a general summary of the modern approach to mythology. But are there any grey areas even concerning the time *before* the flood where it would be right to debate whether something more than just symbolism and myth underlies the relevant texts and traditions? Might they have some basis in fact that, albeit perhaps in only the broadest of senses, can act as a pointer to real historical events? My research has led me to believe these grey areas do exist, particularly with respect to the passages I encountered repeatedly that appear to describe a veiled history of humankind – one only hinted at in Genesis. In particular various ancient cultures right across the globe preserve a tradition of a forgotten antediluvian race that was originally highly spiritual but degenerated until it was wiped out by a major catastrophe. As can be seen from Figure 1 these traditions are far more widespread than is sometimes recognized, and orthodox scholars' attempts to explain them away as mere psychological or sociological constructs can often appear unconvincing at best. Arguably it is therefore time to reappraise them to see if we can unveil the history of our forgotten race from the many common elements, while still appreciating the role played by symbolism and archetypes.

This discovery whetted my appetite considerably. Most of my original research was undertaken in the days before the internet made it so incredibly easy, so I was often spending weeks at a time in the British Library poring over obscure anthropological studies and other rare manuscripts. As I did so the more I was drawn to several other key themes that consistently crop up in these texts and traditions: in particular those dealing with the 'creation of mankind' and the 'origins of the world'. Again their spread is shown in Figure 1, and again orthodox scholars who concentrate on those from our most celebrated historical civilizations tend to oversimplify them by concentrating on the anthropomorphic qualities of the various gods that take center stage. But I have become convinced that, when properly interpreted from a spiritual perspective, these consistent themes reveal that their originators had a highly sophisticated worldview and a common source of spiritual wisdom on which to draw.

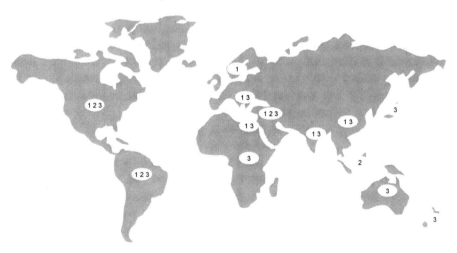

1 A golden age followed by debasement and destruction
2 Multiple attempts to create a successful human race
3 The world created from the void by the supreme deity

Figure 1: The Common Themes in Ancient Texts around the World

I must emphasize that wonderful studies of lesser-known individual cultures have been prepared, and indeed form the source material for much of this work. But a proper appreciation of the legacy left by our forebears *across the globe*, and a reappraisal of the consistent elements of their worldview *from a spiritual perspective*, is long overdue. This just may take us closer to their underlying messages than we have ever been before.

Nevertheless this work could not stand up to scrutiny if it relied solely on the reinterpretation of ancient texts and traditions. In support, first we can turn to archaeology. A mounting body of orthodox artifactual and cultural evidence increasingly suggests modern humans have been around in highly cultured form for somewhat longer than has hitherto been accepted. Second we can bring in the geological evidence that in the relatively recent past the earth has been rocked by at least one major catastrophe, which could easily have wiped out all traces of any advanced culture that prospered before it hit. Some of the older material in this area has proved to be of little value, but important new research keeps recent-catastrophe theory very much alive and kicking.

Ever since the scientific orthodoxy began to properly wrest power from the church in the mid-nineteenth century, a succession of nonreligious mavericks who nevertheless believe that the rationalist materialism of science does not have *all* the answers have continued to question and probe. Generally this can only be seen as healthy. Indeed the number of 'revisionists' who have put forward alternative views of the history of our planet, and in particular of human life thereon, has proliferated dramatically in recent decades – and many of these are the very authors who inspired me to begin my own quest many years ago.

But on closer inspection over the years I have learned that unfortunately many revisionists can be somewhat lacking in scholarship. To make matters worse there has hitherto been an almost complete lack of peer review and constructive criticism among the 'club' of leading revisionists. For this reason I have regularly taken issue with them, not because I like the sound of my own voice or have a point to prove – ok, maybe a little in the early days, but not now – but in the genuine hope that highlighting those theories that are clearly nonsensical will actually advance, at least in some small way, the revisionist movement's general cause and credibility. Of course there are commercial considerations for modern authors under pressure from hard-pressed publishers, but surely the constant underlying aim should be to move together towards a better understanding of the enigmas of our past, and to share this research in an honest and responsible way with the general public. What is more there are a hard core of real enigmas untouched by orthodox scholars that deserve serious study, without us needing to fabricate all sorts of weird and wonderful nonsense.

So in what ways does my approach differ from that of most of my revisionist colleagues? My biggest criticism is that they tend, either explicitly or implicitly, to display a serious lack of respect for the specialists in a number of orthodox disciplines. Although there are exceptions in any walk of life and orthodox scholars in general are by no means infallible, by and large they have not achieved what they have by being narrow-minded imbeciles. Of course some leading revisionists are masters of rabble-rousing, and their followers love to hear them pouring vitriol on anything to do with the orthodoxy. But surely it is time for a new 'rational revisionism' to come to the fore. Such an approach questions aspects of the orthodoxy that deserve reevaluation without blatant disrespect. Even more it does not gloss over or remain ignorant of orthodox arguments, but instead faces them head on.

In particular when postulating a 'forgotten', 'lost' or 'hidden' former race of humans on earth, some revisionists have demonstrated a disturbing lack of understanding of orthodox arguments in three main areas. The first is human evolution, where certain of them provide supposed evidence of great antiquity for modern man; not only is this fatally flawed anyway, but they also fail to place it in any philosophically or scientifically logical context. Meanwhile others propose that extraterrestrial intervention is the only answer to supposed enigmas they have not fully investigated. The second is the role not just of symbolism but also of *context* in myth. So some of them, for example, produce entirely literal translations of specific texts with no regard for the context of similar themes in other cultures. The third is the dating of monuments from our earliest historical civilizations, where again the significant body of *contextual* evidence archaeologists have painstakingly amassed is often disregarded. Nowhere is this latter phenomenon better demonstrated than in attempts to ascribe a far earlier date to the Giza Pyramids and Sphinx, a subject covered in detail in my first book *Giza: The Truth*.

Other revisionists take a different tack and, even if they accept the orthodox view of human evolution and of the dating of ancient monuments, suggest the level of technology displayed by these early civilizations could not possibly have 'developed overnight' – some even arguing that highly advanced technology must have been handed down by survivors from the legendary Atlantis, or again introduced by extraterrestrials. Yet arguably they fail to properly appreciate just how much can be achieved by a civilization with superb organization and focus, but not necessarily high levels of technology in the modern sense of the word. When we understand that there *is* a development period in the archaeological record of these ancient civilizations that they tend to ignore, and we remind ourselves of how rapidly modern Western civilization has developed in only a handful of centuries, these arguments just do not stand up.

By contrast, rather than using the argument that the supposedly advanced technology of our earliest historical civilizations *implies* that previous civilizations must have existed, I would argue there is prima facie textual and to some extent archaeological evidence of humankind's extensive cultural prehistory – although it does *not* suggest these earlier cultures were technologically advanced in the modern sense of the word. They might have constructed settlements of considerable size, but not necessarily with huge structures or advanced techniques, or even durable materials. They might have developed a high state of civilization, but one based primarily on group cooperation, and on knowledge development and education. What is more they might have continued like this for millennia before becoming slaves to the great god of material progress.

Above all, instead of extrapolating the *technical* knowledge of our postdiluvian ancestors back to their antediluvian forebears, we should arguably concentrate on extrapolating their *spiritual* knowledge back. Although many other commentators have explored the symbolism and esoteric wisdom displayed by our earliest historical civilizations, they often seem to fall short of being able to put this into any meaningful metaphysical context. Even more important they seem to have overlooked the fact that this, more than anything else, may be the key to unveiling the hidden messages of the ancient texts and traditions regarding our forgotten antediluvian race. It is their original *spiritual* advancement in a 'golden age', their subsequent debasement through concentration on the material world and forgetting their spiritual roots, and their consequent destruction, that appears to shine through loud and clear.

The first draft of *Genesis Unveiled* – the work on which this rewrite is based – was prepared in the early years of the new millennium, although the research started some years before that. But in early 2003, when my original publishers Virgin had finally been persuaded to take it on, they asked me at the last minute to insert a chapter containing the evidence for spirituality, and especially for reincarnation and karma, to which at that point I was only briefly alluding. As a result I wrote up the information I already had, which mainly concerned children who spontaneously remember past lives, using the research of the celebrated Ian Stevenson as my source. But as part of my hurried research on the internet I then came across the work of Michael Newton, who had spent many years regressing subjects not only into their past lives, but also into their time *between* lives. This struck me as fascinating, and I wrote it up at some length in the new chapter.

But when the book came out it seemed from the feedback that is was this material, more than any of my own ideas about our hidden spiritual history, that readers were most picking up on. So, after a brief period of slight disillusion and confusion about what to do next, I bowed to the unseen forces that in retrospect were clearly guiding me. I had picked up a few hints that Newton was not the only researcher to have investigated the 'interlife' as I would come to call it, and so my research took me down a completely new and at least consciously unforeseen path of purely spiritual research.

This was based on amassing and distilling modern evidence from a variety of sources: to the children's past-life memories already mentioned I added research into near-death experiences, and also into adult's past-life memories. In all of these fields I was searching for those cases involving the recall of verifiable evidence by subjects that was *so obscure* that to ascribe it to anything other than a paranormal source was actually the more *illogical* approach to adopt. To this was added my extensive research into the common elements of the interlife experience – transition and healing, past-life review, soul group interaction, next-life planning and returning – that had been independently stumbled upon by a variety of original pioneers from the late 1960s through to the early 1980s. This latter was particularly important in providing a context with which to understand *why* we reincarnate as individual souls – which, I discovered after much confusion and searching, has little to do with being tied to the 'wheel of karma' and much more to do with experience of every kind, and with soul growth. So, with the publication of the original *Book of the Soul* in late 2004, 'Rational Spirituality' was born. Further research led to this being completely rewritten and published as *The Big Book of the Soul* in 2008 – its simpler, far shorter, story-based counterpart *The Little Book of the Soul* having already come out a year before. In 2007 and 2010 *The Wisdom of the Soul* and *Your Holographic Soul* were also added to this growing collection of complementary spiritual books.

For this reason I have removed the old chapter on evidence for a spiritual worldview from this new version of the book, rather than try to update it by cramming so much research that is already written up elsewhere into a relatively small space. Of course those who are interested in this aspect of my research are strongly urged to consult one or other of these source books, especially because I will be making repeated references to certain aspects of a 'Rational Spiritual worldview' in this work – albeit that in some instances I use this phrase for simplicity even when I am merely reflecting a view also held by modern spiritual seekers of many and diverse persuasions.

Of course other factors too were involved in my decision to completely rewrite this work under a new title. There was some new evidence to bring in, and some old evidence needed to be discarded. I also had a desire to streamline elements that are not so critical to my arguments and move them to my website, making for a somewhat shorter, two-part instead of three-part work.[5] And I wanted to remove from the main chapters all the personal references that unfortunately characterized my earlier style of writing.

Yet probably most crucial to this rewrite was some new research I have been involved in over the last year. It concerns channeled material about 2012 and related topics, and as such will not be to everyone's taste. For that reason I have attempted to isolate everything to do with it in the epilogue so that, for those who would otherwise be put off, the main body of this work stands firm without it. But for me the most significant issue was a new understanding of energy cycles, and in particular of how they have impacted the cultural and spiritual development of the human race. The information we gained shed new light on various aspects of this that I at least had never come across before. But because the messages in *The Future of the Soul*, published earlier this year, are relatively brief, I wanted to expand on certain areas and also to see whether there was any supporting evidence to back up their version of events. I was not disappointed; and for some readers it will be the overlaying of a new understanding of these cycles, and of what happened in previous 'energy shifts' compared to the current one, that will give this new work its greatest relevance.

Ian Lawton
December 2010

FOOTNOTE ON THE DEFINITION OF CULTURE

Because the word *culture* can be used in many different contexts, and its specific meaning in particular instances is of vital importance to the arguments in this work, I intend to use four broad definitions thereof:

- *Primitive culture* includes language, cooperation, the use of fire and a degree of ritualistic behavior, for example in simple burials. It is typified by early hunter-gatherer cultures.

- *Culture proper* includes artistic expression in sculptures and paintings sometimes of high complexity, as well as in music. It is typified by, for example, the Cro-Magnon culture of southern Europe.

- *Advanced culture* includes the development of permanent and sizeable settlements; large-scale agriculture with grain cultivation and possibly animal husbandry; trading and ocean navigation; and an advanced understanding of astronomy. It is typified by, for example, the city-states of ancient Mesopotamia – although note that certain aspects such as building in stone, metalworking and writing need not *necessarily* be included in this stage.

- *Technologically advanced culture* includes the use of sources of power for lighting, heating and tools, of powered vehicles for terrestrial, aerial and even space travel, and all the other developments that typify our modern society.

PART ONE

REVELATIONS

1

MYTHS IN THE MAKING

We face a formidable task in attempting to identify genuine historical pointers in the body of ancient texts and traditions from around the world that are broadly categorized as 'mythical' by the established orthodoxy. Researching opinions across the whole spectrum of mythical analysis, from those of learned specialist scholars to those of the more outrageous revisionists, it soon becomes clear that *everyone* is heavily influenced by their own largely subjective judgments regarding what is possible as history and what is not, and also regarding whether or not to allow for genuine spiritual messages to be involved.

This work starts with the premise that the scholarly consensus about these texts and traditions has been developed under an unduly restrictive paradigm, conditioned by everything from the archaeological to the scientific, metaphysical and sometimes even religious perspectives of the academic establishment. Further that there *are* some aspects of the ancient texts and traditions – particularly those dealing with the time before the catastrophe they all report – that are not only worthy of reappraisal in terms of possible historicity, but are also of the utmost importance in providing us with some context for what is happening in our modern world.

Many revisionists have uttered similar sentiments before, but unfortunately many of them have also proved to have a somewhat inadequate understanding of the body of orthodox interpretation they seek to overthrow. To overcome this deficiency we should attempt to lay out the foundation of the orthodox position before putting forward alternatives. So let us begin by considering the backbone of the consensus attitude toward mythology that now prevails.

A BRIEF HISTORY OF MYTHOLOGY

A variety of definitions of *myth* have been attempted, and they have varying degrees of usefulness. But broadly speaking in the modern world attempts are made to distinguish between historical or canonical records on the one hand and myths, legends, and folklore on the other. Within this context myths are normally held to deal with important metaphysical concepts such as the origins of the world and of humankind, and to involve gods or supernatural beings. Legends by contrast tend to involve human heroes, usually on great quests of one sort or another, while folk tales are pretty much dismissed as localized superstitions of minimal significance. Even these broad categorizations suffer from myriad weaknesses – for example many legends contain important motifs also found in myths, so to exclude them from this study where relevant would be a nonsense. In any case use of the more general words *texts* and *traditions* – the latter usually referring to information still handed down orally in indigenous tribes until anthropologists recorded it – does not have the pejorative connotations of terms such as *myths* and *legends*.

So, accepting a broad definition of the term, let us look at the history of what has been referred to as the 'science of myth'.[1] A number of important contributions are worth noting, starting in 1856 with that of the man regarded as the founder of the discipline of comparative mythology, Max Müller. In his *Essays on Comparative Mythology* he proposed that all myth was an attempt to explain natural phenomena. This was closely followed by the work of Daniel G Brinton, who brought in the burgeoning study of the New World as well as the Old; of Adolf Bastion, who attempted to introduce psychological factors into the study of 'constants' in mythology; and of Edward Burnett Tylor, who used similar methods to analyse animistic motifs. In the late nineteenth century Bronislaw Malinowski kept the psychological theme to the fore in his study of various surviving indigenous cultures, while in 1890 Sir James George Frazer published the first two volumes of what would eventually become his twelve-volume *The Golden Bough,* a landmark work that introduced the importance of the cyclical nature of life as an underlying mythical motif.

In 1889 Leo Frobenius presented a counterargument to the psychological school, positing that a primitive cultural continuum once existed around the equator, so that any similarities in myths result more from transoceanic diffusion than from parallel development. In part this is exactly the view this work seeks to reestablish, except removing the word *primitive* from the mix, because the focus in the twentieth century has remained resolutely on psychological interpretations, most often underpinned by an atheistic perspective that sees psychology and spirituality as stark choices rather than as possibly complementary factors. The most celebrated proponent of this psycho-materialist position was Sigmund Freud, with his emphasis on sexual and relational tensions in the make-up of myth. One notable exception, however, was his collaborator-turned-opponent Carl Jung, whose concept of archetypes was briefly mentioned in the preface. He was one of the few influential figures in the formative years of psychiatry who was hugely interested in all things metaphysical and, although not exactly explicit on the matter, always allowed plenty of room for spiritual interpretations of his work.

Overlapping with Jung, three of the giants of modern mythology took the arguments forward in the 1950s and subsequent decades. We have already mentioned Joseph Campbell and his four-volume masterwork *The Masks of God*, which represents the apogee of general studies of the subject. It contains an incredible breadth and depth of knowledge of myth from all over the world and all ages, combined with detailed and erudite commentary. Mircea Eliade has also made a huge contribution to the study of comparative religion and mythology in a number of works, including *Myth and Reality*, *The Sacred and the Profane*, *Shamanism* and *Patterns in Comparative Religion*. Likewise Claude Levi-Strauss, who has especially attempted to analyse the contradictions and opposites so often found in myth, in works such as *Myth and Meaning* and *The Way of the Masks*.

THE DEVELOPMENT OF MYTH

Any summary of the orthodox approach to the analysis of myth should arguably use Campbell's *Masks* as its primary reference. Although certain aspects have been questioned by some of his successors, it remains the definitive study to this day. The basic starting point is that myths in their purest form evolved primarily because of certain psychological features of the human makeup.[2] Campbell begins by discussing the differences between 'innate' stimuli built into all humans and those that are 'impressed' by cultural influences. This can be best understood if we look at the three basic stages of human growth:

- At the beginning we have the psychological trauma of birth, of switching from the safety and warmth of the womb to the unpredictability of life outside it. Psycho-materialists suggest this innate experience underlies the recurrent mythic theme of the search for nirvana, which they insist is actually only a desire to return to the womb. Then during childhood individual, selfish desires – for sustenance, warmth, and affection – predominate, and most are seen as being satisfied by the mother. Again psycho-materialists suggest this is the cause of the massive importance attached to the mother figure in myth.

- As we move into adulthood the self-oriented behavior of childhood has to be reengineered into a sense of social responsibility, especially in more primitive cultures where the group has to work together just to survive. There can be little doubt that much early myth sprang up to assist this process, because it is the 'sacred lore' into which young adults are initiated even in modern tribal cultures that helps prevent them from disintegrating. These stimuli are culturally impressed and will vary from one group to another.

- Finally with the onset of old age we find ourselves orienting once again toward the individual, universal and innate in our contemplation of death, and Campbell is not alone in suggesting that the human species is the only one that has developed an awareness of its own mortality. It is clear this stimulus perhaps above any other lies at the very heart of myth, leading to the themes of life after death, and sometimes of reincarnation and rebirth, that so predominate in one form or another.

Campbell continues by describing how as primitive humans evolved, especially in recognizing a sense of self, they became increasingly interested in their surroundings; interested, that is, not only in understanding how they would be affected from the practical point of view of food, shelter and survival in the face of changes in weather and climate; but also, increasingly, in their underlying workings from a more abstract or philosophical perspective. For the first time our ancestors started to ask fundamental questions about how the earth, sun, moon, plants, animals, indeed humankind itself, originated, and they tended toward supernatural explanations involving supernatural beings. Of course psycho-materialists tend to leave it at that, without questioning whether some part of this supposedly primitive philosophy actually derives from innate stimuli – which themselves derive from a universal consciousness, as Jung suggested, and therefore have genuine spiritual significance. But this is an argument we must leave to one side for now.

Campbell continues that the aspect of their surroundings that most impressed itself on early humans was the extent to which all of nature is cyclical. They noticed the cycles of the sun and moon, of the seasons, of plant life – all of which implied a continuous cycle of birth, growth, death and rebirth. They also recognized the impact the cycles of the moon had, for example, on female menstruation and on the tides; and they became intrigued by the opposing forces that so often predominate in myth – of night versus day, dark versus light, male versus female, life versus death and so on. These, he says, are the underlying factors that led to the sun and moon in particular playing such a decisive and enduring role in myth. Moreover it was this impetus that led to the more detailed study of the stars and planets, and this in turn would lead eventually to the all-pervasive mythic theme in all advanced cultures that saw the earth as a mirror of what was happening in the skies – 'as above, so below'.

This is necessarily an extremely brief survey of the major psychological and metaphysical stimuli that underpin much of mythology, although it should provide a sufficient backdrop for the analysis to follow. But to complete this backdrop we should consider, again in highly summarized form, the orthodox view of the major mythological motifs of our earliest-known cultures.

To begin with, says Campbell, two major cultural variants developed.[3] On the one hand the primitive planter culture of the equatorial zone depended primarily on protoagriculture and harvesting natural crops, so communities were relatively settled. The emphasis of worship was on Mother Earth as a provider, the culture was typically matriarchal and the serpent was the dominant animal symbol – its ability to periodically shed its skin being representative of death, rebirth and renewal. By contrast the hunter-gatherer culture of the less temperate zones to the north was typically more patriarchal, given their dependence on their menfolk to hunt and kill game, and the dominant animal symbol was the bull.

According to the orthodoxy a combination of these two cultural influences prevailed until civilization proper emerged in Sumer in the latter half of the fifth millennium BCE. The new hieratic city-states, with their fresh hierarchies of kings, priests, merchants and peasants, required an entirely new form of control – indeed needed to create 'order out of chaos', another fundamental theme of myth. This is how Campbell describes the huge impact this had on the development of mythology:[4]

> The new inspiration of civilized life was based, first, on the discovery, through long and meticulous, carefully checked and rechecked observations,

that there were, besides the sun and moon, five other visible or barely visible heavenly spheres (to wit, Mercury, Venus, Mars, Jupiter, and Saturn) which moved in established courses, according to established laws, along the ways followed by the sun and moon, among the fixed stars; and then, second, on the almost insane, playful, yet potentially terrible notion that the laws governing the movements of the seven heavenly spheres should in some mystical way be the same as those governing the life and thought of men on earth. The whole city, not simply the temple area, was now conceived as an imitation on earth of the cosmic order, a sociological 'middle cosmos', or mesocosm, established by priestcraft between the macrocosm of the universe and the microcosm of the individual, making visible the one essential form of all. The king was the centre, as a human representative of the power made celestially manifest either in the sun or in the moon, according to the focus of the local cult; the walled city was organized architecturally in the design of a quartered circle (like the circles designed on the ceramic ware of the period just preceding), centered around the pivotal sanctum of the palace or ziggurat (as the ceramic designs around the cross, rosette, or swastika); and there was a mathematically structured calendar to regulate the seasons of the city's life according to the passages of the sun and moon among the stars – as well as a highly developed system of liturgical arts, including music, the art rendering audible to human ears the world-ordering harmony of the celestial spheres.

As for the effect this had on the symbolism of these new civilizations:[5]

The impression one gets from these is of a considerable hodge-podge of differing mythologies being coordinated, synthesized, and syncretized by the new professional priesthoods. And how could the situation have been otherwise, when it was the serpent of the jungle and the bull of the steppes that were being brought together? They were soon to become melted and fused – recompounded – in such weird chimeric creatures as the bull-horned serpents, fish-tailed bulls, and lion-headed eagles that from now on would constitute the typical apparitions of an extremely sophisticated new world of myth.

THE FUNCTION OF MYTH

To complete our necessarily brief introduction to the orthodox view of mythology, let us finally see what Campbell has to say about the function of myth, and the closely associated activity that puts it into practice – ritual:[6]

Functioning as [an innate] 'way', mythology and ritual conduce to a transformation of the individual, disengaging him from his local, historical

17

conditions and leading him toward some kind of ineffable experience. Functioning as an [impressed] 'ethnic idea', on the other hand, the image binds the individual to his family's system of historically conditioned sentiments, activities, and beliefs, as a functioning member of a sociological organism. This antinomy is fundamental to our subject, and every failure to recognize it leads not only to unnecessary argument, but also to a misunderstanding – one way or the other – of the force of the mythological symbol itself, which is, precisely, to render an experience of the ineffable through the local and concrete, and thus, paradoxically, to amplify the force and appeal of the forms even while carrying the mind beyond them. The distinctive challenge of mythology lies in its power to effect this dual end; and not to recognize this fact is to miss the whole point and mystery of our science.

Campbell's writings are underpinned by a fundamental spirituality, albeit that he seems to have held the broadly agnostic view that all spirituality is a search for an 'unknown force' that is itself 'unknowable'.[7] But despite his erudition and undoubted influence most orthodox scholars still tend to adopt a broadly psycho-materialist view of myth.

CONCLUSION

Mythology is fickle. Every single ancient text or tradition handed down to us from every part of the world has had a multitude of influences brought to bear on its composition. These include psychological, cultural, political, religious and philosophical influences, as well as the potentially historiographical ones with which we are most concerned. One of the simplest and most poignant examples of editing for political and religious purposes, which tends to come as a great surprise to those brought up in a Christian environment, is that there are actually two separate Hebrew words that are translated as 'God' in English versions of the Old Testament: one is Yahweh, a singular proper name and the other Elohim, a plural collective term. Broadly speaking these two words derive from two separate sources known as the Yahwist and Elohist texts. For an accurate translation the latter word would have to be rendered as gods plural, but this would of course contradict the basic monotheism of Christianity. So the simple removal of the s at the end is one of the finest examples of expedient editing of older texts that we have.

To make matters worse it is often difficult to distinguish between the different influences in any given text. We will find, for example, that the traditions of indigenous peoples across the globe contain much that is obviously conditioned by local sociological factors, along with much that is quite clearly allegorical. Does this mean it will be impossible or pointless to attempt to discern any historiographical material they might contain? Not necessarily, but we must tread extremely carefully in attempting to find it.

Another general factor we will have to consider is the way in which traditions that were originally firmly founded on historical fact can be distorted by the passage of time and by geographic diffusion. Campbell himself uses the term *regressed mythology*, and discusses an example of this by tracing certain distorted aspects of the tenth-century *Tales of the Arabian Nights* right back to the now-proven custom of ritual regicide that prevailed in many early cultures:[8]

> So, from what we now know, it can be said with perfect assurance that in the earliest period of the hieratic city state the king and his court were ritually immolated at the expiration of a span of years determined by the relationship of the planets in the heavens to the moon; and that our legend of Kash is, therefore, certainly an echo from that very deep well of the past, romantically reflected in a late story-teller's art.

Such a statement does of course support the case for a historical reevaluation of certain aspects of supposed mythology. But before we become too complacent let us look at the other side of the coin: here he is discussing the 'great traditional books' of history:[9]

> The world is full, also, of great traditional books tracing the history of man (but focused narrowly on the local group) from the age of mythological beginnings, through periods of increasing plausibility, to a time almost within memory, when the chronicles begin to carry the record, with a show of rational factuality, to the present. Furthermore, just as all primitive mythologies serve to validate the customs, systems of sentiments, and political aims of their respective local groups, so do these great traditional books. On the surface they may appear to have been composed as conscientious history. In depth they reveal themselves to have been conceived as myths: poetic readings of the mystery of life from a certain interested point of view. But to read a poem as a chronicle of fact is – to say the least – to miss the point. To say a little more, it is to prove oneself a dolt. And to add to this, the men who put these books together were not dolts but knew precisely what they were doing – as the evidence of their manner of work reveals at every turn.

Strong words that are hard to disagree with, except perhaps in their somewhat black-and-white emphasis. Of course such records were comprehensively and skillfully edited to fulfill all sorts of purposes, and so will never represent strict and detailed chronicles of history. Yet can anyone sensibly dispute that there are grey areas too, and that they *may* carry a germ of underlying factuality in *certain* aspects? It is the possibility that such a germ resides in the passages describing an advanced culture that existed before a great catastrophe that we will examine in the next chapter; and what better place to start than with the biblical Genesis itself.

2

DEBASEMENT AND DESTRUCTION

The book of Genesis is the first book of the Torah, or Pentateuch, which itself constitutes the first five books of the biblical Old Testament and is traditionally attributed to the patriarch Moses himself. Scholars still cannot be sure of the identity of the authors of the books now handed down to us, but we do have access to several early Hebrew and Aramaic forerunners that were in circulation in the first half of the first millennium BCE.[1]

Our focus is on the early chapters in Genesis that deal with the period between the creation of humankind and its destruction in the flood. As we saw in the preface the former event is now regarded as entirely fanciful, while the latter is now seen by many as the point at which the text turns from myth to reality because, apart from the geological evidence that we will consider in Part 2, similar catastrophe traditions exist all over the world.[2] So what are we to make of the biblical account of what happened in between, which suggests that humans lived in relatively civilized circumstances for a long time *before* the flood?

THE ANTEDILUVIAN PATRIARCHS

Ten antediluvian patriarchs are listed in Genesis 5. They are Adam, Seth, Enos, Cainan, Mahalaleel, Jared, Enoch, Methuselah, Lamech and Noah, and they are given lifespans of anywhere from 365 to 969 years. Even though these are clearly unrealistic, some revisionists suggest that this list offers proof positive of a precatastrophe civilization – especially given that it is similar to a number of older 'king lists' from ancient Mesopotamia, Egypt and China?[3] Yet this is one area where the authors had obvious political and religious motives for fabrication, as Garrett Fagan, professor of ancient history at Penn State University, points out:[4]

> In every instance, to my knowledge, the lists start out with the gods. The lists then function to show (a) the antiquity of the regime or culture that composed them and (b) that regime or culture's direct connection with the gods. It is much harder to challenge a divinely ordained system than an admittedly human one.

But even if these king lists from around the globe cannot sensibly be used to support the case for a precatastrophe civilization, there is a great deal of other textual support as we are about to find out.

THE NEPHILIM REAPPRAISED

The first place we find such evidence is in the celebrated and rather more intriguing account of life before the flood in Genesis 6:

> 1. And it came to pass, when men began to multiply on the face of the earth, and daughters were born unto them,
> 2. That the sons of God saw the daughters of men that they were fair; and they took them wives of all which they chose.
> 3. And the Lord said, My spirit shall not always strive with man, for that he also is flesh: yet his days shall be an hundred and twenty years.[5]
> 4. There were giants in the earth in those days; and also after that, when the sons of God came in unto the daughters of men, and they bare children to them, the same became mighty men which were of old, men of renown.
> 5. And God saw that the wickedness of man was great in the earth, and that every imagination of the thoughts of his heart was only evil continually.
> 6. And it repented the Lord that he had made man on the earth, and it grieved him at his heart.
> 7. And the Lord said, I will destroy man whom I have created from the face of the earth; both man, and beast, and the creeping thing, and the fowls of the air; for it repenteth me that I have made them.
> 8. But Noah found grace in the eyes of the Lord.

Who were these 'sons of God' and their 'giant' offspring? Are they mere fictional creations of an earlier age, or was there really a race of culturally advanced humans who lived in a remote time before a great catastrophe wiped them out? The Hebrew word for the biblical giants is 'Nephilim', while their progenitors, the 'sons of God', are often referred to as the 'Watchers' because of the way they are described in the celebrated *Book of Enoch* – a text that holds many clues to their identities as we will shortly see. Perhaps more than any other biblical characters apart from

Jesus himself, these enigmatic figures have fired the imagination of a whole host of theologians, artists and poets down through the ages – as well as, more recently, a host of revisionists. Two main, modern schools of thought stand out, and we should consider any shortcomings in their arguments before attempting to correct them. It is also instructive at this point to get a feel for the full extent to which their hugely popular proponents have misled their massive worldwide readerships.

The first is the 'Ancient Astronaut' school. Although a number of lesser-known writers had gone down this road in the preceding decades, it was Swiss hotelier Erich von Däniken who really captured the public's imagination in 1969 when *Chariots of the Gods* was published for the first time in English. It perfectly reflected the anti-Establishment spirit of the age, and became an overnight and huge success. He did not specifically mention the Nephilim, but he certainly examined some of the relevant Enochian and Mesopotamian literature, provocatively asking: 'Does not this seriously pose the question whether the human race is not an act of deliberate "breeding" by unknown beings from outer space?'[6]

Unfortunately, however much modern revisionists owe a debt of gratitude to this trailblazer, there are obvious flaws in his work. A fine example is his suggestion that one part of the infamous 'Nazca lines' in Peru, an enigma he admittedly did much to put on the map, is 'reminiscent of the aircraft parking bays of a modern airport'. Even the most casual inspection of photographs of the lines reveals that they are huge drawings of various animals and insects, and he must surely have known that his parking bays were in fact a depiction of the tail feathers of a bird. Admittedly these pebble sculptures laid out on a flat desert plain can only really be appreciated from the air, and their construction from scale drawings as a tribal offering to the gods is a wonderful piece of ingenuity. But aircraft runways they are not. Meanwhile other questions such 'why should ancient gods be associated with the stars?' only serve to demonstrate his lack of understanding of myth and symbolism.[7]

After a few sequels von Däniken disappeared amid typical allegations of a conspiracy to silence him.[8] But the public imagination had been fired. Into the fray stepped journalist Zecharia Sitchin, who rocketed to fame in 1976 with *The Twelfth Planet,* then followed it up with a number of sequels to form his *Earth Chronicles* series. He *was* intrigued by the Nephilim specifically, proposing that they were a race of high-longevity beings, originating from an undiscovered planet in our solar system with a highly eccentric orbit, who came to earth and genetically engineered the human race. This latter aspect gave rise to that special breed within the Ancient Astronaut school known as 'Interventionists', while also having clear echoes of von Däniken that Sitchin does not appear to acknowledge.

In any case he too has attracted a huge, worldwide army of fanatical supporters who regard him as nothing less than a guru, and it is worth reiterating that both of these revisionist pioneers should be commended for introducing huge numbers of people to ancient texts, monuments, artwork and artifacts of which they might otherwise have remained largely ignorant.[9] Nevertheless Sitchin's scholarship has proved no more reliable than von Däniken's, to such an extent that his translations and interpretations of many ancient Mesopotamian texts can really only be viewed as entertaining fiction. There is indisputable, scholarly evidence that they display a fundamental lack of knowledge not only of basic Sumerian and Akkadian grammar and linguistics but also, once again, of mythological symbolism.[10] Unfortunately this has not stopped others following Sitchin's lead and using his work to develop further ill-founded theories; and the process continues to this day, with authors who should know better still referencing his work without checking it.[11]

Does that mean that the Ancient Astronaut or even Interventionist hypotheses as inherently implausible? No. What is clear, however, is that the textual and physical evidence used to support them has been misinterpreted and distorted. Of course none of this would matter much were it not for the fact that these theories tend to suggest that we as humanity are under the control of an extraterrestrial master race rather than masters of our *own* fate, which is an incredibly important distinction, especially at such a crucial stage in our cultural and spiritual evolution. Furthermore such obvious shortfalls in scholarship have provided an easy target for the Establishment, and helped to blacken the name of revisionist research in general.

The second revisionist school is that of the 'Redating' movement, whose prime modern movers include John Anthony West, Graham Hancock and Robert Bauval. From the mid-1990s they began to use much of the same evidence of supposedly advanced technology and so on first brought to our attention by von Däniken, Sitchin and others to postulate the existence of an advanced antediluvian civilization – but *not* one of extraterrestrial origin. Crucial to much of their work was a revision to the age of the Great Sphinx of Giza and its associated temples but, while this monument may indeed be older than orthodox scholars allow, it is almost certainly not of the antiquity they suggest. Of course this work too postulates a forgotten antediluvian race but, as indicated in the preface, without the emphasis on high technology and redating of known monuments – for which, so far at least, no convincing evidence has been produced. We will return to these issues in Part 2.

One author who has done more than most to restore a decent standard of scholarship to the revisionist movement is Andrew Collins. In his 1996 work *From the Ashes of Angels* he suggests that the Watchers and Nephilim were remnants of a more advanced culture that migrated from Egypt around 9000 BCE and introduced civilization to areas of Anatolia and Kurdistan, from where it spread in due course into Mesopotamia and Egypt again. He argues that these people were of different physical appearance to their Near Eastern subjects, being taller, with elongated heads, emasculated white faces, narrow slitlike eyes and long white hair – although exactly where this racial type is supposed to have originated is never made clear. He further suggests they were primarily a shamanic people that identified with the vulture, serpent and goat and wore long robes made of feathers; and that the cause of their supposed fall and subsequent demonization was that certain of their number left their isolated enclave in the Kurdish mountains to live among the indigenous people of the surrounding plains, where they took wives and taught the more advanced aspects of their culture.

Unfortunately there are a number of potential problems with this 'out of Egypt' hypothesis. The first is that Collins' postulation of the migration of an Egyptian 'elder culture' was originally founded on the mistaken redating of the age of the Sphinx already discussed. The second is that the texts clearly state that the Watchers and Nephilim lived *before* the flood. He attempts to overcome this problem by postulating *two* floods – a devastating global event that caused the migration out of Egypt and another more localized one around 5000 BCE, which is the one Noah survived – although he admits there is little evidence for the latter.[12]

Perhaps the greatest shortcoming of all of these revisionist theories, however, is their failure to acknowledge the clear existence in the Near Eastern traditions, and in all the others from around the world, of the theme of the *debasement* of a forgotten race that resulted in its destruction. Arguably it is this key facet that lies at the heart of a proper understanding of the Watchers and Nephilim.

A TALE OF TWO CITIES

One clue to what is going on in Genesis 6 lies in a less frequently discussed preceding passage. The first two chapters describe God's creation of the world, of all animals and of Adam and Eve, while the third deals with their 'first fall' having tasted the forbidden fruit in Eden, and their expulsion from it. The early part of the fourth chapter commences with the birth of their first two sons, Cain the farmer and Abel the shepherd, and describes how the former slew the latter in a jealous rage, for which he was rejected by God and banished to the 'land of Nod', east of Eden. Then we get to the heart of the matter, because the remainder of the chapter is devoted to a genealogy of *Cain's* descendants who, although their lifespans are not given, are named as Enoch, Irad, Mehujael, Methusael, Lamech and his sons Jabal, Jubal and Tubalcain. We are also told briefly that Cain built a city that he named after his son Enoch and that Lamech, like his forefather, was guilty of murder – although these two are clearly not meant to be the same as the celebrated patriarchs descended from Adam's third son Seth, as listed previously from Genesis 5.

So here we have another line of preflood ancestors who appear to have coexisted with the line descending from Adam via Seth; and while Cain's line was damned as evil and murderous, Seth's was regarded as God-fearing and righteous. In his *Ancient History of the Jews* the first-century historian Flavius Josephus provides more useful details, describing how Cain 'built a city named Nod' and 'only aimed to procure every thing that was for his own bodily pleasure', becoming 'a great leader of men into wicked courses'.[13] Even more intriguingly, we find that:

> He also introduced a change in that way of simplicity wherein men had lived before; and was the author of measures and weights. And whereas they lived innocently and generously while they knew nothing of such arts, he changed the world in to cunning craftiness.

The venerated Saint Augustine's fourth-century biblical commentary, *The City of God,* gives us a further insight into the sparse Genesis narrative:[14]

> When the human race, in the exercise of this freedom of will, increased and advanced, there arose a mixture and confusion of the two cities by their participation in a common iniquity. And this calamity, as well as the first [fall], was occasioned by woman, though not in the same way; for these women were not themselves betrayed, neither did they persuade the men to sin, but having belonged to the earthly city and society of the earthly, they had been of corrupt manners from the first, and were loved for their bodily beauty by the sons of God, or the citizens of the other city which sojourns in this world.

God's wrath and his decision to destroy humankind in Genesis 6 therefore appears to have arisen because a highly spiritual and simple race, here represented by the 'other city' containing Seth's descendants, was gradually perverted and swallowed up by a far more materialistic and decadent race, the descendants of Cain residing in their 'earthly city'. So can we shed any more light on the underlying causes and significance of this 'second fall'; and on why the composers-cum-editors of the Old Testament decided to massively condense the more comprehensive source material available to them?

ENOCHIAN CONFUSION

To answer these questions we should turn to the aforementioned *Book of Enoch*, which contains far fuller details of the passage in Genesis 6. Although it is attributed to the enigmatic preflood patriarch it is impossible for scholars to say with any certainty when it was originally compiled, albeit that a version of it was undoubtedly regarded as part of the genuine divine revelation of early Judaism.[15] But its existence was clearly something of an embarrassment to the founders of the Christian Church because, along with other lesser-known texts from that time that have been discovered in the modern era, it describes a messiah figure who acts in very similar ways to Jesus, but clearly predates or at least is not the same person as him. This of course casts severe doubt on their insistence that he was the uniquely divine 'savior of humankind'.

So, instead of being given canonical status when the Old Testament was compiled in its current form in the fourth century, this text was rejected as part of the Apocrypha – meaning 'of questionable authenticity', although whether they understood the irony that the original Greek word means 'something that is hidden' is unclear. As a result of this deliberate prejudice it remained almost unknown in the West for nearly fifteen hundred years until three manuscripts were discovered in Ethiopia in 1773 by James Bruce. Like his more famous ancestor Robert he was a leading Scottish Freemason, and had almost certainly gone looking for it deliberately because it plays a huge part in Masonic tradition. But even then the main public copy lay forgotten in the Bodleian Library in Oxford until 1821, when Archbishop Richard Laurence translated it into English for the first time – at which point this long-hidden text caused an immediate sensation.

So what are the explosive secrets that have generated so much controversy? Because it is so important the most relevant verses are reproduced in full, starting with the seventh chapter:[16]

1. It happened after the sons of men had multiplied in those days, that daughters were born to them, elegant and beautiful.

2. And when the angels, the sons of heaven, beheld them, they became enamored of them, saying to each other, Come, let us select for ourselves wives from the progeny of men, and let us beget children.

3. Then their leader Samyaza said to them; I fear that you may perhaps be indisposed to the performance of this enterprise;

4. And that I alone shall suffer for so grievous a crime.

5. But they answered him and said; We all swear;

6. And bind ourselves by mutual execrations, that we will not change our intention, but execute our projected undertaking.

7. Then they swore all together, and all bound themselves by mutual execrations. Their whole number was two hundred, who descended upon Ardis, which is the top of mount Armon.

8. That mountain therefore was called Armon, because they had sworn upon it, and bound themselves by mutual execrations.

9. These are the names of their chiefs: Samyaza, who was their leader, Urakabarameel, Akibeel, Tamiel, Ramuel, Danel, Azkeel, Saraknyal, Asael, Armers, Batraal, Anane, Zavebe, Samsaveel, Ertael, Turel, Yomyael, Arazyal. These were the prefects of the two hundred angels, and the remainder were all with them.

10. Then they took wives, each choosing for himself; whom they began to approach, and with whom they cohabited; teaching them sorcery, incantations, and the dividing of roots and trees.

11. And the women conceiving brought forth giants,

12. Whose stature was each three hundred cubits. These devoured all which the labor of men produced; until it became impossible to feed them;

13. When they turned themselves against men, in order to devour them;

14. And began to injure birds, beasts, reptiles, and fishes, to eat their flesh one after another, and to drink their blood.

15. Then the earth reproved the unrighteous.

The following chapter continues the theme:[17]

1. Moreover Azazyel taught men to make swords, knives, shields, breastplates, the fabrication of mirrors, and the workmanship of bracelets and ornaments, the use of paint, the beautifying of the eyebrows, the use of stones of every valuable and select kind, and of all sorts of dyes, so that the world became altered.

2. Impiety increased; fornication multiplied; and they transgressed and corrupted all their ways.

3. Amazarak taught all the sorcerers, and dividers of roots:

4. Armers taught the solution of sorcery;
5. Barkayal taught the observers of the stars;
6. Akibeel taught signs;
7. Tamiel taught astronomy;
8. And Asaradel taught the motion of the moon.
9. And men, being destroyed, cried out; and their voice reached to heaven.

There are sufficient similarities between this and Genesis 6 that there can be little doubt they share a common origin, except this time those who err are described as 'angels' or 'sons of heaven' rather than 'sons of God'. But before we consider any new spiritual interpretation of these passages, let us pause to consider the more prosaic possibilities. Could they simply be in the king list mould, attempting to tie Judaic bloodlines back to great antiquity and to a divine source? Surely not, because then it would be counterproductive to include such a strong debasement theme. Alternatively do they act as nothing more than a warning that materialism and sin are heavily punished? Again surely not, because this time attributing the debased behavior to the sons of God or angels would make no sense.

Theological commentators down the ages have interpreted these passages as meaning that the angels, who were normally incorporeal beings, took some sort of temporary physical form in order to consort with the daughters of men. But this is hardly the most logical of interpretations. So what is the alternative? A strong argument can be made that these passages contain two separate themes that have been distorted, condensed and interwoven; and that it is only when they are disentangled that we can gain a proper perspective.

First we have in both Enoch 7 and 8 a description of the angels teaching sorcery, divination and astronomy to their human counterparts, which can arguably be seen as a perfectly constructive development, even if here it is confused with other less savory practices. The same argument could be made concerning Josephus' description of Cain introducing the use of 'measures and weights'. All this seems to fit perfectly with the positive theme of 'divine beings' who teach the 'arts of civilization' and reveal various other 'secret' knowledge to humankind, which is widespread in other traditions that we will consider in the next chapter – but remember it is all happening *before* the flood, so the idea of more advanced survivors does not come into play yet. From a Rational Spiritual perspective this can, therefore, be interpreted as reflecting the commonly understood idea that highly experienced souls, who no longer *have* to continue with the cycle of earthly incarnation because they have gained all they need from it, can still choose to come back to help the rest of us to develop.[18] Although it seems that more often than not they actually adopt low-key lives, the most obvious examples are spiritual leaders such as Buddha, Jesus and Mohammed. So arguably these passages are merely reflecting the same process occurring in antediluvian times. Indeed in the next few chapters we will encounter the suggestion that the incarnation of highly experienced souls in these early stages of human cultural development produced a 'golden race' with a high degree of spiritual awareness, although this aspect is largely omitted from the biblical and Enochian literature. So there is a strong argument that this theme of education or 'knowledge transfer' should actually be seen in an entirely positive light.

Second, of course, in both Enoch 7 and 8 there is a clear echo of the debasement theme in the biblical commentaries, this time with rampant materialism joined by excessive fornication, greed, cannibalism and impiety of all kinds. Furthermore it seems this did involve the loss of the spiritual worldview with which the golden race had originally been imbued, to such an extent that only a few remembered, appreciated and honored the real truth about their spiritual roots. Indeed the fact that the race who fell from grace are so often seen as somehow angelic surely reflects the very spirituality they originally possessed.

So was our forgotten race really destroyed, and was this really a punishment from God?

THE DELUGE

The version of the flood story in Genesis 6–8 is well enough known. Noah and his wife and various animals are the only survivors on the infamous ark, which eventually comes to rest on Mount Ararat as the waters subside. So how is it described in the *Book of Enoch*? It is referenced in a number of places, yet with virtually none of the same details. It emerges for the first time in Enoch 10, starting with God instructing an angel to visit Noah to warn him of the deluge that is about to occur.[19] But it then goes on to explain how only the fallen angels and their offspring are to be slaughtered in various ways. In fact the text explicitly states that 'all the sons of men shall not perish', so it is clear that no universal obliteration is intended, and there is no mention at this point of a deluge.[20]

This sort of confusion actually persists throughout the text. In a much later chapter Enoch himself has a vision of the earth sinking into a great abyss, and as a result begs God 'that a posterity may be left to me on earth, and that the whole human race may not perish'.[21] This is supposedly Enoch himself speaking and, while the word *abyss* is used, there is no direct mention of a flood. Is this somehow a distorted echo of an earlier destruction separate from the more celebrated flood? This prospect is perhaps increased when, in another chapter, we find Enoch reporting the following:[22]

> 6. For I know, that oppression will exist and prevail on earth; that on earth great punishment shall in the end take place; and that there shall be a consummation of all iniquity, which shall be cut off from its root, and every fabric raised by it shall pass away. Iniquity, however, shall again be renewed, and consummated on earth. Every act of crime, and every act of oppression and impiety, shall be a second time embraced.
> 7. When therefore iniquity, sin, blasphemy, tyranny, and every evil work, shall increase, and when transgression, impiety, and uncleanness also shall increase, then upon them all shall great punishment be inflicted from heaven.

There exists another version of the *Book of Enoch* that was found in Slavonic Russia;[23] and the idea of multiple destructions is echoed therein.[24] Yet we should not become too carried away by this possibility because the various Enochian manuscripts contain so many variations of themes and contradictions that they are clearly composite creations from various earlier sources, so to be unduly literal or pedantic in their interpretation would be a mistake. This confusion is compounded by the fact that the tenses are often confused, and that we are often skipping between prophetic visions and historical events. There are also suggestions that Enoch may actually represent a *generic* name for a multitude of different seers, in which case not all references may be to the same person.

In the Ethiopian *Book of Enoch*, after one brief description of the flood God repents and, swearing that he will never act in the same way again, says he will 'place a sign in the heavens' as a token of his covenant.[25] In Genesis itself this is taken to mean a rainbow after the flood, but was there originally some deeper meaning.[26] Another chapter contains a most intriguing description of how Noah saw that 'the earth became inclined, and that destruction approached', of how 'the earth labored, and was violently shaken', and of how God reports that 'respecting the moons have they [humankind] enquired, and they have known that the earth will perish'.[27] Could these be descriptions of some sort of catastrophic axial tilt of the earth that would cause all heavenly bodies to shift in the sky? And if, for example, this were caused by the impact of a comet, could it be that at least some members of our forgotten race had some sort of advance warning?

This is not all. Even more enigmatic descriptions are provided in another chapter: 'In the days of sinners the years shall be shortened... the rain shall be restrained, and heaven shall stand still... the moon shall change its laws, and not be seen at its proper period... many chiefs among the stars of authority shall err, perverting their ways and works... all the classes of the stars shall be shut up against sinners.'[28]

Of course these latter could just be symbolic descriptions of order being temporarily overtaken by chaos again, but at the very least all this is fascinating stuff, and we will return to the potential nature of the catastrophes that may have affected our planet in the past in Part 2. In the meantime let us now go in search of other texts that support the theme of the debasement and destruction of a forgotten race.

HERMETIC PROPHECIES

The *Hermetica* are a body of texts dating to the second century although, just as with the *Book of Enoch*, the suggestion that they contain divine revelations made to the Greek god of wisdom Hermes – the equivalent of the Egyptian Thoth and arguably of Enoch too – has led some commentators both ancient and modern to argue for their far greater antiquity. They are of Greco-Egyptian origin and separated into two broad categories, the 'philosophical' and the 'popular' or 'technical' treatises. Although certain texts appear to contain elements of both, broadly speaking the latter include astrological, alchemical and magical works.[29] However it is the philosophical texts that are of most interest to us, comprising the 17 treatises of the Greek *Corpus Hermeticum* plus the Latin *Asclepius*.[30]

Unfortunately there are considerable inconsistencies between the various texts, and these must surely have arisen not just through their repeated editing in antiquity but also because of a somewhat haphazard approach to their compilation as one body of work. In particular it seems likely that the versions we now have were based on shorter works that were repeatedly added to in the form of commentary. However in general they do contain some wonderful glimpses of metaphysical wisdom.

That having been said they make only a brief reference to our current theme, the idea that a loss of spiritual roots led to a previous catastrophe: 'choosing the lesser [path] has been humankind's destruction'.[31] But they are worth introducing at this point because they also contain an intriguing prediction of a supposed repeat performance at some point in the future:[32]

> They will not cherish this entire world, a work of god beyond compare, a glorious construction, a bounty composed of images in multiform variety... They will prefer shadows to light, and they will find death more expedient than life. No one will look up to heaven. The reverent will be thought mad, the irreverent wise; the lunatic will be thought brave, and the scoundrel will be taken for a decent person. Soul and all teachings about soul (that soul began as immortal or else expects to attain immortality) as I revealed them to you will be considered not simply laughable but even illusory.

Is this not, to some extent at least, exactly the state of affairs produced by our increasingly materialist preoccupation over the last century or so?

GNOSTIC ABOMINATIONS

Staying with the Near East, rather more significant support for our interpretation of the biblical and Enochian texts is provided by the Gnostics. They were a separate sect with roots in both Judaism and Christianity who broke away to plough a lone furrow. The largest source of their traditions is a cache of scrolls found buried in a jar in Nag Hammadi, Upper Egypt, in 1945. It comprises 52 tractates written in Coptic script – Egyptian written in the Greek alphabet – although they are clearly translations from Greek originals. The texts as we have them date to the middle of the fourth century.[33] They are similar to the *Hermetica* in that as a body of literature they contain many inconsistencies, and the close link between the two is proved by the fact that the Gnostic texts include four Hermetic tractates.[34]

This is about as far as the comparisons with the *Hermetica* go, however, because, as much as the two are often spoken about in the same reverential tones, the Gnostic texts are arguably far less sophisticated. They are dominated by the idea that one particular 'lesser god' created the physical world and everything in it because of his arrogant assumption that he was the ultimate creative power, and due to his ignorance of the true power above him.[35] Accordingly they regard the entire physical world as a mistake and an abomination that should never have arisen, and unfortunately this oppressively negative view pervades the whole Gnostic corpus.[36] As a result their entire focus is on the achievement of 'gnosis' – the Greek word for knowledge – in order to escape the bonds of the physical. By contrast a Rational Spiritual worldview sees the physical plane, and incarnation on earth in particular, as one of the most testing but valuable experiences a soul can have – and any enlightenment achieved is seen not as a fixed, one-off goal but instead as an ongoing contribution to the growth process.[37]

In any case the most important Gnostic passage for our current purposes comes from the *Apocryphon of John*, which describes the behavior of the fallen angels thus:[38]

> They brought gold and silver and a gift and copper and iron and metal and all kinds of things. And they steered the people who had followed them into great troubles, by leading them astray with many deceptions. They became old without having enjoyment. They died, not having found truth and without knowing the God of truth. And thus the whole creation became enslaved forever, from the foundation of the world until now. And they took women and begot children out of the darkness according to the likeness of their spirit. And they closed their hearts, and they hardened themselves through the hardness of the counterfeit spirit until now.

It is quite clear from this that once again our two themes have been mixed up. The entirely constructive knowledge transfer process is only hinted at in the first sentence, with the golden race omitted as is usual with Judaeo-Christian material. Meanwhile the theme of debasement is described as prevailing 'right from the outset until now', but this is hardly surprising given the Gnostic view of the entire physical world.

Perhaps rather more interesting is this text's explicit assertion that the account of the flood in Genesis is wrong, and that there were multiple survivors:[39]

> It is not as Moses said, 'They hid themselves in an ark', but they hid themselves in a place, not only Noah but also many other people from the immovable race.

However it could easily be argued that this was just the Gnostics' way of proving that their entire lineage, the 'immovable race', had survived even the flood itself.

THE NOISE OF HUMANKIND

The most obvious place to continue our quest is ancient Mesopotamia, originally located between the Tigris and Euphrates rivers in what is now Iraq. The Sumerian civilization first developed here in the latter half of the fifth millennium BCE, more than a thousand years before the dynastic era commenced in ancient Egypt at the beginning of the third millennium BCE, and it revolved around city-states with advanced religious, political and legal systems. The Sumerians dominated the region for several millennia, but increasing political upheaval meant their power was eventually usurped, first by the Akkadians in about 2300 BCE, and more conclusively by the Assyrians who established their capital at Babylon in about 1750 BCE.

Apart from biblical references this Mesopotamian civilization remained largely unknown until the middle of the nineteenth century, when the diligent efforts of numerous explorers and archaeologists – Paul Emil Botta, Sir Austen Henry Layard, Stephen Langdon and Sir Leonard Woolley notable among them – led to the ruins of cities such as Eridu, Nippur, Lagash, Uruk, Shuruppak, Ashur, Ur, Babylon and Nineveh being unearthed from the desert sands that had smothered them for millennia. Not only did these excavations confirm that a number of biblical sites previously thought to be fictitious were real, but they also unearthed a multitude of fragments of delicate clay tablets inscribed with a variety of scripts.

With incredible dedication scholars including Sir Henry Rawlinson, Edward Hincks and Julius Oppert set about the painstaking task of not only reassembling but also deciphering them. In terms of scripts they commenced with Sumerian pictographs and progressed to Sumerian and then Akkadian cuneiform, named after its distinctive wedge-shaped characters. Now a huge variety of texts are available to us, including historical and administrative ones such as votive inscriptions detailing a ruler's major achievements, law codes, court decisions and royal letters. But for our purposes the literary texts are far more fascinating. As per the convention they are divided into the myths of the gods and the legends of the epic heroes, and in reflecting the warriorlike nature of a patriarchal society they are full of descriptions of ferocious battles – although they do have a more subtle side as well.[40]

They contain a plethora of gods, referred to collectively as the Anunnaki or sometimes Igigi. The chief members of the original Sumerian pantheon were An (Anu in Akkadian texts), residing in heaven; Enlil (Ellil), the chief god of the earth often portrayed especially in later texts as somewhat harsh on humankind, who is associated with air; Enki (Ea), who is usually represented as the god who brought civilization to humankind and is associated with water; Ninhursag (Ninmah), the Mother Earth goddess; Inanna (Ishtar), the goddess of love; Nanna (Sin), the moon god; Utu (Shamash), the sun god; Ninurta (Ningirsu), the war god; Ishkur (Adad), the storm god; and Nergal (Erra), the plague god and ruler of the underworld with his consort Ereshkigal. But as in many other ancient cultures these names changed over time, so that in later Akkadian texts in particular we often find localized gods elevated to the main pantheon in certain areas. A case in point is the relatively late emergence of the preeminent Babylonian god Marduk.[41]

Perhaps the most stunning discovery of all was that some of these texts were the clear precursors for key passages in the book of Genesis – especially the three main compositions that include the flood tradition. The most detailed is the Akkadian *Atrahasis*, named after its flood hero, the oldest version of which is thought to date to around 1700 BCE. It contains themes repeated throughout Mesopotamian literature and is comprised of three tablets. The first describes how the gods rebelled against their excessive workload in digging and maintaining the irrigation canals that were so fundamental to the area, how they asked that humans be created to assist them, and how their request was granted. This all takes place in a clearly mythical epoch that has little relevance to the current enquiry, although we will return to it in chapter 7. The second tablet goes on to describe how the new creations proliferate, but Enlil protests that 'the noise of humankind has become too much', so he sends first a plague of sickness, then a drought – towards the end of which the people are so hungry they resort to cannibalism – and then, when neither appears to work properly, he decides to destroy humankind in its entirety with a flood. The third tablet describes how Enki warns Atrahasis of the impending flood and how to survive it; the flood itself; and finally the argument and subsequent rapprochement between the brothers Enlil and Enki when the former finds out that Atrahasis and his family have survived.[42]

It is only the second tablet that interests us here, but even then there is precious little information about life before the flood. The only message we find repeatedly in these texts is that it was sent because humankind made too much *noise*. Is this some distorted echo of the idea that humankind was becoming more degenerate?

The next text that contains a description of the flood is the *Eridu Genesis* and, although the earliest version found is thought to date to only around 1600 BCE, it is written in Sumerian script and is therefore likely to be of earlier provenance. The tablets that survive are far more fragmented and as a result shorter than *Atrahasis* but its tone is quite similar, with the hero here called Ziusudra.[43] Again, however, little survives about life before the flood other than a brief description of the building of the early

36

cities of Eridu, Bad-Tibira, Larak, Sippar and Shuruppak, as if they had been constructed *before* the flood. This suggests either that this aspect of the account is fictitious, or that the flood described is only a local and relatively recent event that has perhaps been confused with a more widespread, earlier event. Incidentally, the global spread of flood traditions militates against any suggestion that this is a satisfactory explanation for them all.[44]

The third main text to mention the flood in any detail is the Akkadian *Epic of Gilgamesh*, which is thought to represent a lengthy composite of a number of Sumerian originals. The flood story is recounted to the hero Gilgamesh by its main survivor, this time called Utnapishtim, in the first part of the eleventh tablet. But again, although it is broadly consistent with the other accounts, it contains little information about what happened before.[45]

So far, apart from a clear flood tradition, the better-known Mesopotamian texts have added little to our body of evidence. But important additional information is contained in one of the lesser-known Akkadian compositions entitled *Erra and Ishum*. Although this only dates to around the eighth century BCE it is thought to be based on far older traditions, and the version we have appears to be mainly politically inspired, reflecting the instability of the time. It mostly consists of a series of rhetorical, warmongering speeches by Erra, the god of the underworld and of plagues, and his rival, the chief Babylonian deity Marduk, interspersed with placatory comments by the lesser-known deity Ishum.

Nevertheless it also contains clear echoes of the Judaeo-Christian fallen angels with its brief reference to the seven 'divine sages' sent by Enki to teach the 'arts of civilization' to humankind before the flood.[46] Intriguingly, after the flood they anger Enki in some way – although here his place is usurped by Marduk – and as a result are banished back to the 'Apsu' from which they originally came.[47] Although the idea of banishment is a negative one, in general even in this relatively late text the sages are described in a positive light. Indeed their place of banishment is described as 'a domain of sweet, fresh water beneath the earth', and remember this is also their place of origin.[48] Surely this suggests that the late Mesopotamian texts started the process of confusion that the later Judaeo-Christian traditions thoroughly completed – that of merging the two originally separate themes of knowledge transfer, and of debasement and punishment.

We also find in this text clear echoes of *Atrahasis* in that once again plagues and a flood are sent against humans, but this time there is far greater emphasis on them not revering their gods. The events are somewhat jumbled but we are told that: 'The people abandoned justice and took to atrocities. They deserted righteousness and planned wickedness.'[49] Erra also declares that he will 'make their words wicked, and they will forget their god, will speak great insolence to their goddess', and that 'the belt of god and man is loosened and cannot be retied'.[50] These passages provide far more support for our theme of debasement and destruction.

There are several more interesting passages in this text that deal with the more prosaic phenomenon of the flood itself. One again suggests that, instead of just one survivor and his family, Erra 'left a remnant'.[51] In another Marduk, who this time is usurping the original role of Enlil, recalls sending the flood against humankind:[52]

> A long time ago, when I was angry and rose up from my dwelling and arranged for the Flood... the control of heaven and earth was undone. The very heavens I made to tremble, the positions of the stars of heaven changed, and I did not return them to their places.

Could this short extract again represent a memory of a shift in the earth's axis that somehow managed to survive the ravages of time? Or are we again merely in the realms of chaos-instead-of-order symbolism?

THE EYE OF RE

Let us now turn to the wealth of ancient Egyptian literature that has been bequeathed to us. This comprises literally thousands of inscriptions inside burial chambers, on sarcophagi, on temple walls and on stone steles, as well as on clay tablets and later papyri. The subject is rendered more complex because, although early Sumerian pictographic script is difficult to interpret, Egyptian hieroglyphs are arguably even more so – despite the popular fascination with them and the massive amount of time devoted to their study in the last century and a half.[53] So although scholars have made commendable attempts to provide translations for us they can still only guess at the significance of some of the enigmas, and nowhere is an appreciation of symbolism more crucial.

The ancient Egyptian pantheon includes Nun, the primeval waters; Ra or Re, the sun god; Ptah, also known as Amon and Atum, the creator god and his sister and spouse Sekhmet, goddess of war and destruction; Shu, the air god and his spouse Tefnut, the goddess of water or moisture; Geb, the earth god and his spouse Nut, the sky goddess; Osiris, the god of the underworld, his spouse Isis and their son Horus; Seth and his spouse

Nepthys; Thoth, the god of wisdom; and Ma'at, the goddess of truth and justice.

There are a number of main compositions that were clearly of great importance, including what are now known as the *Book of What is in the Duat*, the *Book of Gates*, the *Book of the Dead* and the *Pyramid Texts* and *Coffin Texts*.[54] Some of these date at least as far back as the end of the Fifth Dynasty around 2350 BCE. But many other lesser-known texts are referenced by commentators and, to make matters worse, they often describe various ancient Egyptian traditions without even identifying the relevant source.

One celebrated composition that is crucial for our current purposes is *The Story of Re*:[55]

Then Re took on the shape of a man and became the first Pharaoh, ruling over the whole country for thousands and thousands of years, and giving such harvests that for ever afterwards the Egyptians spoke of the good things 'which happened in the time of Re'.

But, being in the form of a man, Re grew old. In time men no longer feared him or obeyed his laws. They laughed at him, saying: 'Look at Re! His bones are like silver, his flesh like gold, his hair is the color of lapis lazuli!'

Re was angry when he heard this, and he was more angry still at the evil deeds which men were doing in disobedience to his laws. So he called together the gods whom he had made – Shu and Tefnut and Geb and Nut – and he also summoned Nun. Soon the gods gathered about Re in his Secret Place, and the goddesses also. But mankind knew nothing of what was happening, and continued to jeer at Re and to break his commandments. Then Re spoke to Nun before the assembled gods: 'Eldest of the gods, you who made me; and you gods whom I have made: look upon mankind who came into being at a glance of my Eye. See how men plot against me; hear what they say of me; tell me what I should do to them. For I will not destroy mankind until I have heard what you advise.'

Then Nun said: 'My son Re, the god greater than he who made him and mightier than those whom he has created, turn your mighty Eye upon them and send destruction upon them in the form of your daughter, the goddess Sekhmet.'

Re answered: 'Even now fear is falling upon them and they are fleeing into the desert and hiding themselves in the mountains in terror at the sound of my voice.'

'Send against them the glance of your Eye in the form Sekhmet!' cried all the other gods and goddesses, bowing before Re until their foreheads touched the ground.

This is clearly the theme of debasement and destruction rearing its head again. Having said that we should note that the destruction subsequently wrought by Sekhmet is only described as being local to Egypt. Not only that but a flood is only mentioned as part of a ruse involving beer, adopted by Re to stop her before everyone was wiped out.

THE VEDIC ASURAS

If we now move further east and turn our attention to India, we find in its earliest texts an intriguingly similar theme of debasement. According to the orthodox view a sophisticated civilization suddenly emerged in northwest India in the middle of the third millennium BCE. The two most celebrated sites of this high Indus culture are at Harappa, on the River Ravi in the Punjab, and at Mohenjo-daro, on the Indus in Sind.

Although they had developed a script that appears on their stamp seals, for example, it has yet to be deciphered and we have no real written texts from this period. But we do know from the cultural remains that, while they exhibit a degree of Western influence from Mesopotamia, they also exhibit clear strains of an indigenous culture that is assumed to have already developed in India by this time – perhaps in the east in the Ganges delta and Bengal areas, or perhaps in the Dravidian south. This indigenous culture appears to have been more spiritually advanced than any other of the time, arguably including that of the Egyptians whose Old Kingdom dynasties were by this time in full flower. This is no more clearly demonstrated than in the meditative Yogic poses found for the first time in this era again on various stamp seals.[56]

The two main cities seem to have remained largely unchanged for something like a thousand years. At this point they were overcome and destroyed by the incursion of largely nomadic Aryan or Indo-European warriors from the West, who had by now mastered the art of horsemanship and developed the wheeled chariot. According to the orthodoxy this marks the start of the so-called Vedic Age, around 1500 BCE, which represents something of an enigma. This is the era of the first written Sanskrit records of India, by far the most important of which are the *Vedas*. Joseph Campbell and other Western scholars – presumably allowing their arguments to be dominated by the essentially negative and regressive influence of the invaders – have suggested that the Vedic religion was largely exoteric, and that the indigenous traits were not reestablished until some five hundred years later in the Brahmanic Age.[57]

Other commentators disagree with this view, however, instead arguing that the *Vedas* represent the earliest written embodiment of a largely indigenous and highly esoteric Eastern philosophy that had probably been passed down verbally for many millennia beforehand. In fact in their 1995 study *In Search of the Cradle of Civilization* Georg Feuerstein, Subhash Kak and David Frawley go as far as to suggest that the Vedic Age should be properly dated to 3000 BCE or even earlier, and that the 'Aryan invasion' never happened. They also present a strong case for the level of metaphysical sophistication of the *Vedas*.[58] In part they were following up on the views of Ganga Prasad, who in 1927 in *The Fountainhead of Religion* argued that the *Vedas* influenced the development of all the other major religions, which only emerged *after* them:[59]

> We have seen that the principles of Mahommedanism and Christianity are derived from Judaism, those of Christianity being partly traceable also to Buddhism, that the doctrines of Judaism can be deduced from Zoroastrianism, and further that both Zoroastrianism and Buddhism are directly traceable to the Vedic religion. Can we similarly trace the teachings of the Vedas to any other religion? No; for history does not know of any older or prior religion.

This is not intended to be a definitive study of comparative religion, and the whole question of the interplays between the three most ancient historical civilizations of India, Egypt and Mesopotamia is infinitely complex. Nevertheless the point seems to be well made that we find in the *Vedas* a level of esoteric sophistication that seems highly unlikely to have derived from either of the other two. So it is either indigenous or the legacy of a more universal, possibly even antediluvian, wisdom. We will return to this possibility in chapter 8.

The Sanskrit word *veda* also means knowledge or wisdom, and there are four main Vedic texts: the *Rig Veda*, *Yajur Veda*, *Sama Veda* and *Atharva Veda*. As with most Indian literature they are extremely lengthy, to the point that English translations provide only excerpts – although that did not deter the Brahman priests who held such enormous influence from memorizing them word for word, as their forebears would have done when there were no written records. Later on various commentaries known as the *Brahmanas* were developed to help to explain their contents.

So much for the background. We find in the *Vedas* that the major gods such as Indra, Varuna, Agni, Savitri, Rudra and Shiva are all originally described as Asuras, and that this term translates as 'breather or giver of life', or alternatively 'spiritual, signifying the divine, in opposition to human nature'.[60] But the tradition of the Asuras is more complex than this, because scholars are united in suggesting that in later texts the term also came to be associated with demons or devas, the enemies of the true gods.[61] This must surely be seen as related to the fallen angel motif we have already encountered, but can we shed any light on what caused this fall in Vedic tradition? Prasad's commentaries on the Asuras are highly illuminating in this respect:[62]

> In later Sanskrit the word has come to be used in a bad sense being a synonym of Rakshasa, an evil being. The idea then is 'one who takes pleasure in, or enjoys, his present life disregarding the next or future life; one who only cares for his body and not for the spirit.'

Of course the suggestion here is that the Asuras' context changes according to the age of the texts in which they appear, and not that the change describes genuine events in remote antiquity. Still it seems likely that this is an oversimplification. For example in one hymn from the highly celebrated *Rig Veda* entitled 'Indra Lures Agni from Vrtra', the nature of the Asuras and of their relationship to the various gods is already unclear.[63] It even seems to be attempting to describe the conflict between two sets of gods, in which the 'good' set 'has the sacrifice' and has 'regained the power of kingship', while the 'bad' set have 'lost their magic powers'. It also makes a brief reference to Varuna 'letting the waters flow', which could be indicative of an original destruction theme related to these events.

We must always remember the rules of engagement when dealing with all these texts, and it would clearly be foolish to attempt too literal an interpretation of this enigmatic hymn. But arguably there are echoes of the fallen angel and debasement theme in the Vedic traditions of the Asuras; and this suggestion is strengthened by the fact that later Indian traditions clearly support the idea of an original golden race, as we will see in chapter 4. Meanwhile there is a flood tradition in India too, with the survivor, Manu, told to build a boat by a magic fish.[64]

KARMIC CATASTROPHE

We will not be investigating the potential nature of the catastrophe until Part 2. But whether it resulted from huge earthquakes and volcanic eruptions, or a comet or asteroid impact, or a combination of the two, it was surely just a natural phenomenon. The idea that it was divinely inspired is preposterous to the rational mind. Or is it? Perhaps it is not that simple?

Here we need to delve a little into a Rational Spiritual worldview.

Broadly speaking under the monotheistic religions that predominate in the West – that is Christianity, Judaism and Islam – God tends to be seen as an all-powerful individual who is separate from and external to each of us, and is able to exert total control over our destinies. Indeed Campbell sees the 'mythic dissociation' of God and humans as underlying the theme of the first fall in Genesis 3, when Adam and Eve eat the forbidden fruit of the 'tree of the knowledge of good and evil' at the serpent's suggestion, and God banishes them from Eden.[65] Unfortunately it would appear that this idea of a separate God was deliberately invented and introduced at a relatively late stage, along with the idea of punishment in hell, as an essentially political control mechanism designed to keep the common people in their place.

By contrast many modern spiritual seekers adopt what the far older Eastern view that essentially 'we are all *part of* God' or even that 'we *are all* God' period. To give this its full Rational Spiritual context, the concept of the holographic soul was designed to show that our soul energy or consciousness, as well as being a full holographic representation of the universal consciousness of 'source', also has an individual aspect whose aim is to experience and grow by reincarnating repeatedly.[66] We are both unity and individuality all at the same time. So the idea that a separated, even vindictive God might decide to destroy the human race because of its shortcomings is anathema to a Rational Spiritual worldview.

But what if there exist highly experienced souls who oversee what happens on our planet? What if, even though we have individual free will, there is nevertheless a 'grand earth plan', aspects of which sometimes come into play and with which we as individual souls agree to go along?[67] So if at some point in our history we did go somewhat off the rails, forgetting our true spiritual nature and immersing ourselves in materialism and greed, might we not all have agreed that action was called for; perhaps drastic action, such as a massive clear-out of the human population so that, as souls incarnating once again on a less-populated earth, we could start again with a clean slate? This would in no sense represent a punishment, but rather a collective decision made using our soul rather than human perspective. We will discuss these ideas more in the epilogue.

In the meantime, as hinted at in the preface, the concept of karma that is normally coupled with reincarnation is much misunderstood, associated as it so often is with ideas of punishment and even retribution. So arguably it is usually far more useful to think in terms of experience and growth, pure and simple.[68] But in this instance it is hard to think of a better word to describe the underlying spiritual dynamics of the flood catastrophe.

Of course there are alternative interpretations. The first is that serious natural catastrophes have repeatedly ravaged the earth, even if the modern human race has only been affected by the more recent ones. For example, as we will discuss further in Part 2 it is now universally agreed that a massive comet impact wiped out the dinosaurs, and that such events are relatively commonplace although of varying scale. Does that mean they have all been karmically driven? We cannot properly answer that, except to say a Rational Spiritual worldview strongly suggests that everything tends to happen for a reason – whether individual or more universal, whether crucial or apparently more trivial, and even if we do not always understand the dynamics at the time.

The second is that not only have such catastrophes occurred repeatedly during the life of our planet, but also they occur at regular intervals. Were this to be the case it would be hard to argue they were karmically driven, especially because – and this is a crucial point that is often misunderstood – karma involves choice and *not* predestiny. But as we will see in chapter 5 the Eastern religious traditions that hold to the idea of the cyclical destruction of the earth and of humanity are almost certainly misguided applications of earlier, more esoteric ideas about cycles involving the entire universe.

The third alternative is the psycho-materialist interpretation that, even if the flood catastrophe did occur and did wipe out the bulk of the human population, the simplistic reaction of the survivors would be to assume their forebears had done something wrong for the gods to want to inflict such serious punishment. This would indeed be plausible were it not for the more general context of the various worldwide texts and traditions. As we will shortly see many of them contain descriptions of the original golden race that are full of spiritual insight, and even more impressively esoteric material about the origins of the world. So the idea that the people who compiled them in whatever form were operating under the spell of relatively primitive superstition simply does not hold water.

Overall then there is good reason to suggest that the catastrophe reported in the various texts we have considered was karmically driven – albeit with a slight twist that we will discuss in the epilogue.

CONCLUSION

The Near and Far Eastern texts of varying antiquity that we have considered in this chapter are not the easiest to decipher. But we have started with them because they are some of the best known, and are all to varying degrees germane to our central theme of a highly spiritual forgotten race who became so debased that the forces of universal karma dictated their destruction. Of course if this were the only evidence available to support this theme it would be fair to regard our case as possibly interesting though hardly conclusive. But in due course we will find it echoed, often with far more clarity, in various other texts and traditions from around the world that have a rather different main context.

3

THE ARTS OF CIVILIZATION

In the previous chapter we discussed various texts that describe angels, demigods or sages appearing to introduce humanity to mathematics, astronomy, divination and various other magical practices. We also saw that this theme of knowledge transfer tended to be mistakenly interwoven with that of debasement. So now we will turn to other traditions that preserve the original meaning rather better.

KNOWLEDGE TRANSFER

We have already briefly encountered the Mesopotamian tradition of Enki sending seven sages to teach the arts of civilization to humankind. This theme is not fully developed in any of the original Mesopotamian source texts so far discovered, but it survives mainly through the writings of Berossus, a Babylonian historian-priest of the third century BCE. Although his original *Babyloniaca* has not survived, much of it has been preserved for us in the commentaries of subsequent historians such as Alexander Polyhistor, Abydenus and Apollodorus. Polyhistor's account opens by informing us of the records that Berossus said existed in his time:[1]

> He mentions that there were written accounts preserved at Babylon with the greatest care, comprehending a term of fifteen myriads [ten thousands] of years. These writings contained a history of the heavens and the sea; of the birth of humankind; also of those who had sovereign rule; and of the actions achieved by them.

He then goes on to describe how the sages' leader Oannes – referred to in the original Mesopotamian sources as Adapa – 'emerged from the

Erythraean sea', how he was part-man, part-fish, how his voice was 'articulate and human' and how 'a representation of him is preserved even to this day'. This latter is born out by depictions of a man wearing fish scales as a headdress in multiple Mesopotamian and Babylonian reliefs. In addition the lesser-known historian Helladius reports that 'some accounts say that... he was actually a man, but only seemed a fish because he was clothed in the skin of a sea creature'.[2] All this tends to suggest that the sages were not monstrous amphibious creatures, nor for that matter extraterrestrials as some would have us believe, but real humans. It may even be that the fish motif is symbolic of wisdom, given that Enki himself is associated primarily with both water and wisdom.[3]

Berossus, via Polyhistor, continues as follows:

This Being in the day-time used to converse with men; but took no food at that season; and he gave them an insight into letters and sciences, and every kind of art. He taught them to construct houses, to found temples, to compile laws, and explained to them the principles of geometrical knowledge. He made them distinguish the seeds of the earth, and shewed them how to collect fruits; in short, he instructed them in every thing which could tend to soften manners and humanize humankind. From that time, so universal were his instructions, nothing has been added material by way of improvement.

We can see that this has none of the negative tone of the accounts in the previous chapter. We do not know what Berossus' source was for this particular information, but it must have been old enough to have avoided the late-Mesopotamian distortions we encountered previously in *Erra and Ishum*. Moreover Polyhistor goes on to report that 'after this there appeared other animals like Oannes, of which Berossus promises to give an account when he comes to the history of the kings'. Were there indeed a number of these sages, and did they perhaps assist their peers over a prolonged period?

Although none of the Mesopotamian texts that we now have completely mirrors Berossus' account, certain of them do reveal important details that considerably predate the Babylonian tradition. The introduction to the short and incomplete Akkadian text *Adapa*, which dates to around 1500 BCE, reveals the following about him:[4]

Ea made broad understanding perfect in him, to disclose the design of the land. To him he gave wisdom, but did not give eternal life. At that time, in those years, he was a sage, son of Eridu. Ea created him as a protecting spirit among humankind. A sage – nobody rejects his word – clever, extra-wise, he was one of the Anunnaki.

This description of Adapa as 'extra-wise' is in fact the same as the epithet given to the flood heroes Atrahasis, Ziusudra and Utnapishtim, while they all have the additional epithet 'far-distant'.[5] As for the other six sages, unsurprisingly we find that in *Erra and Ishum* they are all described in similar terms as 'the holy carp, who are perfect in lofty wisdom like Ea their lord.'[6] It is surely not going too far to suggest that these descriptions are intended to convey a high degree of spiritual insight?

There exists an even older, Sumerian text entitled *Inanna and Enki: The Transfer of the Arts of Civilization from Eridu to Erech*. The title itself is revealing, although we should appreciate that the text has an obvious political message in that it attempts to justify the ascendancy of Inanna's ancient city of Erech over that of Enki in Eridu. Nor does it contain any details of who bestowed these gifts on humankind in the first place. Yet it does include a detailed description of more than one hundred of these so-called arts – an approximate translation of the Sumerian word *me*. In his 1963 work *The Sumerians* Mesopotamian scholar Samuel Noah Kramer points out that 'only some sixty-odd are at present intelligible, and some of these are only bare words which, because of lack of context, give but a hint of their real significance'.[7] But as well as more mundane arts such as those of the metalworker, smith, leatherworker, builder and basket weaver, the list includes words and phrases that have been translated as godship, kingship, truth, ascent from and descent into the netherworld, various unidentified priestly offices, law, art, music, scribeship, wisdom, attention, judgment and decision. If the less politicized elements of the traditions of Adapa and various flood heroes are correct, it suggests that these skills were indeed introduced to humanity at some time in our *antediluvian* past.

What is more these accounts of knowledge transfer are by no means restricted to the Near East. For example Chinese tradition reports that the Yellow Emperor, Huang Ti:[8]

> ...taught the arts of divination and mathematics, composed the calendar, invented musical instruments of bamboo, taught the use of money, boats and carriages, and the arts of work in clay, metal, and wood. He established the rituals of address to *shang ti,* built the first temple and the first palace, studied and taught the properties of healing herbs.

As an isolated case this could of course be interpreted entirely prosaically as a political text extolling the virtues of the culture's main ancestors. Yet there are accounts from other parts of the world that back up the idea of knowledge bringers *from afar,* a celebrated example being the tradition of Quetzalcoatl of the Mexican Toltecs.[9] However sometimes it appears that they are catastrophe survivors rather than original antediluvian civilizers. Indeed we might go as far as to suggest that the association of Oannes-Adapa with a fish emerging from the sea gives him a hint of the same context, even if in their broader context the Oannes-Adapa traditions point towards the antediluvian transfer of knowledge to the golden race.

This factor somewhat complicates our interpretation of knowledge transfer traditions, in as much as they may relate to vastly different periods in our history. So let us attempt to build on the scenario presented in the previous chapter. Those with a clearly *antediluvian* context provide support for the suggestion made previously that, at various points in early human history, highly experienced souls deliberately incarnated to help the 'civilization' process move forwards. Of course this would not have been a one-off process but more likely a gradual one that was repeated over a lengthy period.

On the other hand we have seen that there are hints this knowledge transfer process also carried on *after* the catastrophe. From this perspective we can construct a further scenario. There is good reason to believe that the most culturally advanced elements of our antediluvian race would have lived in coastal areas, especially if their whole system of trade relied on ocean navigation. Of course these would have been the very areas worst affected by any global catastrophe that involved tsunamis, so most pockets of survivors would have been inland farmers or still nomadic hunter-gatherers who led a more basic existence. But it is also highly likely that a few people from the more culturally advanced settlements would have survived, for example because they were at sea in the deep ocean when disaster struck, or because they were in a less affected part of the globe. These are all issues that we will examine more fully in Part 2. But the key point here is that, although all survivors would probably have had a hard time for several generations, if those who were more culturally advanced then came into contact with those who were less so they might well have been seen as 'educating gods' of some sort. At the very least they would have had a sufficiently significant impact on the 'receiving' culture that they would have become highly prominent in its traditions.

This kind of speculation is based on the 'cargo cult' theory that many revisionists have promoted for decades, and it may well have a role to play in the interpretation of some of these knowledge transfer traditions. But the story is unlikely to end there, because there is every reason to suspect that more experienced souls also continued to incarnate after the catastrophe to assist the rebuilding and reeducation process – perhaps in particular to ensure that the spiritual worldview that had been lost was reintroduced. On that basis a variety of different interactions at different times may well underlie these traditions.

KNOWLEDGE PRESERVATION

By way of contrast we also find accounts of knowledge being *preserved* for the future by our ancient forebears, and sometimes these two types of tradition tend to overlap and become confused too. As an example a number of flood accounts contain this idea. In Berossus' Babylonian version the hero Xisuthros is asked by the deity to 'commit to writing a history of the beginning, procedure, and final conclusion of all things, down to the present term'.[10] The same idea is found in Josephus' biblical commentary when he describes how the descendants of Adam's favored son Seth took precautions before the onset of the flood:[11]

> And that their inventions might not be lost before they were sufficiently known, upon Adam's prediction that the world was to be destroyed at one time by the force of fire, and at another time by the violence and quantity of water, they made two pillars; the one of brick, the other of stone: they inscribed their discoveries on them both, that in case the pillar of brick should be destroyed by the flood, the pillar of stone might remain, and exhibit those discoveries to humankind; and also inform them that there was another pillar of brick erected by them. This remains in the land of Siriad to this day.

It is not entirely obvious why the church fathers decided to omit this aspect of the flood story from Genesis. As to there Josephus obtained this information we know that before writing his account he spent time at Qumran in the company of another breakaway sect known as the Essenes.[12] They were the authors of the Dead Sea Scrolls, discovered in various caves there in 1947, and most scholars accept they had a rather more esoteric take on the Judaic and other material available to them than the founders of the Christian church. We also find that the Gnostic literature contains many texts that extol Seth as the father of the bloodline of the immovable race, and one in particular entitled *The Three Steles of Seth* is clearly based on the same theme, although unfortunately the contents are not particularly revealing.[13]

Intriguingly this idea of knowledge preservation is not found in the Ethiopian version of the *Book of Enoch*, although it is implicit that the information recorded therein constitutes its own 'preserved revelation'. However the Slavonic version does make it clear that Enoch was instructed to record everything that the archangels showed and taught him during his visionary trip to the 'seven abodes of heaven':[14]

> And now, my children, I know all things from the lips of the Lord; for my eyes have seen from the beginning to the end. I know all things and have written all things in the books.

The list of the 'things' that follows mainly includes details of astronomy, calendars and the seasons. Yet there has always been a strong suspicion that the original Enochian material contained far more esoteric knowledge that was hidden from the masses but preserved in Masonic tradition, as suggested by Manley P Hall in his wide-ranging 1928 work *The Secret Teachings of All Ages*:[15]

> He [Enoch] also constructed an underground temple consisting of nine vaults, one beneath the other, placing in the deepest vault a triangular tablet of gold bearing upon it the absolute and ineffable Name of Deity. According to some accounts, Enoch made two golden deltas. The larger he placed upon the white cubical altar in the lowest vault and the smaller he gave to into the keeping of his son, Methusaleh, who did the actual construction work of the brick chambers according to the pattern revealed to his father by the Most High... According to Freemasonic symbolism, Enoch, fearing that all knowledge of the sacred Mysteries would be lost at the time of the Deluge, erected the two columns mentioned in the quotation [that is, of Josephus]. Upon the metal column in appropriate allegorical symbols he engraved the secret teaching and upon the marble column placed an inscription stating that a short distance away a priceless treasure would be discovered in a subterranean vault. After having thus successfully completed his labors, Enoch was translated from the brow of Mount Moriah. In time the location of the secret vaults was lost, but after the lapse of ages there came another builder – an initiate after the order of Enoch [presumably King Solomon] – and he, while laying the foundations for another great temple to the Great Architect of the Universe, discovered the long-lost vaults and the secrets contained within.

These accounts are echoed in other traditions. For example in the *Hermetica* Hermes is said to have inscribed 'knowledge of all' on certain tablets.[16] Meanwhile Eve Reymond, former professor of Egyptology at the University of Manchester, has this to say about the *Edfu Documents* that date to the last half of the first millennium BCE in her 1969 work *The Mythical Origin of the Egyptian Temple*:[17]

The introduction of the first Edfu cosmogonical record discloses the tradition that the contents of these records were the words of the Sages. We are told that this sacred book was believed to be a copy of writings which Thoth made according to the words of the Sages of Mehweret.

This appears to have parallels with the Mesopotamian knowledge transfer tradition of the seven sages. Then, sticking with Egypt, we also have the Arab accounts preserved by the ninth-century writer Abd al Hokm. These describe an antediluvian king named Saurid who supposedly built the three pyramids of Giza *before* the flood to secrete and preserve knowledge of the 'profound sciences... of astrology, arithmetic, geometry and physics', and also 'the commentaries of each priest... concerning what was done in his time, and what is, and what shall be, from the beginning of time, to the end of it'.[18] But as we will see in Part 2 there is overwhelming evidence that these monuments were indeed built only around 2500 BCE as orthodox scholars suggest. So what about the many other accounts from Egyptian, Greek and Roman sources that suggest some sort of secret knowledge of the remote past was preserved in Egypt in particular?[19] These eventually led to the now celebrated suggestion that a 'Hall of Records' awaits discovery somewhere in Egypt, and perhaps also elsewhere.

Such intriguing possibilities have provided massive incentives to a variety of researchers and explorers who have devoted their lives to attempting to locate such records, and perhaps even caches of artifacts developed using lost technology. However it seems likely that the bulk of these traditions have built up from the sort of rumor and exaggeration that has always been associated with the Giza plateau especially.[20] To take the most celebrated example there is no genuine evidence whatsoever for hidden chambers underneath the Sphinx;[21] and in any case as we will see in Part 2 everything points towards it being of at least similar age to the pyramids. Indeed there is a strong argument that, rather than a physical repository containing evidence of our forgotten race, the Hall of Records is far better seen as a spiritual concept similar to that of the 'akashic records' of every soul's many lives, which are said to exist in the collective consciousness.[22]

Yet, despite all this, does the possibility remain that historical records of a highly cultured antediluvian race survive that are far more detailed than those currently in the public domain? Rumors abound of caches of ancient documents being secreted away in hidden vaults in the Vatican or remote hideaways in Tibet. But so far that is all they are... rumors.

CONCLUSION

It is surely reasonable to suggest that, taken all together, the various knowledge transfer traditions do point towards an underlying reality: that the development of human culture and civilization has received a significant boost from the catalyst of the incarnation of highly experienced souls at various times throughout our history, which means both before and after any worldwide catastrophe. This is coupled with the more prosaic possibility of more advanced catastrophe survivors educating their more primitive fellows.

As for the knowledge preservation traditions, if they have any validity at all they do provide general support for the idea that a cultured antediluvian race existed. However with these traditions in particular this validity is more than usually questionable.

4

THE GOLDEN AGE

We have now started to build up a picture of a forgotten race who were originally highly aware of their true spiritual roots, but then began to concentrate unduly on the material. This led to their destruction in a karmic catastrophe that was universally agreed at a soul level. But we have also seen that the traditions so far studied tend to omit or only hint at any description of what life was really like before the process of degeneration commenced. So we will now turn to those that fill in this gap, with their widespread references to an antediluvian 'golden age'.

PARADISE IN EDEN

A few gaps can be filled in even from the Judaeo-Christian traditions. Although the details of the biblical Eden are sparse and fairly prosaic in Genesis, only mentioning an abundance of food for humans and animals, since time immemorial it has been regarded as a paradise from which Adam and Eve were expelled after the first fall.[1] Does this represent a thinly veiled reference to a golden age in the distant past? A passage from the Slavonic version of the *Book of Enoch* describes the conditions God provided for Adam in Eden as follows:[2]

> I made for him the heavens open that he should perceive the angels singing the song of triumph. And there was light without any darkness continually in paradise.

This 'continual light' should clearly not be taken literally, so is it a veiled reference to the idea that Eden was filled with 'spiritual light'? Meanwhile Josephus, as well as reporting how 'evil' Cain altered the 'simple and innocent lives that men lived before', goes on to describe 'good' Seth's descendants as follows:[3]

All these proved to be of good dispositions. They inhabited the same country without dissensions, and in a happy condition, without any misfortunes falling upon them, till they died. They were the inventors of that peculiar sort of wisdom which is concerned with the heavenly bodies, and their order.

So perhaps, even in the often-distorted Judaeo-Christian traditions, we can perceive the message that our antediluvian ancestors originally lived in a 'paradisial' spiritual state.

As we saw previously the Mesopotamian texts too are not exactly forthcoming on this issue, but one at least gives us some reason to assume that the Judaic traditions were once again informed by these far earlier predecessors. *Enki and Ninhursag* has been dubbed 'A Sumerian Paradise Myth' and, although the version we now have was composed primarily to entertain visiting merchants from Dilmun – or the island of Bahrain – it was clearly composed from at least two separate original sources. Both of these appear to have been ruthlessly culled judging by the contextual jumps that remain, yet the opening stanzas contain a description of a paradisial state that may originally have been much longer and more detailed, and not associated with Dilmun at all. It is described as a 'pure' and 'virginal' land, where there was no disease.[4]

THE FIRST OCCASION

Most scholars do not emphasize the idea that a golden age formed part of ancient Egyptian tradition, but one of the few who does is R T Rundle Clark, a former professor of Egyptology at the University of Birmingham. In his 1959 study *Myth and Symbol in Ancient Egypt* he provides this description of *tep zepi,* or the 'first time':[5]

> The basic principles of life, nature and society were determined by the gods long ago, before the establishment of kingship. This epoch – '*Tep Zepi*' – 'the First Time' – stretched from the first stirring of the High God in the Primeval Waters to the settling of Horus upon the throne and the redemption of Osiris. All proper myths relate events or manifestations of this epoch.
>
> Anything whose existence or authority had to be justified or explained must be referred to the 'First Time'. This was true for natural phenomena, rituals, royal insignia, the plans of temples, magical or medical formulae, the hieroglyphic system of writing, the calendar – the whole paraphernalia of the civilization...
>
> All that was good or efficacious was established on the principles laid

down in the 'First Time' – which was, therefore, a golden age of absolute perfection – 'before rage or clamor or strife or uproar had come about'. No death, disease or disaster occurred in this blissful epoch, known variously as 'the time of Re', 'the time of Osiris', or the 'time of Horus'.

The Golden Age was disturbed. The entry of evil was generally thought to have happened when the eye of the High God grew angry seeing that it had been supplanted by another in its absence. The partial restoration of this Golden Age – *hetep* – is the chief theme of the ritual. Hence the emphasis on the constraint of evil forces and the defeat of the powers of chaos. After the triumph of the Osiris cult the chief disturber of cosmic harmony was Seth.

Rundle Clark's work is heavily relied on by a number of revisionists, especially Robert Bauval and Adrian Gilbert in their best-selling 1995 work *The Orion Mystery*, and Bauval and Graham Hancock in the follow-up *Keeper of Genesis*. But it stands somewhat alone because, although the concept of the first time displays clear parallels with the original 'dream time' of indigenous peoples in Australasia and elsewhere, the main reference books on Egyptian mythology and the main texts listed above do not seem to contain much in the way of references to it or to a golden age. The only other possibly relevant source is the *Edfu Documents*, which have also been referenced extensively by various revisionists because they include a number of apparently cosmogonical records. According to a former professor of Egyptology at the University of Manchester, Eve Reymond, these appear to represent highly edited extracts from original compositions perhaps of extreme antiquity, which were not specifically associated with Edfu but unfortunately have not survived.[6] Yet, even though the first of these is entitled *Sanctified God Who Came into Being at the First Occasion*, we should recognize that Reymond's commentary on these texts has very little to say about the 'first occasion', and nowhere do either she or the texts themselves elaborate on this as a golden age. It is merely described as a time when the earliest gods inhabited the earth.

But whatever we make of these lesser-known sources the idea of a golden age is very definitely hinted at in the celebrated *Story of Re* as reproduced in chapter 2, even if only briefly, with its allusion to 'the good things in the time of Re'.

THE DAYS OF DASA-RATHA

We saw in chapter 2 how Brahmanism emerged in India around the start of the first millennium BCE. Then in the middle of this millennium the teachings of one of the archetypal 'world saviors', Gautama Buddha, led to the emergence of Buddhism in northern India. The two main strands that developed were the broad-based Mahayana school and the more orthodox Hinayana school, and their teachings were recorded for the first time in writing late in the first millennium BCE – the former in a number of sutras, the most important of which is the *Avatamsaka Sutra*, and the latter in the *Pali Canon*. But while Buddhism then spread to the Orient in the early centuries of the first millennium, in northern India Hinduism developed out of a resurgent Brahmanism.

The two main Sanskrit epics of Indian literature are the Hindu *Mahabharata* and *Ramayana*. The former is described by Joseph Campbell as the 'chief mythological document of the Indian golden age... much of the material of which is indefinitely old, perhaps ante 400 BC, but of which the final style and tone are rather of around AD 400 and thereafter.'[7] Both epics are lengthy and full of references to a golden age, although it tends to be placed in the context of multiple ages as we will see in the next chapter. But for now here is an example taken from a translation of extracts from the *Ramayana*, undertaken by Romesh C Dutt at the beginning of the twentieth century. It is a lengthy passage from the first book entitled 'The Bridal of Sita', but to paraphrase or edit it would be to miss out on the beautiful poetry of Dutt's translation:[8]

Rich in royal worth and valor, rich in holy Vedic lore,
Dasa-ratha ruled his empire in the happy days of yore,
Loved of men in fair Ayodhya, sprung of ancient Solar Race,
Royal rishi in his duty, saintly rishi in his grace,
Great as Indra in his prowess, bounteous as Kuvera kind,
Dauntless deeds subdued his foemen, lofty faith subdued his mind!
Like the ancient monarch Manu, father of the human race,
Dasa-ratha ruled his people with a father's loving grace,
Truth and Justice swayed each action and each baser motive quelled,
People's Love and Monarch's Duty every thought and deed impelled,
And his town like Indra's city – tower and dome and turret brave –
Rose in proud and peerless beauty on Sarayu's limpid wave!
Peaceful lived the righteous people, rich in wealth in merit high,
Envy dwelt not in their bosoms and their accents shaped no lie,
Fathers with their happy households owned their cattle, corn, and gold,
Galling penury and famine in Ayodhya had no hold,
Neighbors lived in mutual kindness helpful with their ample wealth,
None who begged the wasted refuse, none who lived by fraud and stealth!
And they wore the gem and earring, wreath and fragrant sandal paste,

And their arms were decked with bracelets, their necks with nishkas graced,
Cheat and braggart and deceiver lived not in the ancient town,
Proud despiser of the lowly wore not insults in their frown,
Poorer fed not on the richer, hireling friend upon the great,
None with low and lying accents did upon the proud man wait!
Men to plighted vows were faithful, faithful was each loving wife,
Impure thought and wandering fancy stained not holy wedded life,
Robed in gold and graceful garments, fair in form and fair in face,
Winsome were Ayodhya's daughters, rich in wit and woman's grace!
Twice-born men were free from passion, lust of gold and impure greed,
Faithful to their Rites and Scriptures, truthful in their word and deed,
Altar blazed in every mansion, from each home was bounty given,
Stooped no man to fulsome falsehood, questioned none the will of Heaven.
Kshatras bowed to holy Brahmans, Vaisyas to the Kshatras bowed,
Toiling Sudras lived by labor, of their honest duty proud,
To the Gods and to the Fathers, to each guest in virtue trained,
Rites were done with true devotion as by holy writ ordained.
Pure each caste in due observance, stainless was each ancient rite,
And the nation thrived and prospered by its old and matchless might,
And each man in truth abiding lived a long and peaceful life,
With his sons and with his grandsons, with his loved and honored wife.
Thus was ruled the ancient city by her monarch true and bold,
As the earth was ruled by Manu in the misty days of old.

Although this passage does not deal with the original golden age itself, which is presumably the time when 'the earth was ruled by Manu in the misty days of old', it is nevertheless attempting to describe a period of rule in which it was supposedly recreated. Having said that it is reasonably prosaic and moralistic in tone, apart from its reference to 'twice-born' men, which broadly speaking means those who have been initiated into spiritual wisdom. But we will find plenty more esoteric wisdom to back this up in the broader and earlier Indian material covered in forthcoming chapters.

THE AGE OF PERFECT VIRTUE

We have not yet considered the important Chinese texts and traditions. The first formalized religion to emerge in China was Confucianism around the middle of the first millennium BCE. Its main texts include the *Shu King* or 'Book of History', which commences with the 'Canon of Yeo' who ruled around 2300 BCE; the *Shih King*; the *Hsiao King*; the *Yi King*, the basis for the I Ching system of divination; and the *Li Ki*. Its emergence was accompanied by a purge of earlier literature and traditions that culminated in the 'burning of the books' by the emperor Shih Huang Ti in 213 BCE, at about the same time the Great Wall was constructed. But after this the rulers of the Han dynasty set about reinventing their early traditions, so scholars have found it extremely difficult to piece back together the original traditions of the earliest historical dynasties of Shang and Chou. Meanwhile Taoism emerged shortly after Confucianism, its main texts being the *Tao Teh King* and the *Writings of Kwang Tze*. As previously mentioned, Buddhism did not come to China until some time in the first half of the first millennium.

Translations of and commentaries on all of these main texts are available in a monumental forty-volume compilation entitled *The Sacred Books of the East*, compiled in the late nineteenth century by Max Müller – specifically in the subset entitled *The Sacred Books of China* prepared by the leading contemporary Orientalist James Legge.[9] His translation of the Taoist *Writings of Kwang Tze* contains a number of excellent descriptions of the nature of man in the 'Age of Perfect Virtue':[10]

> In the age of perfect virtue they attached no value to wisdom, nor employed men of ability. Superiors were (but) as the higher branches of a tree; and the people were like the deer of the wild. They were upright and correct, without knowing that to be so was Righteousness; they loved one another, without knowing that to do so was Benevolence; they were honest and loyal-hearted, without knowing that it was Loyalty; they fulfilled their engagements, without knowing that to do so was Good Faith; in their simple movements they employed the services of one another, without thinking that they were conferring or receiving a gift. Therefore their actions left no trace, and there was no record of their affairs.

And again:[11]

> In the age of perfect virtue, men lived in common with birds and beasts, and were on terms of equality with all creatures, as forming one family; how could they know among themselves the distinctions of superior men and small men? Equally without knowledge, they did not leave (the path of) their natural virtue; equally free from desires, they were in the state of pure simplicity. In that state of pure simplicity, the nature of the people was what it ought to be.

To add to this picture we have extracts from another Taoist text, this time translated by Evan Morgan of the University of Wales in his *Essays from Huai Nan Tzu*. One entitled 'Beginning and Reality' contains the following description:[12]

The ancients lodged within the realm of the Tao; desire was controlled and passion mastered; and, in consequence, the spirit did not wander into the extraneous. They derived repose from the calm of creation: they were not disturbed by the baneful effects of comets and the tail of the Great Bear. Though noxious, they refused to be disturbed by their appearances.

During this period, the people were in a state of Arcadian simplicity; they ate and rambled about: they smacked their stomachs and rejoiced. All together enjoyed the blessings of heaven and ate of the fruits of the earth. They did not wrangle in mutual recriminations, nor dispute over rights and wrongs. Peace and plenty existed. This may be called the Ideal Rule...

The perfect man of ancient time stood in the very root and centre of being, the foundations of Heaven and Earth themselves, and wandered at will, unhasting and free, in this central seat of being. He cherished and diffused virtue, he enkindled the spirit of harmony of existence and thus enabled creation to come to full maturity.

A lengthy passage in another essay, 'Natural Law', reinforces the point:[13]

The rule of the T'ai Ch'ing was in accord with Heaven, and beneficial to creation. Nature was constant, the spirit simple and centered. The mind had no appetites: it was quiescent: it was active, not stagnant. Mental activities were consistent with the Tao, and outward activities were in agreement with right. The activities of the mind worked artistically; action was correct with benefit to things. Words were prized and in accord with reason. Actions were simple and direct, in accordance with nature. The mind was contented and without cunning. Actions were simple and without ostentation. So there was no recourse to horoscopy and divination of the eight signs and the tortoise. There was no thought of where to begin and how to end. Action took place when it was demanded. Principles were embodied: the spirit of Yin and Yang were envisaged. All was in conformity with the four seasons. All was bright and clear as the sun and moon: man was a fit mate of the Creator. Hence Heaven overshadowed them with grace, and Earth sustained them with life. The four seasons did not lose their order, nor did the wind and rain fall with violence. The sun and moon were limpid and lucent, shining in their brightness, and the five planets moved in their orbits without error.

During these periods the primal fluid was surpassingly glowing (in men of the period) and transmitted its brilliancy.

These are all highly eloquent descriptions of a golden race whose mode of being can now *only* be interpreted in spiritual terms. But the latter essay continues with a description of the decadence that resulted when the way of the Tao was eventually forsaken:

When we arrive at the decadent age, we find that men dug into the mountains for precious stones. They wrought metal and jade into cunning vessels and broke open oysters in search of pearls: they melted brass and iron; the whole of nature withered under the exploitation. They ripped open the pregnant and slew the young, untimely (in order to get skins and furs). The Chilin, as a result, did not visit the land. They broke down nests and despoiled birds that had not lain, so that the phoenix no longer hovered around. They drilled wood for fire: they piled up timber to make verandas and balustrades: they burnt forests to drive out game and drained the waters for fish. In spite of this, the furniture at the service of the people was not enough for their use, whilst the luxuries of the rulers were abundant. Thus, the world of life partially failed and things miscarried so that the larger half of creation failed of fruition.

The classes made mounds and built on high grounds: they fertilized their land and sowed their corn: they dug the land for wells, to drink from, and opened up irrigation channels, for their enrichment. They laid foundations for their cities, so that they were munitioned. Captured wild beasts were domesticated: thus, there was grievous rupture of the Yin and Yang, and the succession of the four seasons failed. Thunder-bolts wrought havoc, and hailstones fell with violence. Noxious miasma and untimely hoarfrosts fell unceasingly, resulting in atrophy and the failure of nature to bear abundantly. Luxuriant grass and thick brushwood were cut down in order to get land. They cut down the jungle in order to grow ears of corn. The plants and trees that died before germination, flowering and bearing fruit, were innumerable.

Does this message of the fall of our forgotten race strike a cord as it reaches out to us across the millennia?

THE RACE OF GOLD

Whenever the idea of a golden age is discussed the primary reference is to classical Greek tradition, although as with India this tends to place it within the context of multiple ages that we will examine in the next chapter. But this is what one of their earliest historians, Hesiod, had to say about it in the middle of the eighth century BCE in his *Works and Days*:[14]

> The race of men that the immortals who dwell on Olympus made first of all was of gold. They were in the time of Kronos, when he was king in heaven; and they lived like gods, with carefree heart, remote from toil and misery. Wretched old age did not affect them either, but with hands and feet ever unchanged they enjoyed themselves in feasting, beyond all ills, and they died as if overcome by sleep. All good things were theirs, and the grain-

giving soil bore its fruits of its own accord in unstinted plenty, while they at their leisure harvested their fields in contentment amid abundance. Since the earth covered up that race, they have been divine spirits by great Zeus' design, good spirits on the face of the earth, watchers over mortal men, bestowers of wealth: such is the kingly honor that they received.

This theme persisted in Greek literature for nearly a thousand years, with Ovid repeating it in *Metamorphosis* at the start of the first century:[15]

Golden was that first age which unconstrained,
With heart and soul, obedient to no law,
Gave honor to good faith and righteousness.
No punishment they knew, no fear; they read
No penalties engraved on plates of bronze;
No suppliant throng with dread beheld their judge;
No judges had they then, but lived secure.
No pine had yet, on its high mountain felled,
Descended to the sea to find strange lands afar;
Men knew no shores except their own.
No battlements their cities yet embraced,
No trumpets straight, no horns of sinuous brass,
No sword, no helmet then – no need of arms;
The world untroubled lived in leisured ease.

These Greek accounts are also similar to some Indian compositions in their somewhat prosaic tone, and the original spiritual message seems to have been left behind. Nevertheless Hesiod's description of how the golden race went on to become 'divine spirits' hints at it. There is also a basic Greek flood myth, in one version of which the Titan Prometheus is punished for stealing the gift of fire from the gods and giving it to the human race, as a result of which he instructs his son Deucalion to build a boat so that he might survive along with his wife Pyrrha.[16] Meanwhile other versions of this myth are more consistent with the theme of human sinfulness generally.

Moving north in direction and forwards in time, Snorri Sturluson's *Edda* is one of the earliest surviving compilations of Scandinavian tradition, dating to the beginning of the thirteenth century. Although it is extremely difficult to follow, the first part, 'The Deluding of Gylfi', contains a clear reference to a golden age. It describes how their chief god Odin set up his temple in Asgard; how everything within it was made of gold; and how he 'saw over the whole world and what everyone was doing, and he understood everything he saw'.[17] This latter seems to be a surviving reference to the 'awareness' that we encounter in other traditions from around the world but unfortunately, again, it is about the only vestige of a spiritual message that remains.[18]

THE DIVINE ATLANTEANS

Although the bulk of the classical Greek writers failed to retain the original spiritual message of the golden age, there is one notable exception: the celebrated philosopher Plato. Revisionists have spent a great deal of time analyzing his *Timaeus* and *Critias* dialogues, written in the fourth century BCE, because they contain a detailed description of the location and layout of Atlantis – a subject to which we will return in Part 2. Much less well known yet arguably far more important, at least for our current purposes, are the passages at the very end of *Critias*, in which he provides a detailed description of the nature of the Atlantean people. Although it actually stops in mid-sentence, apparently because he was getting old and suddenly decided to switch to his last book, the *Laws*, what a revelation it is:[19]

For many generations, so long as the divine element in their nature survived, they obeyed the laws and loved the divine to which they were akin. They retained a certain greatness of mind, and treated the vagaries of fortune and one another with wisdom and forbearance, as they reckoned that qualities of character were far more important than their present prosperity. So they bore the burden of their wealth and possessions lightly, and did not let their high standard of living intoxicate them or make them lose their self-control, but saw soberly and clearly that all these things flourish only on a soil of common goodwill and individual character, and if pursued too eagerly and overvalued destroy themselves and morality with them. So long as these principles and their divine nature remained unimpaired the prosperity which we have described continued to grow.

But when the divine element in them became weakened by frequent admixture with mortal stock, and their human traits became predominant, they ceased to be able to carry their prosperity with moderation. To the perceptive eye the depth of their degeneration was clear enough, but to those whose judgment of true happiness is defective they seemed, in their pursuit of unbridled ambition and power, to be at the height of their fame and fortune. And the god of gods, Zeus, who reigns by law, and whose eye can see such things, when he perceived the wretched state of this admirable stock decided to punish them and reduce them to order by discipline.

He accordingly summoned all the gods to his own most glorious abode, which stands at the centre of the universe and looks out over the whole realm of change, and when they had assembled addressed them...

Whatever we may think of the Atlantis myth itself, how can we ask for a clearer elucidation of our main theme of a highly spiritual, antediluvian race who became debased? It has often been suggested that Plato spent a number of years in the company of Egyptian priests who initiated him into their sacred mysteries, and that his writings were a coded 'story' version of what he learned – coded because, like other initiates, he was not allowed to reveal the full extent of his knowledge to the common people. Whether or not this is the case, this final passage appears to provide an extremely clear and lucid account of the nature and fate of our forgotten race. In fact there is a strong argument that any coding and fabrication applies far more to the prosaic details of Plato's account of Atlantis, that is its location and layout, than to its spiritual content.

The only possible criticism would be of the idea that the original Atlanteans' divine nature was diluted by 'admixture with mortal stock', suggesting they were somehow a different order of divine being rather than mortal humans imbued with a high degree of spiritual awareness. But as we have seen this was something of a confusing and grey area for many early writers who seem to have forgotten the real, underlying, spiritual dynamics of what they were describing.

CONCLUSION

In chapter 2 we briefly considered and argued against a purely psycho-materialist interpretation of the flood tradition. But we must now do the same for the broader theme of a golden age that came to an end. Of course it is easy to suggest that this stems from the reactionary and arguably innate human tendency to view the past through rose-tinted spectacles, and to hark back to simpler times before progress ruined everything. To some extent the idea of a golden age is also consistent with the cyclical worldview that will come more into play in the next chapter, whereby all things are born or created and then degenerate until they are destroyed or die. Perhaps we could even see in these traditions a relatively simplistic attempt to account for how evil entered the world – especially when so many people even today are troubled by the apparent conundrum of how an all-powerful God could allow terrible things to happen.

There is also the possibility that the psychology of politics and control fuelled these traditions, just as it did the separation of God and man as we saw in chapter 2. If common people acted as their priests or shaman told them to, in accordance with whatever 'divine laws' they deemed appropriate for that culture and that time, they would recreate the golden age. If not, and they continued with their debased ways, they too would ultimately be destroyed. Indeed this is merely a more collective alternative to the personal threat of a hellish realm. What is more, this time psycho-materialists do not need to dismiss the composers of these texts as simplistic; instead they can assert that their attempts to use a religious or spiritual message to exert control over the masses were ingenious and imaginative.

There is much to be said for these alternatives, and they surely do have *a* part to play. Nevertheless there is one overriding argument against them, and that is again the depth of spiritual and esoteric wisdom displayed in at least some of these texts and traditions that have been less ravaged by editorial distortions. Psycho-materialist interpretations can only work off the assumption that any underlying spirituality within them is complete nonsense, whereas our prima facie approach is to place them in what is arguably their correct context of a Rational Spiritual worldview.

That being said we have now collated a significant body of evidence that there was a time when humankind possessed a high degree of awareness and adopted a simple and predominantly spiritual approach to life. Indeed we have now come nearly full circle around the globe in our review of these traditions, with the exception that we have yet to discuss the indigenous American variants. But we will find in the next chapter that they too strongly exhibit this theme.

5

WORLD AGES AND UNIVERSAL CYCLES

The theme of multiple world eons exists in a number of cultures and can be split into two main categories, although these sometimes overlap. On the one hand we have the world *ages* traditions that are most obviously found in ancient Greece, Scandinavia and the Americas, which tend to be relatively unstructured. On the other we have the world *cycle* traditions found primarily in the East that are based on regulated long term cycles.

We will examine each in turn and then consider how they can best be interpreted, and whether any aspects of them provide any sort of support for the themes already developed.

OF SILVER, BRONZE AND IRON

We have already seen that Greek traditions are best known for their descriptions of multiple world ages and, for example, Hesiod's account continues from the previous chapter's description of a golden age by recording four further races of humankind that succeeded it. As usual we will look at the extract in full to try to obtain a proper perspective:[1]

> A second race after that, much inferior, the dwellers on Olympus made of silver. It resembled the golden one neither in body nor in disposition. For a hundred years a boy would stay in the care of his mother, playing childishly at home; but after reaching adolescence and the appointed span of youthful manhood, they lived but a little time, and in suffering, because of their witlessness. For they could not restrain themselves from crimes against each other, and they would not serve the immortals or sacrifice on the sacred altars of the blessed ones, as is laid down for men in their various homelands. They were put away by Zeus son of Kronos, angry because they

did not offer honor to the blessed gods who occupy Olympus. Since the earth covered up this race in its turn, they have been called the mortal blessed below, second in rank, but still they too have honor.

Then Zeus the father made yet a third race of men, of bronze, not like the silver in anything. Out of ash-trees he made them, a terrible and fierce race, occupied with the woeful works of Ares and with acts of violence, no eaters of corn, their stern hearts being of adamant; unshapen hulks, with great strength and indescribable arms growing from their shoulders above their stalwart bodies. They had bronze armor, bronze houses, and with bronze they labored, as dark iron was not available. They were laid low by their own hands, and they went to chill Hades' house of decay leaving no names: mighty though they were, dark death got them, and they left the bright sunlight.

After the earth covered up this race too, Zeus son of Kronos made yet a fourth one upon the rich-pastured earth, a more righteous and noble one, the godly race of the heroes who are called demigods, our predecessors on the boundless earth. And as for them, ugly war and fearful fighting destroyed them, some below seven-gated Thebes, the Cadmean country, as they battled for Oedipus' flocks, and others it led in ships over the great abyss of the sea to Troy on account of lovely-haired Helen. There some of them were engulfed by the consummation of death, but to some Zeus the father, son of Kronos, granted a life and home apart from men, and settled them at the ends of the earth. These dwell with carefree heart in the Isles of the Blessed Ones, beside deep-swirling Oceanus: fortunate Heroes, for whom the grain-giving soil bears its honey-sweet fruits thrice a year.

Would that I were not then among the fifth men, but either dead earlier or born later! For now it is a race of iron; and they will never cease from toil and misery by day or night, in constant distress, and the gods will give them harsh troubles. Nevertheless, even they shall have good mixed with ill. Yet Zeus will destroy this race of men also, when at birth they turn out grey at the temples. Nor will father be like children nor children to father, nor guest to host or comrade to comrade, nor will a brother be friendly as in former times. Soon they will cease to respect their ageing parents, and will rail at them with harsh words, the ruffians, in ignorance of the gods' punishment; nor are they likely to repay their ageing parents for their nurture. Fist-law men; one will sack another's town, and there will be no thanks for the man who abides by his oath or for the righteous or worthy man, but instead they will honor the miscreant and the criminal. Law and decency will be in fists. The villain will do his better down by telling crooked tales, and will swear his oath upon it. Men in their misery will everywhere be dogged by the evil commotions of that Envy who exults in misfortune with a face full of hate. Then verily off to Olympus from the wide-pathed earth, veiling their fair faces with white robes, Decency and Moral Disapproval will go to join the family of the immortals, abandoning humankind; those grim woes will remain for mortal men, and there will be no help against evil.

Like most of the other world age traditions we will encounter this heady concoction is not easy to interpret. We can see that the silver race is to some extent credited with the lengthy lifespans that we encountered in the main biblical list of antediluvian patriarchs, which is a common feature of many traditions. Their successors, the bronze race, appear to reflect the fixation with a race of giants that, as we also saw earlier, came to infect the Judaic traditions of the offspring of the fallen angels, the Nephilim. After these apparently regressive races we have a somewhat more progressive shift to the 'demigods', who were 'more righteous and noble' yet still manage to perish through 'ugly war and fearful fighting'. Finally we come to the iron race, apparently our own, which appears destined to be as debased as any of its predecessors.

What are we to make of this? Probably not a great deal. Although it is a relatively early text it appears to be heavily infected by distortions that we know have little basis in reality. The silver race does exhibit the spiritual debasement we have already encountered on numerous occasions, but apart from that Hesiod's account provides little credible support for the idea that multiple races of humans have existed on earth, each in turn destroyed. In fact the clear message that these races were 'created' makes this account in some respects comparable with the multiple-creation-of-man traditions that we will consider in chapter 7 – albeit that in these, by contrast, the last-created race tends to be the most perfect.

Ovid's much later account contains a number of major differences.[2] The silver and bronze races are dealt with swiftly and do not differ substantially from Hesiod. The demigods are then omitted, which leaves a clear path for the even more regressive iron race that is no longer our own, as in Hesiod, but whose members are this time actually destroyed for their debased behavior. As a result there is another race thereafter, unnamed but presumably our own, which unfortunately is just as bad. Of course it could be argued that if we omit the silver race from this account it is consistent with our main themes, in that we have a golden age followed by a developing debasement that ends in the destruction of the iron race, with our own modern race then arguably repeating the same mistakes. But it is just as easy to maintain there is so much confusion in these classical Greek traditions of multiple world ages that for our current purposes they deserve little credence.[3]

SOLON'S SOJOURN

Just as in the previous chapter Plato takes a somewhat different tack from the other Greek traditions when he discusses the theme of world ages. The *Timaeus* and *Critias* dialogues remain his most relevant works for this, but first we need to understand their structure because it is somewhat confusing and often poorly explained. Although, unusually for Plato, each is primarily a monologue by the two title characters, *Timaeus* commences in his more usual style with a dialogue between these two, Socrates and Hermocrates. It opens with Critias describing a world age tradition told to him by his grandfather, also called Critias, who in turn received it from Solon. This is the celebrated Platonic figure who, with echoes of the Mesopotamian sages, is described as 'the wisest of the seven wise men', and here we find him in the company of some Egyptian priests at Sais on the Nile delta:[4]

> And a very old priest said to him, 'Oh Solon, Solon, you Greeks are all children, and there's no such thing as an old Greek.'
>
> 'What do you mean by that?' enquired Solon.
>
> 'You are all young in mind', came the reply: 'you have no belief rooted in old tradition and no knowledge hoary with age. And the reason is this. There have been and will be many different calamities to destroy humankind, the greatest of them by fire and water, lesser ones by countless other means. Your own story of how Phaethon, child of the sun, harnessed his father's chariot, but was unable to guide it along his father's course and so burnt up things on the earth and was himself destroyed by a thunderbolt, is a mythical version of the truth that there is at long intervals a variation in the course of the heavenly bodies and a consequent widespread destruction by fire of things on the earth.'

Plato is clearly suggesting that multiple catastrophes have plagued the earth, and that these occur in cycles related to variations 'in the course of the heavenly bodies'. At this point it will be useful to introduce the phenomenon of precession, in as much as this could be what he is referring to. Because the polar axis around which the earth rotates has a wobble akin to that of a spinning top, the stars appear to move in the sky over prolonged periods.[5] This rate of precession changes slightly over time, and currently it is estimated that it takes around 2150 years for the earth to move through each of the 12 zodiacal constellations, producing a complete cycle of around 25,765 years. This is why people refer to us moving out of the Age of Pisces into the Age of Aquarius, although the point at which one age ends and another begins relies on rough observation alone and cannot be accurately pinpointed.[6] But even if Plato did mean to tie his concept of world ages into the precessional cycle there is no obvious mechanism by which the latter might produce regular catastrophes. We should also note that these timescales are orders of magnitude shorter than those of the Eastern world *cycle* traditions we will consider shortly, which usually stretch to millions or even billions of years.

In any case this passage is followed by another in which the Egyptian priest describes how they managed to preserve far more ancient records than the Greeks:

'On such occasions those who live in the mountains or in high and dry places suffer more than those living by rivers or by the sea; as for us, the Nile, our own regular savior, is freed to preserve us in this emergency. When on the other hand the gods purge the earth with a deluge, the herdsmen and shepherds in the mountains escape, but those living in the cities in your part of the world are swept into the sea by the rivers; here water never falls on the land from above either then or at any other time, but rises up naturally from below. This is the reason why our traditions here are the oldest preserved; though it is true that in all places where excessive cold or heat does not prevent it human beings are always to be found in larger or smaller numbers.

But in our temples we have preserved from earliest times a written record of any great or splendid achievement or notable event which has come to our ears whether it occurred in your part of the world or here or anywhere else; whereas with you and others, writing and the other necessities of civilization have only just been developed when the periodic scourge of the deluge descends, and spares none but the unlettered and uncultured, so that you have to begin again like children in complete ignorance of what happened in our part of the world or in yours in early times.

So these genealogies of your own people which you were just recounting are little more than children's stories. You remember only one deluge, though there have been many, and you do not know that the finest and best race of men that ever existed lived in your country; you and your fellow citizens are descended from the few survivors that remained, but you know nothing about it because so many succeeding generations left no record in writing. For before the greatest of all destructions by water, Solon, the city that is now Athens was preeminent in war and conspicuously the best governed in every way, its achievements and constitution being the finest of any in the world of which we have heard tell.'

Apart from Plato's clear political message of the preeminence of the earliest Athenian civilization at the end of this passage, it also shows some interesting parallels to the scenario painted in chapter 3 of who might survive and what might happen after a major flood catastrophe. These ideas are echoed further in a later reprise in *Critias*:[7]

> Their names have been preserved but what they did has been forgotten because of the destruction of their successors and the long lapse of time. For as we said before, the survivors of the destruction were an unlettered mountain race who had just heard the names of the rulers of the land but knew little of their achievements. They were glad enough to give their names to their own children, but they knew nothing of the virtues and institutions of their predecessors, except for a few hazy reports; for many generations they and their children were short of bare necessities, and their minds and thoughts were occupied with providing for them, to the neglect of their earlier history and tradition. For an interest in the past and historical research came only when communities had leisure and when men were already provided with the necessities of life. This is how the names but not the achievements of these early generations came to be preserved.

Returning to *Timaeus*, Plato continues from where we left off by providing a clue as to when the 'greatest of all destructions by water' actually occurred:

> Solon was astonished at what he heard and eagerly begged the priests to describe to him in detail the doings of these citizens of the past. 'I will gladly do so, Solon', replied the priest, 'both for your sake and your city's, but chiefly in gratitude to the Goddess to whom it has fallen to bring up and educate both your country and ours – yours first, when she took over your seed from Earth and Hephaestus, ours a thousand years later. The age of our institutions is given in our sacred records as eight thousand years, and the citizens whose laws and whose finest achievement I will now briefly describe to you therefore lived nine thousand years ago; we will go through their history in detail later on at leisure, when we can consult the records.'

Of course many revisionists have seized on this and, assuming that if Solon really did visit Egypt it would have been around 500 BCE, suggested the flood must have occurred some time before 9500 BCE. Can we take this at all literally? It is difficult to say. There is no clear psychological or symbolic interpretation of these numbers and, even if many of the specifics of the Atlantis and early Athenian traditions were fabricated by Plato, it does not mean that the general theme of a debased race being destroyed by flood, perhaps around that time, can have no basis in fact. But we will have to reserve judgment until we examine the geological evidence in Part 2.

To sum up, Plato's general theme of multiple catastrophes seems to be contextually quite different from his description of the divine Atlanteans who were destroyed in a single major catastrophe. Indeed to the extent that their context is more cyclic it is perhaps difficult to interpret them as having any real historical value, with the exception of a possible *sporadic* link between the precessional cycle and catastrophes that we will examine in the epilogue.

DEPARTURE FROM TAO

We saw in the previous chapter that the Chinese Taoists had a flourishing tradition of a golden age that was terminated by debasement. We find hints that this too is mixed in with a tradition of world ages, for example from Donald Mackenzie in his *Myths of China and Japan* published in 1923 – even if his association of it with Indian world *cycle* traditions is probably incorrect:[8]

> Here we touch on the doctrine of the World's Ages. Like the Indians of the Brahmanic period, the Chinese Taoists believed that the first age was a perfect one, and that humankind gradually deteriorated.

This is to some extent substantiated by a brief passage from the *Tao Teh King*:[9]

> In the highest antiquity, the people did not know that there were rulers. In the next age they loved and praised them. In the next they feared them; in the next they despised them.

Accounts such as these that do not explicitly involve multiple and especially cyclic catastrophes could be argued to support the proposition that there was a gradual increase in debasement over a prolonged period. But it is difficult to remove them completely from the more general global context of catastrophic endings to each age.

THE FOUR WORLDS

The most abundant sources of world age traditions are indigenous American cultures, every one of which appears to have some sort of variant thereof. The finest example of the North American genre comes from the Hopi of northern Arizona. Although never written down in antiquity their traditions were handed down orally from generation to generation for centuries, and kept a closely guarded secret from the outside world. That is until 1963 when the elders allowed them to be recorded for the first time by

Frank Waters, who had since childhood cultivated close ties with various indigenous cultures. Working from the information provided by 30 elders, and especially Oswald White Bear Fredericks, his *Book of the Hopi* has gained widespread acclaim. Its contents in general demonstrate the deep erudition and spirituality of these people, and anyone who reads it must surely question the long-held view that indigenous tribes around the world are backward or primitive, and that modern technological progress makes us superior.

The Hopi commence by describing the creation of the earth by the god Sotuknang, acting under instructions from the all-powerful creator Taiowa, and then of the first humans by the creator goddess Spider Woman – which themes we will return to in chapters 7 and 8 respectively. They then proceed to describe how the human race multiplied and spread out over the earth during the first 'world', Topkela:[10]

> The First People knew no sickness. Not until evil entered the world did persons get sick in the body or head... they understood themselves... were pure and happy... they felt as one and understood one another without talking.

This is yet another revelation of the 'awareness' of our earliest ancestors, this time including the concept of telepathy. But the golden age did not last:

> Gradually there were those who forgot the commands of Sotuknang and the Spider Woman to respect their Creator. More and more they used the vibratory centers of their bodies solely for earthly purposes, forgetting that their primary purpose was to carry out the plan of Creation... It was then that animals drew away from people... In the same way, people began to divide and draw away from one another – those of different races and languages, then those who remembered the plan of Creation and those who did not.

We can see that this account is even more explicit in its confirmation that the debasement was based on a loss of spiritual roots that departed from the 'plan of creation'. In any case, as the situation worsened Sotuknang decided to destroy the first race by fire and volcano, but not before he had selected an untainted group to survive and father a new race. These were secreted under the earth with the 'ant people'. Then Sotuknang created the second world, Tokpa, 'changing its form completely, putting land where the water was and water where the land had been'. When the second race first emerged they 'multiplied rapidly, spreading... even to the other side of the world'. But 'this did not matter, for they were so close together in spirit they could see and talk to each other from the centre on top of their head'. Ultimately, however, they too fell into wicked ways:

> More and more they traded for things they didn't need, and the more goods they got, the more they wanted... they forgot to sing joyful praises to the Creator and soon began to sing praises for the goods they bartered and stored. Before long it happened as it had to happen. The people began to quarrel and fight, and then wars between villages began.

We can see that this second debasement clearly emphasizes the dominance of materialism, and again Sotuknang was forced to destroy the world except for a chosen few survivors hidden under the ground. This time the Hopi's description of the destruction seems to suggest a monumental shift of the earth's axis:

> The world, with no one to control it, teetered off balance, spun around crazily, then rolled over twice. Mountains plunged into seas with a great splash, seas and lakes sloshed over the land; and as the world spun through cold and lifeless space it froze into solid ice.

For many years the earth lay frozen and dormant, and the survivors remained underground. Finally Sotuknang created the third world, Kuskurza, and after they emerged the third race 'multiplied in such numbers and advanced so rapidly that they created big cities, countries, a whole civilization'. But we can now guess what happened next:

> More and more of them became wholly occupied with their own earthly plans. Some of them, of course, retained the wisdom granted them upon their Emergence. With this wisdom they understood that the farther they proceeded on the Road of Life and the more they developed, the harder it was. That was why their world was destroyed every so often to give them a fresh start... some of them made a *patuwvota* (shield made of hide) and with their creative power made it fly through the air. On this many of the people flew to a big city, attacked it, and returned so fast no one knew where they came from. Soon the people of many cities and countries were making *patuwvotas* and flying on them to attack one another. So corruption and war came to the Third World as it had to the others.

Once again Sotuknang called for destruction, this time by flood, although a select group was again to be saved, this time by being sealed inside hollow reeds:

> He loosed the waters upon the earth. Waves higher than mountains rolled in upon the land. Continents broke asunder and sank beneath the seas. And

still the rains fell, the waves rolled in.

When the survivors emerged into the fourth world, Tuwaqachi, all they could see was water. Having crossed a number of seas and islands, heading eastward, they arrived at the land in which Sotuknang wanted them to settle. At this point he instructed them to look west and south, at the way they had come, and then he made all the islands disappear:

'I have washed away even the footprints of your Emergence: the stepping-stones which I left for you. Down on the bottom of the seas lie all the proud cities, the flying *patuwvotas,* and the worldly treasures corrupted with evil, and those people who found no time to sing praises to the Creator from the tops of their hills. But the day will come, if you preserve the memory and the meaning of your Emergence, when these stepping-stones will emerge again to prove the truth you speak... What you choose will determine if this time you can carry out the plan of Creation on it or whether it must in time be destroyed too. Now you will separate and go different ways to claim all the earth for the Creator. Each group of you will follow your own star until it stops. There you will settle. Now I must go. But you will have help from the proper deities, from your good spirits. Just keep your own doors open and always remember what I have told you.'

According to the Hopi this is the world in which we now live. There is much in this narrative that is clearly symbolic and cannot be taken literally, for example the subterranean ant people. The apparently advanced technology of the third race too can probably be taken with a pinch of salt, as we will see in Part 2. But an interesting aspect of the Hopi world age tradition is that each time the race that emerges is 'given a fresh start' and so has its spirituality or awareness initially restored. Does any of this provide us with any genuine support for our main themes of a golden age followed by debasement and destruction? We are given no timescales for any of this, so for now let us reserve judgment.

THE FIVE SUNS

If we turn to Central America, and specifically to the Aztecs of Mexico, we have a number of texts written in alphabetic script that date to the middle of the sixteenth century, after the Spanish conquest. The primary source for their world age traditions is the three-part *Codex Chimalpopoca,* translated by John Bierhorst in his *History and Mythology of the Aztecs.* One part, the *Leyenda de los Soles* or 'Legend of the Suns', is summarized in Figure 2:[11]

These periods are actually extremely short and fall well within our known historical epoch. The first age apparently began 2513 years before its composition in 1558 – that is in 956 BCE – so, given that the first four ages total 2028 years, we would have been 485 years into the current age even by the time it was written. If the other periods are anything to go by the volcanic destruction promised for our current race should have occurred at the latest by the middle of the eighteenth century. Of course 364, the length in years of the wind age, is roughly the number of days in a year, while the length of every age is a multiple of 52, the number of weeks in the year but also the length of a Mayan century as we will shortly see. What is more the length of the second and third ages combined is the same as that of the first and of the fourth. So we can probably assume that these numbers have some calendrical rather than factual significance.

Age/Sun	Details
Jaguar	Lasted 676 (13 x 52) years. This age ended with all the people being devoured by jaguars.
Wind	Lasted 364 (7 x 52) years. This age ended when everything was swept away by the wind.
Rain	Lasted 312 (6 x 52) years. This age ended when everything was destroyed by a rain of fire.
Water	Lasted 676 (13 x 52) years. This age ended when everything was destroyed by flood; 'the skies came falling down... all the mountains disappeared'.
Movement	Because of its name, it is assumed that an earthquake will bring this, our current age, to an end.

Figure 2: The Aztec Legend of the Suns

Another section of the codex, the *Anales de Cuauhtitlan*, is even less revealing in that it contains no durations and, although the details are broadly the same, the ages are in the different order of water, jaguar, rain, wind and movement.[12] Meanwhile in a separate source called the *Historia de Colhuacan y de Mexico*, discussed by Eric Thompson in his *Maya Hieroglyphic Writing*, the four preceding ages once again total 2028 years.[13]

Some researchers have found it tempting to speculate that the length of these ages can be tied into the phenomenon of precession, but no argument to this effect really stands up.[14] What is more a further Mexican source known as the *Codex Rios* – also referred to as *Codex 3738* and *Codex*

Vaticanus A – provides completely different numbers, with each age lasting 4008, 4010, 4801 and 5042 years respectively for a total of 17,861 years.[15] This text also contains the following interesting passage about the survivors of the first destruction by flood:[16]

> Others say that not only the two inside the tree survived the flood, but that other people found refuge in certain caves, and after the flood they came out and they parted from each other spreading all over the world, and the following populations worshipped them as Gods, each in his nation.

This is very much a part of the postcatastrophe survivor scenario put forward in chapter 3. But the remainder of this text contains a number of superimposed Christian distortions, including an early race of giants, a 'tower of Babel' and a 'virgin birth'.

Moving down to South America, the world age traditions of the Peruvian Incas were recorded by a number of their own scholars in the sixteenth century. They are summarized as follows by Hartley Burr Alexander in his Latin American volume of *The Mythology of All Races* – a monumental thirteen-volume work dating to the early part of the twentieth century, which is an invaluable source of traditions from all over the world:[17]

> Molina, Cieza de Leon, Sarmiento, Huaman Poma tell of the making of sun and moon, and of the generations of men, associating this creation with the lake of Titicaca, its islands, and its neighborhood. Viracocha is almost universally represented as the creator, and the story follows the main plot of the genesis narratives known to the civilized nations of both Americas – a succession of world eons, each ending in cataclysm. As told by Huaman Poma, five such ages had preceded that in which he lived. The first was an age of Viracochas, an age of gods, of holiness, of life without death... the second was an age of skin-clad giants, the Huari Runa, or 'Indigenes', worshippers of Viracocha; third came the age of Puron Runa, or 'Common Men', living without culture; fourth, that of the Auca Runa, 'Warriors', and fifth that of the Inca rule, ended by the coming of the Spaniards. As related by Sarmiento the first age was that of a sunless world inhabited by a race of giants, who, owing to the sin of disobedience, were cataclysmically destroyed.

Although we can see that these various Central and South American traditions do contain a degree of support for our main themes, in general they are inconsistent even amongst each other, relatively brief, highly symbolic and have been significantly distorted by intrusive Christian influences.

COUNTING LONG

So far we have only made passing reference to the celebrated Mayan culture that flourished in Central America from Mexico right across to the Yucatán. They too have a world ages tradition of sorts contained in their most famous surviving text, the *Popol Vuh*, but it slants much more towards the multiple-creation-of-man theme so we will not discuss it until chapter 7. In the meantime this culture represents a point of crossover between the world age and world cycle traditions, because the Maya also developed an extremely sophisticated calendar that incorporated the notion of long-term cycles. Unlike many of their counterparts in other parts of the Americas, the Maya had an extensive literature and a sophisticated form of pictographic writing that used distinctive glyphs. Three main hieroglyphic texts survived the Spanish conquest in the early sixteenth century, during which almost all copies of such texts were avidly sought out and destroyed, and they are named after the cities in whose institutions they reside:[18]

- The *Dresden Codex* mainly contains almanacs of complex and accurate astronomical and calendrical data, for example on lunar cycles and the heliacal rising of Venus.

- The *Madrid Codex*, also known as the *Codex Tro-Cortesianus* and made up of several parts including the *Troano Codex*, merely contains divinations.

- The *Paris Codex* shares similarities with the others but is not fully translatable because incomplete.

The *Dresden Codex* is thought to date to the twelfth century because its latest dates for astronomical calculations are for this period, while the other two appear to be somewhat later compositions. The only other Mayan texts of note are the *Books of Chilam Balam*, various versions of which have been found because each town had its own copy. Although they are in alphabetic script they are similar to the codices, but are somewhat distorted by being interwoven with later Christian infusions.

From all these written texts and various inscriptions on steles and temples, scholars have been able to establish the details of the Mayan calendrical system. Their short-count calendar had two types of year – a sacred one of 260 days called a tzolkin, and a normal one of 365 days. Any given day was identified by both systems, so that the calendar lasted 52 years or 73 tzolkins before it repeated itself, and this was the Mayan equivalent of a century. It was therefore supplemented by a long-count calendar in which 20 days or kins made up a 20-day month or uinal; 18 uinals made up a 360-day year or tun; 20 tuns made up a katun of approximately 20 years; 20 katuns made up a baktun of 394.3 years; and longer cycles of 13 and 20 baktuns are also referenced, representing 5125 and 7886 years respectively.[19] It is because the long-count calendar is generally reckoned to have a starting date of 11 August 3114 BCE under our Gregorian system that some people have focused on the start of a new era after 13 baktuns have passed, that is on 21 December 2012, as such a key date. There is also much discussion about whether Mayan cycles are terminated by catastrophes, and all these are subjects to which we will return in the epilogue.

The Mayan system leads us neatly on to the most complex world cycle traditions of all – those of the Far East.

DAYS AND NIGHTS OF BRAHMA

The Indian concept of world cycles does not really come to the fore in the Vedic literature, although it would surely be a mistake to suggest that it was newly created in the Hindu epics in which it is most clearly expounded. This time we will concentrate on the *Mahabharata*, which contains 18 main books or 'parvas' including the celebrated 'Bhagavad-Gita'. The full epic was meticulously translated by Chandra Ray over a period of ten years at the end of the nineteenth century and in book 3, the 'Vana Parva', we find the following:[20]

> After the dissolution of the universe, all this wonderful creation again comes into life. Four thousand years have been said to constitute the Krita Yuga. Its dawn also, as well as its eve, hath been said to comprise four hundred years. The Treta Yuga is said to comprise three thousand years, and its dawn, as well as its eve, is said to comprise three hundred years. The Yuga that comes next is called Dwapara, and it hath been computed to consist of two thousand years. Its dawn, as well as its eve, is said to comprise two hundred years. The next Yuga, called Kali, is said to comprise one thousand years, and its dawn, as well as eve, is said to comprise one hundred years. Know, O king, that the duration of the dawn is the same as that of the eve of a Yuga. And after the Kali Yuga is over, the Krita Yuga comes again. A cycle of the Yugas then comprises a period of twelve thousand years. A full thousand of such cycles would constitute a day of Brahma. O tiger among men, when all this universe is withdrawn and ensconced within its home the Creator himself, that disappearance of all things is called by the learned to be Universal Destruction.

With echoes of our main themes except in a clearly cyclical context, the text goes on to describe in great detail how each age becomes successively less enlightened and more debased; how depravity overtakes humankind toward the end of the 'dark' kali age; how it is destroyed by drought, then fire, then flood; and how the new 'golden' krita age then dawns again.[21]

Later in book 12, the 'Santi Parva', we find the same details but with more added.[22] First we are told that 'a year is equal to a day and night of the gods', which Hindu scholars regard as a 'divine year' of 360 'human years' for reasons we will come to shortly. We are then told that:

> With the commencement of Brahman's day the universe begins to start into life. During the period of universal dissolution the Creator sleeps, having recourse to yoga-meditation. When the period of slumber expires, He awakes. That then which is Brahman's day extends for a thousand such Yugas. His night also extends for a thousand similar Yugas.

In the succeeding passages we are given detailed descriptions of the processes of creation and destruction at the beginning and end of each day and night of Brahma. So under this schema humanity on earth is wiped out to start again at the end of each four-yuga cycle lasting 4.3 *million* human years, while the universe as a whole is completely 'reabsorbed' back into its primal state at the end of each day of Brahma lasting 4.3 *billion* human years, after which it lies dormant for an equivalent period.

Age or Yuga	Dawn	Age	Twilight	Total	Total
				Divine Years	Normal Years
Krita	400	4000	400	4800	1,728,000
Treta	300	3000	300	3600	1,296,000
Dwapara	200	2000	200	2400	864,000
Kali	100	1000	100	1200	432,000
Maha				12,000	4,320,000
Manvantara (approx)				0.86 million	0.3 billion
Kalpa or Day/Night of Brahma (1000 maha yugas/14 manvantaras)				12 million	4.32 billion
Year of Brahma (720 kalpas)				8.64 billion	3.11 trillion
Life of Brahma (72,000 kalpas)				864 billion	311 trillion

Figure 3: The Hindu World Cycles

If we now turn to the later *Puranas* that were compiled mainly in the middle of the first millennium, again there are 18 major works in this group, although most record similar information. Perhaps the best known is the *Vishnu Purana*, and here we find the same cycles but with some new information and also some major amendments.[23] With echoes of other cultures' traditions of races of giants and of longer lifespans, it reports that in each yuga humankind's longevity and stature – as well as virtue – decrease. Then in terms of time cycles it explicitly confirms that each divine year is the equivalent of 360 human years; it introduces new terminology in that a complete cycle of the four yugas is referred to as a maha yuga, and the length of a day or night of Brahma as a kalpa; and it introduces the new concept that each day of Brahma is divided into 14 manvantaras, each of which lasts approximately 71 maha yugas or 308 million years. But the most profound change is the introduction of a *year* of Brahma, made up of 360 days and nights of Brahma, or 720 kalpas, or 3 trillion human years; and of a *life* of Brahma, which is made up of 100 years of Brahma, or 72,000 kalpas, or 311 *trillion* human years. According to the Puranic model, it is only at the end of *this* almost inconceivably long period that complete reabsorption of the universe takes place.

From all this we can piece together the various details in Figure 3. But what are we to make of it all? Arguably to give these cycles any sort of meaningful context we need to split them into two and consider each separately. First we have the yuga or what we might term *world* cycles, but even their time periods are ridiculously lengthy in the context of what we know about human history on earth, even if there was only one cycle. For this reason various modern commentators have attempted to shorten them, with varying degrees of scholarship and success, and even to identify where in the cycles we currently stand. The most important issue is whether or not the years mentioned are normal or divine, because if the former – as suggested by, for example, the Vana Parva – then the time periods become reasonable again. We will return to this issue in the epilogue.

But we must then contend with the fact that they seem to describe how the earth is completely subsumed by the 'waters' at the end of each yuga cycle, leading to the apparently complete annihilation of humanity even if not of earth itself, and its subsequent reemergence in a new krita age with no period of evolutionary development – again, and again, and again. This must surely be seen as going against all the evidence of multiple disciplines, from archaeology through to geology and beyond. Yet we can surely argue that, if the cyclical element is removed, in general they do provide some degree of support for our main themes of a golden age followed by progressive debasement.

We then have the ostensibly separate concept of far longer *universal* cycles that deal with the dissolution and reemergence of the entire universe at the end of a day, year or even life of Brahma. But in the Vana Parva we not only encounter the theme of how the waters subsume the earth at the end of each yuga cycle, but also of the lotus-boy who is the only thing left and whose stomach contains all the potential for reemergence and recreation – remembering that this flower closes its petals at night and draws back into the water, only to reemerge and unfold in the dawn.[24] All this seems to bear more than a passing resemblance to the ideas about the emergence of the universe as a whole that are found not only in Vedic but other origin traditions too, as we will see in chapter 8. Indeed in Ray's translation these passages seem to swap seamlessly between the words *earth* and *universe* with little rhyme or reason. So there seems to be a good deal of overlap between the two sets of cycles, at least in the Vana Parva. Indeed a strong argument can be presented that in fact the yuga *ages* have much more in common with the other *non-cyclical* world age traditions we have discussed, while the concept of *universal cycles* should be seen as entirely separate.

Indeed in theoretical rather than strict calendrical terms these universal cycles themselves are highly significant, as we will shortly see. But what is more *if* the concept of divine years is a late and distortive introduction then a year of Brahma lasts only around 8 billion years, as compared with the best estimate of the current age of the universe of around 14 billion years. We would then at least be in roughly the right area in terms of orders of magnitude.

THE WHEEL OF TIME

We have not yet considered the Jain religion, which emerged in India at about the same time as Buddhism in the latter half of the first millennium BCE, and was of similar influence. Its tradition of world cycles is similar to that of the Hindus that we have just considered, but with an interesting twist. It is described briefly by A Berriedale Keith in his Indian volume of *The Mythology of All Races*:[25]

> To the Jain time is endless and is pictured as a wheel with spokes... normally with twelve, divided into two sets of six, one of which belongs to the avasarpini, or 'descending', and the other to the utsarpin, or 'ascending'.

In the first of these eras good things gradually give place to bad, while in the latter the relation is reversed. Of these eras the fifth 'spoke', or ara, of the avasarpini is that in which we live.

This seems to represent a similar idea to that of the fourteen manvantaras within a day of Brahma, except with only twelve. Moreover we again find that the periods involved are incredibly lengthy, while the theme of progressively reducing lifespans and human stature recurs.[26] Yet the Jain tradition can clearly be differentiated in that it suggests that only the first half of the cycle is one of progressive debasement, while the second half is one of upward spiritual progression. This is an important issue to which we will return shortly.

We might also note that a less specific cyclic theme exists in ancient Egyptian tradition. For example modern Egyptologists John Baines and Geraldine Pinch make the following observation in their essay in *World Mythology*:[27]

> The cosmos would not last forever, the Egyptians believed. The time would come when the creator would grow so weary that he and all his works would dissolve back into chaos. Then the cycle of creation would recommence.

More confusing is the contribution made by the Zoroastrian religion, which dominated the mighty Persian Empire at its height in the first millennium BCE and had a significant influence on the development of Judaism.[28] In their most sacred text, the *Zend Avesta*, we find that their cycle is unique in that it contains only two non-repeated rounds of 12,000 years each; the first is dominated by the benign deity Ahura Mazda and the second by his evil counterpart Angra Mainyu.[29]

CONCLUSION

These different types of traditions can broadly be split into three categories of non-repeating *world ages*, and repeating *world* or even *universal cycles*. We need to look carefully at each in turn because there are a number of different ways of interpreting them. But before we do it will be useful to consider the nature of cycles at the various levels of existence.

The nature of all life at the microcosmic level is cyclical. Individual cells divide and multiply then die off. On a broader scale all lifeforms go through a cycle of death and rebirth. In the case of vegetable life the cycle is physically obvious in the progression from seed to plant to death to rebirth as seed again. With animals, including humans, any spiritual worldview based on some form of recycling or reincarnation of soul energy will see the same sort of pattern occurring on a less physical level. But these cycles do not conform to any fixed time pattern and each one is, in relative terms, of extremely short duration.

If we then jump to the macrocosmic scale of the universe as a whole, modern cosmologists are by no means united on whether the universe operates cyclically. Because there is strong support for the idea that at the fundamental level of nonphysical reality time does not exist at all, some would argue that even the idea of cycles is a nonsense. This might mean there is just one universe that 'just is', or it might imply infinite numbers of universes with no beginning and end all coexisting. In terms of the latter, some would argue that these are only minutely differentiated and play out all variations of any human decision, for example. Meanwhile others concentrate on the idea that they contain all combinations of the three dozen or so 'fundamental constants' like the speed of light that govern their very nature, and ours just happens to be the lucky one in which these are incredibly finely-tuned to the development of physical life. But there is also a strong argument for the idea of a 'metaverse', that is an intelligent, consciousness that underlies a never-ending cycle of progressively evolving universes that build on the experience of what has gone before; and because this is arguably the most philosophically elegant and spiritually pleasing solution it is the one we will be following here.[30] We might refer to it as the 'evolution-by-experience' model.

On that basis it is logical to argue that the primarily Hindu *universal cycle* traditions are describing exactly this process, whereby each universe emerges into manifestation on a huge variety of nonphysical and physical planes, the latter taking the form of galaxies and stars and planets and all the lifeforms that evolve on them. Then, after an immense time span, the whole ensemble dissolves and is reabsorbed back into its primal state. This suggestion will gain even more support when we look at the origin traditions from around the world in chapter 8.

But let us now turn to the *world cycle* traditions of the Hindus and Jains. On the face of it these seem to involve the mesocosm of stars and planets, that is the middle ground between the two extremes of the microcosm of the individual lifeform and the macrocosm of the universe as a whole. Of course it goes against all modern reason to support the idea that physical planets themselves might go through any sort of cycle of repeated creation and destruction, as part of a subcycle within the universal cycle. So how did this distortion come about? It is entirely possible that it resulted from a desire to reflect the microcosm in the macrocosm and at all levels in between, so that the entirely sensible cyclical principles of the two extremes were mistakenly applied to the mesocosm as well. On the other hand its originators may simply have incorrectly merged the authentic themes of human debasement and destruction, and of universal cycles.

There is a more profound interpretation, especially of the Jain cycle of regression-descent then progression-ascent. A Qabalistic take would be that various groups of souls or 'monads' are attached to a particular solar system, and that each group descends through a series of 'incarnations' in progressively less subtle and more physical planes, and then gradually reascends back through these same realms until its members are once again at one with the solar 'logos'.[31] To go somewhat further, we are judging all this in the context of our current scientific understanding of how the universe developed, how time operates and so on and so forth. But if all that is just waiting to be blown apart by new discoveries then the sky is probably the limit in terms of how we reappraise these traditions. For example we might find that somehow there are multiple versions of our solar system existing within the context of the 'current universe', and that these may not be discrete entities but instead may exist concurrently and even have some sort of feedback loop between them. The same may even, of course, be true of multiple universes themselves – even if *not* as an infinite number of only minutely differentiated versions. But we are now in extremely theoretical and mind-stretching territory, and in the context of this work we should probably leave it there.

So what are we to make of the less rigidly cyclical *world age* traditions from Europe and the Americas? We have seen that they do contain a number of clear distortions, sometimes with a late Christian influence. We might conjecture that they too have arisen because somewhere along the line the original themes of universal cycles and debasement and destruction became mixed up and interwoven, although this time the distortion was ameliorated by them reporting only one cycle. On the other hand we have already mentioned that it is now generally accepted that the earth has been rocked by repeated major catastrophes in its history. In particular as we will see in Part 2 the peaks and troughs of the last ice age would have produced significant instability and upheaval on a local, continental and even global scale. So it is just possible that some of these traditions reflect that reality, although when reported the timescales for these multiple destructions tend to be way too short.

In conclusion these various traditions are clearly a minefield of confusion. However it is to be hoped that we have been able to give them some sort of context that does not simply dismiss them all as useless distortions or as purely symbolic. Above all it does seem reasonable to argue that they provide at least some support for our main themes of a golden age followed by debasement and destruction.

6

TAKING ON THE EXPERTS

In each of the last four chapters we have discussed the more obvious psycho-materialist interpretations that could be used to dismiss the idea that the themes we have been considering might have some historical authenticity. But if we now turn specifically to the opinions of the experts in comparative mythology, it is something of a surprise to find they do not have a great deal to say about these important themes, despite the considerable quantity of worldwide detail we can now see exists.

CAMPBELL AND CYCLES

If we start with the eminent Joseph Campbell, he reviews the biblical themes of the fall of Adam and Eve and of the flood in some detail, but the fall of the angels that sits in between – a narrative that is arguably of the utmost importance – receives barely a mention. In fact he hardly comments in any detail on our main themes, despite the huge depth and breadth of his studies. To the extent that he does he has a tendency to dismiss them as 'part and parcel of the heritage of civilization itself'.[1] His attitude towards them is also very much angled towards a cyclical interpretation, the principles behind which were introduced in the opening chapter. Nowhere does he emphasize this more than when he discusses the flood theme in *The Masks of God*:[2]

> The whole idea of the Flood rather as the work of a god of wrath than as the natural punctuation of an eon of say 432,000 years seems, indeed, to be an effect of later, secondary, comparatively simple cerebration.
>
> Thus the evidence from a number of quarters suggests very strongly that in the earliest known Sumerian mythological texts the basic, mathematically inspired priestly vision has already been overlaid by an intrusive anthropomorphic view of the powers that motivate the world, far more

primitive than that from which the earliest high civilization had emerged; so that the myths that have survived to us represent a certain drop or devolution of tradition, which was either intentional, in the way of all devotional popularization, or else unintentional following a loss of realization. And the latter is the more likely, since, as Professor Poebel has let us know, the Sumerian idiom of these texts 'is no longer that of the classical period'. They are already of a late, epigonous age.

I would suggest, therefore, that the mathematics still evident in certain of the earliest known, yet late, Sumerian documents suffice to show that during the formative period of this potent tradition (which has by now reshaped humankind) an overpowering experience of order, not as something created by an anthropomorphic first being but as itself the all-creative, beginningless, and interminable structuring rhythm of the universe, supplied the wind that blew its civilization into form. Furthermore, by a miracle that I have found no one to interpret, the arithmetic that was developed in Sumer as early as around 3200 BCE, whether by coincidence or by intuitive induction, so matched the celestial order as to amount in itself to a revelation. The whole archaic Oriental world, in contrast to the earlier primitive and later Occidental, was absolutely hypnotized by this miracle. The force of number was of far greater moment than mere fact; for it seemed actually to be the generator of fact. It was of greater moment than humanity; for it was the organizing principle by which humanity realized and recognized its own latent harmony and sense. It was of considerably greater moment than the gods; for in the majesty of its cycles, greater cycles and ever greater, more majestic, infinitely widening cycles, it was the law by which gods came into being and disappeared. And it was greater even than being; for in its matrix lay the law of being.

For what it is worth, though, we can see from this that Campbell supports the idea that the concept of universal cycles was first developed in the Vedic age. In fact he also regards them as having not just a symbolic but also a practical significance, because he attempts with some success to establish links between their numbers and those used for the precessional cycle.[3] We will return to this subject in the epilogue.

ELIADE AND RENEWAL

Mircea Eliade is a much more specialized commentator, so the fact that he fails to consider our main themes in any great depth is less surprising. In *Myth and Reality* he follows a similar tack to Campbell but with a few differences. His most pertinent comments come when, after discussing the rituals of annual or seasonal renewal at some length, he attempts to apply this to the idea of world ages:[4]

> In other words, the End of the World in the past and that which is to take place in the future both represent the mythico-ritual system of the New Year festival projected on the macrocosmic scale and given an unusual degree of intensity... But now we no longer have what might be called the 'natural end' of the World... there is a real catastrophe, brought on by Divine Beings. The symmetry between the Flood and the annual renewal of the World was realized in some very few cases (Mesopotamia, Judaism, Mandan). But in general the Flood myths are independent from the mythico-ritual New Year scenarios. This is easy to understand, for the periodic festivals of regeneration symbolically reenact the cosmogony, the creative work of the Gods, not the destruction of the old world; the latter disappeared 'naturally' for the simple reason that the distance that separated it from the 'beginnings' had reached its extreme limit.

As a corollary in his separate work *The Sacred and the Profane* he suggests that flood myths, especially of the submerged and lost continent type, can be compared to the concept of initiatory death and rebirth through baptism.[5]

CONCLUSION

Apart from the fact that his work on hero myths was the inspiration for George Lucas' *Star Wars* films, Campbell's contribution to the study of comparative mythology is second to none. Yet in terms of our current themes his work surely leaves something to be desired. In particular his interpretation of catastrophe traditions can be summed up as 'early cyclical models good, later anthropomorphic models bad'. This is still largely psychological and surely somewhat simplistic, in that it effectively suggests that the bulk of the later traditions left to us can contain nothing of any value in terms of possible pointers to a real hidden history. To be more specific he clearly argues that the idea of a single worldwide flood must be seen as an anthropomorphized distortion of the previously dominant cyclic view. He does not even entertain the possibility that the two themes should actually be seen as entirely separate: the latter deriving from an original, highly esoteric wisdom about the workings of the universe as a whole, while the former just might be an echo of a genuine historical event on earth.

Eliade too has much to offer and his observations about global catastrophe traditions quoted above appear highly erudite. Yet if we look behind the façade surely the obscure, symbolic, psychological explanations he pursues with such determination are rather less than convincing?

Above all, as with most modern experts in this field, their dismissal of any possibility that the body of supposedly mythic texts and traditions from around the world that contain our key themes might have some genuine historical content seems to be at least partly based on a lack of awareness of the equally genuine spiritual wisdom that underpins much of it – and of the sort of modern, Rational Spiritual worldview that allows us to make real sense of it. Whether or not the alternative interpretations put forward in this work stand up, either partially or fully, surely the shortcomings of the experts' approach to these traditions are there for all to see – however much their broader erudition is not in doubt.

There are, moreover, two further themes in the texts and traditions that arguably strengthen our spiritual interpretations. We find these new pieces of the puzzle in yet more veiled secrets that our ancestors have bequeathed to us, in their descriptions of the creation of humankind and of the origins of the world. It is to these we will now turn.

7

THE CREATION OF MAN

Although most of the widespread accounts of the creation of humankind appear to be purely symbolic in describing how the first humans were fashioned from dust, clay or earth, some are more complex and just may provide a meaningful insight to add to our growing understanding of the history of the soul.

To provide some context for this we again need a little Rational Spiritual theory. The whole concept of the holographic soul introduced in chapter 2 is that everything in the universe, both animate and supposedly inanimate, has its own soul energy or consciousness that is an aspect of the universal consciousness of source. But if we subscribe to the evolutionary theory that we as humankind are descended from our ape cousins, then a hugely fascinating question that we *must* logically ask arises: is there anything different about our 'human' soul energy? Modern evidence suggests that each species of animal tends to have a more collective soul consciousness compared to a fully individuated human soul consciousness.[1] So this in turn *must* logically lead us to ask: when was it that this kind of fully individuated soul consciousness first started to incarnate on earth?

Of course not only was the evolution of modern *Homo sapiens sapiens* a gradual process, but there was a considerable buildup via earlier *Homo* strains. In Part 2 we will examine the evidence to attempt to establish roughly when our forebears made the dramatic cultural leap forward that the successful incarnation of a more evolved, individuated consciousness would surely produce. But for now there is another question we can ask: would this necessarily have been a simple, one-off process? We will see in Part 2 that the evolution of our species may well have been an intelligently led process driven from the soul rather than human plane, which formed part of the much greater 'grand earth plan'. Yet in as much as it involved evolution it almost certainly involved an element of trial and error too. If so might some experienced, individuated souls residing in the ethereal realms have been tempted to 'try out' the earlier hominid forms they could see developing on our planet? Might there even have been some disagreement as to whether or not this was too early? Might there even have been some unsuccessful early experiments? As far-fetched as this might sound to some, perhaps it is indeed what some of the traditions are hinting at.

IN HIS OWN IMAGE

If we start in the Near East we saw in chapter 2 that, in the early verses of chapter 7 of the Ethiopian *Book of Enoch*, not only do the angels decide to take 'wives from among the progeny of men' but also there is some consternation among them about this approach. What is more the Slavonic version seems to suggest there were two or even three groups of fallen angels, and that they fell at different times and suffered different fates.[2] But it is hard to state with any certainty that these relate to the current theme.

Equally difficult is the following extract from the *Hermetica*, although it *could* be interpreted as describing the cultural leap when the first individuated souls incarnated in human form:[3]

> ...when the man saw in the water the form like himself as it was in nature, he loved it and wished to inhabit it; wish and action came in the same moment, and he inhabited the unreasoning form.

Meanwhile the Gnostic text *On the Origin of the World* contains several intriguing accounts involving multiple versions of Adam:[4]

> And when they had finished Adam, he abandoned him as an inanimate vessel, since he had taken form like an abortion, in that no spirit was in him... He left his modeled form forty days without soul, and he withdrew and abandoned it.

> Sophia sent her daughter Zoe, being called Eve, as an instructor in order that she might make Adam, who had no soul, arise so that those whom he should engender might become containers of light.

> Now the first Adam, Adam of Light, is spirit-endowed and appeared on the first day. The second Adam is soul-endowed, and appeared on the sixth day, which is called Aphrodite. The third Adam is a creature of the earth, that is, the man of the law, and he appeared on the eighth day... which is called Sunday.

Again it is almost impossible to discern exactly what these probably distorted passages are supposed to convey, except there does seem to be a hint of experimentation, while the importance of Adam's offspring being 'containers of light' could be interpreted as meaning physical beings capable of successfully playing host to an experienced, individuated soul energy.

Moving back in time, some of the most detailed accounts of the creation of humankind are to be found in the Mesopotamian texts. The most explicit is the Sumerian *Birth of Man*, the version we have dating to some time in the second millennium BCE.[5] As we have seen so often this appears to be a composite of two original texts that have been merged none too seamlessly. Furthermore, just as we saw previously in the Akkadian *Atrahasis*, in the first part we find the gods deciding to create humankind to relieve them of their excessive workload in digging and maintaining their extensive network of irrigation and drainage canals.[6] As a result:

> To his mother Namma he [Enki] called out:
> 'When you have drenched even the core of the Apsu's fathering clay...
> O mother mine, when you have determined its mode of being, may Ninmah put together the birth-chair
> And when, without any male, you have built it up in it, may you give birth to humankind!'
> Without the sperm of a male she gave birth to offspring, to the embryo of humankind.

The orthodox view is that this passage extols the symbolic role of the archetypal Earth Mother in producing humankind from her own self – that is, the earth or clay. The second part goes on to describe how Enki and Ninmah get drunk together, apparently to celebrate their creation. She boasts that she controls the 'build of men', be it good or bad, and he responds with the challenge that he can mitigate any 'badness' she produces. So she makes a variety of beings, described as the 'man-unable-to-close-the-shaking-hand-upon-an-arrow-shaft-to-send-it-going', the 'one-handing-back-the-lamp-to-the-men-who-can-see', the 'hobbled-by-twisting-ankles', the 'moron, the-engenderer-of-which-was-a-Subarean', the 'man-leaking-urine', the 'woman-who-is-not-giving-birth' and the 'man-in-the-body-of-which-no-male-and-no-female-organ-was-placed'. He is then able to find a position in society for all these creations and, after creating his own being that is literally an abortion because it is not gestated properly in the female womb, the text ends with them agreeing that both men and women have vital roles to play in the reproductive process.

We can see from the full context that it is hopelessly inappropriate for Zecharia Sitchin to suggest that this passage describes genetic experimentation, when in fact it is clearly a polemic on the roles of man and women in reproduction and on that of the disabled in society. Nor for that matter does this text provide any support for our current theme of *soul* experimentation, but it does allow a fuller understanding of the context and background of the Mesopotamian creation accounts.

In the hope of more interesting revelations let us turn to the Akkadian texts that deal with the creation of humankind, the most important of which is *Atrahasis*:[7]

Enki made his voice heard
And spoke to the great gods,
'On the first, seventh, and fifteenth of the month
I shall make a purification by washing.
Then one god should be slaughtered.
And the gods can be purified by immersion.
Nintu shall mix clay
With his flesh and his blood.
Then a god and a man
Will be mixed together in clay.
Let us hear the drumbeat forever after,
Let a ghost come into existence from the god's flesh,
Let her proclaim it as his living sign,
And let the ghost exist so as not to forget (the slain god).'
They answered 'Yes!' in the assembly,
The great Anunnaki who assign the fates.
On the first, seventh, and fifteenth of the month
He made a purification by washing.
Geshtu-e, a god who had intelligence,
They slaughtered in their assembly.

Here we encounter the novel idea that humankind was not just created *by* the gods, but *from mixture with* at least one of them. In particular the parts of the god that humans receive are his 'ghost' and his 'intelligence'. Is this a veiled reference to humankind receiving an individuated soul consciousness for the first time? Support for this interpretation comes from the celebrated *Epic of Creation* or *Enuma Elish*, which dates to the first half of the first millennium BCE, in which a brief reference to the creation of humankind asserts that the 'blood' of one of the gods was involved:[8]

They bound him [the chosen god, Qingu] and held him in front of Ea, imposed the penalty on him and cut off his blood. He created humankind from his blood.

Can this too be taken as a metaphor for 'godlike soul energy' entering humankind for the first time? Certainly Berossus seems to support such an interpretation in his later commentary on this text, suggesting that it is 'on this account that men are rational and partake of divine knowledge'.[9] Of course in the first chapter of Genesis all this is distilled into the suggestion that humankind was created in 'the image of God', but perhaps we now have a different perspective on this brief and veiled reference.[10]

Another fascinating aspect of Mesopotamian accounts comes from the continuation of the above passage in *Atrahasis*:

Mami made her voice heard
And spoke to the great gods,
'I have carried out perfectly
The work that you ordered of me.
You have slaughtered a god together with his intelligence.
I have relieved you of your hard work,
I have imposed your load on man.
You have bestowed noise on humankind.
I have undone the fetter and granted freedom.'

This is of course the same 'noise of humankind' that, when it became excessive, caused the gods to destroy their creation – which we struggled to interpret in chapter 2. If it was 'bestowed' on humans from the beginning, are we referring to the proper development of the power of speech and of intelligent communication? In any case the goddess then 'pinches off fourteen pieces of clay' and, with the assistance of the 'womb-goddesses', creates the first men and women – seven of each.[11] Meanwhile the *Epic of Gilgamesh* contains a brief reference to the creation of humans, again involving 'purification' and 'clay', but we find that the being created is Gilgamesh's eventual companion, Enkidu, who is described as follows:[12]

She created a (primitive man), Enkidu the warrior: offspring of silence...
His whole body was shaggy with hair...
He knew neither people not country; he was dressed as cattle are.
With gazelles he eats vegetation,
With cattle he quenches his thirst at the watering place.

The reference to him being the 'offspring of silence' is surely in direct opposition to the idea of bestowing noise on humankind. So, although the context of this composite text is completely confused, was this originally a reference to earlier beings that did not have the power to communicate properly?

THE MAKER, MODELER, BEARER, BEGETTER

Moving over to the Americas, the Mayan *Popol Vuh* contains a lengthy description of how a variety of beings were created and destroyed before a successful human emerged, which is highly comparable to and yet in some ways very different from the world age traditions discussed in chapter 5.[13] It is thought to have been compiled by indigenous scholars in the middle of the sixteenth century, and the following extracts are taken from the translation by Dennis Tedlock.[14]

First, the creator deities referred to collectively as the 'Maker, Modeler, Bearer, Begetter' fashioned various animals, but they were unable to speak properly to praise them:

> And then the deer and birds were told by the Maker, Modeler, Bearer, Begetter:
> 'Talk, speak out. Don't moan, don't cry out. Please talk, each to each, within each kind, within each group', they were told – the deer, birds, puma, jaguar, serpent.
> 'Name now our names, praise us. We are your mother, we are your father... speak, pray to us, keep our days', they were told. But it didn't turn out that they spoke like people: they just squawked, they just chattered, they just howled. It wasn't apparent what language they spoke; each one gave a different cry.

So the deities experimented again, this time:

> ...working with earth and mud. They made a body, but it didn't look good to them. It was just separating, just crumbling, just loosening, just softening, just disintegrating, and just dissolving. Its head wouldn't turn, either. Its face was just lopsided, its face was just twisted. It couldn't look around. It talked at first, but senselessly. It was quickly dissolving in the water.

And so the first human creation was destroyed:

> So then they dismantled, again they brought down their work and design. Again they talked:
> 'What is there for us to make that would turn out well, that would succeed in keeping our days and praying to us?' they said. Then they planned again.

After various further consultations, a new human was devised from wood:

> The moment they spoke it was done: the manikins, woodcarvings, human in looks and human in speech.

This was the peopling of the face of the earth.

They came into being, they multiplied, they had daughters, they had sons, these manikins, woodcarvings. But there was nothing in their hearts and nothing in their minds, no memory of their mason and builder. They just went and walked wherever they wanted. Now they did not remember the Heart of Sky.

And so they fell, just an experiment and just a cutout for humankind. They were talking at first but their faces were dry. They were not yet developed in the legs and arms. They had no blood, no lymph. They had no sweat, no fat. Their complexions were dry, their faces were crusty. They flailed their legs and arms, their bodies were deformed.

And so they accomplished nothing before the Maker, Modeler who gave them birth, gave them heart. They became the first numerous people here on the face of the earth...

They were not competent, nor did they speak before the builder and sculptor who made them and brought them forth, and so they were killed, done in by a flood.

So again this race was destroyed, this time by the ubiquitous flood, and a detailed and gory description of the revenge taken on them by the deities they had not praised and the animals they had not respected ensues. This is followed by a highly suggestive passage:

Such was the scattering of the human work, the human design. The people were ground down, overthrown. The mouths and faces of all of them were destroyed and crushed. And it used to be said that the monkeys in the forests today are a sign of this. They were left as a sign because wood alone was used for their flesh by the builder and sculptor. So this is why monkeys look like people: they are a sign of a previous human work, human design – mere manikins, mere woodcarvings.

Manikins and woodcarvings that resemble monkeys: what can the authors have meant? We have already seen that the ancient texts and traditions place great emphasis on how the golden race paid due homage to their gods or, in more philosophical terms, appreciated and respected their spiritual roots. But here this idea is placed in an entirely different context, with an emphasis on early creations that are unable to speak to 'keep our days and pray to us'. In purely practical terms the prerequisites for a golden race would have been sufficient *intelligence* to be able to think about and appreciate their spiritual roots, and the necessary corollary of *communication* that went far beyond the rudiments required for mere survival, allowing real culture to blossom for the first time. So were the Maya describing the idea that experienced, individuated souls may have tried to incarnate *before* the human form was sufficiently advanced along the evolutionary path to make the experiment viable?

Let us return to the text to see if they give us any more clues. As a final resort, the creators decided to fashion humankind proper from corn:

> 'The dawn has approached, preparations have been made, and morning has come for the provider, nurturer, born in the light, begotten in the light. Morning has come for humankind, for the people of the face of the earth', they said...
>
> And then the yellow corn and white corn were ground, and Xmucane did the grinding nine times. Food was used, along with the water she rinsed her hands with, for the creation of grease; it became human fat when it was worked by the Bearer, Begetter, Sovereign Plumed Serpent, as they are called.
>
> After that, they put it into words: the making, the modeling of our first mother-father, with yellow corn, white corn alone for the flesh, food alone for the human legs and arms, for our first fathers, the four human works.

This time the experiment was more of a success:

> And these are the names of our first mother-fathers. They were simply made and modeled, it is said; they had no mother and no father. We have named the men by themselves. No woman gave birth to them, nor were they begotten by the builder, sculptor, Bearer, Begetter. By sacrifice alone, by genius alone they were made, they were modeled by the Maker, Modeler, Bearer, Begetter, Sovereign Plumed Serpent. And when they came to fruition, they came out human:
>
> They talked and they made words.
>
> They looked and they listened.
>
> They walked, they worked.
>
> They were good people, handsome, with looks of the male kind. Thoughts came into existence and they gazed; their vision came all at once. Perfectly they saw, perfectly they knew everything under the sky, whenever they looked. The moment they turned around and looked around in the sky, on the earth, everything was seen without any obstruction. They didn't have to walk around before they could see what was under the sky; they just stayed where they were.
>
> As they looked, their knowledge became intense. Their sight passed through trees, through rocks, through lakes, through seas, through mountains, through plains. Jaguar Quitze, Jaguar Night, Not Right Now, and Dark Jaguar were truly gifted people.

This is surely yet another eloquent description of the spiritual awareness humankind displayed in the golden age, after the first fully conscious, individuated souls were successful in incarnating in modern human form. As a result it arguably adds weight to the suggestion that underneath all the symbolism the previous passages are describing unsuccessful previous attempts.

THE DAWN OF CREATION

While the Maya appear to have merged the themes of multiple creations and of world ages, the Hopi tradition of world ages discussed in chapter 5 is preceded by a separate and complementary account of the creation of humankind that again involves multiple attempts:[15]

So Spider Woman gathered earth, this time of four colors, yellow, red, white, and black; mixed with *tuchvala,* the liquid of her mouth; moulded them; and covered them with her white-substance cape which was the creative wisdom itself. As before, she sang over them the Creation Song, and when she uncovered them these forms were human beings in the image of Sotuknang. Then she created four other beings after her own form. They were *wuti,* female partners, for the first four male beings.

When Spider Woman uncovered them the forms came to life. This was at the time of the dark purple light, Qoyangnuptu, the first phase of the dawn of Creation, which first reveals the mystery of man's creation.

They soon awakened and began to move, but there was still a dampness on their foreheads and a soft spot on their heads. This was at the time of the yellow light, Sikangnuqa, the second phase of the dawn of Creation, when the breath of life entered man.

In a short time the sun appeared above the horizon, drying the dampness on their foreheads and hardening the soft spot on their heads. This was the time of the red light, Talawva, the third phase of the dawn of Creation, when man, fully formed and firmed, proudly faced his Creator.

'That is the Sun', said Spider Woman. 'You are meeting your Father the Creator for the first time. You must always remember and observe these three phases of your Creation. The time of the three lights, the dark purple, the yellow, and the red reveal in turn the mystery, the breath of life, and warmth of love. There comprise the Creator's plan of life for you as sung over you in the Song of Creation.'

The First People of the First World did not answer her: they could not speak.

This is clearly the same concept of creations that cannot speak. The account continues:

Spider Woman explained. 'As you commanded me, I have created these

First People. They are fully and firmly formed: they are properly colored; they have life: they have movement. But they cannot talk. That is the proper thing they lack. So I want you to give them speech. Also the wisdom and the power to reproduce, so that they may enjoy their life and give thanks to the Creator.'

So Sotuknang gave them speech, a different language to each color, with respect for each other's difference. He gave them the wisdom and the power to reproduce and multiply.

Then he said to them, 'With all these I have given you this world to live on and to be happy. There is only one thing I ask of you. To respect the Creator at all times. Wisdom, harmony, and respect for the love of the Creator who made you. May it grow and never be forgotten among you as long as you live.'

So the First People went their directions, were happy, and began to multiply.

The idea that once they had been 'given the power of speech' it allowed them to 'respect the creator' is clearly the same as the Mayan tradition too, again suggesting that humankind had at last advanced sufficiently along the evolutionary path to be ready to successfully receive the individuated souls that had been waiting in the wings. The account ends as follows:

With the pristine wisdom that had been granted them, they understood that the earth was a living entity like themselves... Thus they knew their mother in two aspects which were often synonymous – as Mother Earth and the Corn Mother.

In their wisdom they also knew their father in two aspects. He was the Sun, the solar god of their universe. Yet his was but the face through which looked Taiowa, their Creator.

These universal entities were their real parents, their human parents being but the instruments through which their power was made manifest. In modern times their descendents remembered this...

The First People, then, understood the mystery of their parenthood. In their pristine wisdom they also understood their own structure and functions – the nature of man himself.

What more eloquent expression of the dual lineage of our bodies from our earthly parents, and of our souls from the universal and ethereal, could we desire?

SILENT CREATIONS

Further examples of multiple creation attempts from the other side of the world can be found in the traditions of various Indonesian tribes, described by Roland Burrage Dixon in his Polynesian volume of *The Mythology of All Races*:[16]

> A somewhat different form of origin-myth describes a series of attempts at creation in which different materials are tried, the first trials being failures, although success is finally achieved. Thus the Dyaks of the Baram and Rejang district in Borneo say that after the two birds, Iri and Ringgon, had formed the earth, plants, and animals they decided to create man. 'At first, they made him of clay, but when he was dried he could neither speak nor move, which provoked them, and they ran at him angrily; so frightened was he that he fell backward and broke all to pieces. The next man they made was of hard wood, but he, also, was utterly stupid, and absolutely good for nothing. Then the two birds searched carefully for a good material, and eventually selected the wood of the tree known as Kumpong, which has a strong fiber and exudes a quantity of deep red sap, whenever it is cut. Out of this tree they fashioned a man and a woman, and were so well pleased with this achievement that they rested for a long while, and admired their handiwork. Then they decided to continue creating more men; they returned to the Kumpong tree, but they had entirely forgotten their original pattern, and how they executed it, and they were therefore able only to make very inferior creatures, which became the ancestors of the Maias (the Orang Utan) and monkeys.
>
> A similar tale is found among the Iban and Sakarram Dyaks, only reversing the order, so that after twice failing to make man from wood, the birds succeeded at the third trial when they used clay. Farther north, among the Dusun of British North Borneo, the first two beings 'made a stone in the shape of a man but the stone could not talk, so they made a wooden figure and when it was made it talked, though not long after it became worn out and rotten; afterwards they made a man of earth, and the people are descended from this till the present day.'

We can see even from such summaries that they contain similar themes, especially the pervasive idea of the inability of the earliest creations to talk.

THE VEIL OF AMNESIA

There is a passage in the Hermetic *Kore Kosmu* that describes Hermes as follows:[17]

> When he [the divine creator] decided to reveal himself, he breathed into certain godlike men a passionate desire to know him, and bestowed on their minds a radiance ampler than that which they already had within their breasts, that so they might first will to seek the yet unknown God, and then

have power to find him. But this… it would not have been possible for men of mortal breed to do, if there had not arisen one whose soul was responsive to the influence of the holy Powers of heaven. And such a man was Hermes, he who won knowledge of all. Hermes saw all things, and understood what he saw, and had power to explain to others what he understood.

Again this seems to be describing the time when fully conscious, individuated souls first incarnated successfully. Yet the accompanying suggestion seems to be that even they would not have had sufficient awareness of their spiritual roots to kickstart the golden age without the assistance of a far more experienced soul or souls.

This harks back to the knowledge transfer traditions we discussed in chapter 3, and to understand it we need to understand the concept of the 'veil of amnesia. This is designed to make our human experience richer and more fulfilling by ensuring that we incarnate with no knowledge of our previous lives or of any life plans we might have made as a soul before incarnating, or even any memory of our true spiritual nature. One reason for this is that if we were to 'take our exams with the answers already given to us' we would not learn very much. Another is to avoid homesickness for the unconditional love of our true spiritual home, as summed up by another passage in the *Kore Kosmu* that contains a plea from the first souls to incarnate on earth:[18]

> Ordain some limits to our punishment… make us forget what bliss we have lost, and into what an evil world we have come down, and so release us from our sorrow.

So, if the 'ordinary' individuated souls who came down to populate the golden race suffered from this amnesia, then certain highly experienced 'angelic' souls who transcended this limitation would have been required to bring a spiritual worldview into the physical plane. This is clearly how Hermes is described in the first passage.

On the other hand an enigmatic passage follows the extracts from the Mayan *Popol Vuh* above, which perhaps refers to the imposition of the veil not at the outset but only some time later. It describes how the deities decide that the golden race they have created is *too* good and a potential threat:[19]

> 'What our works and designs have said is no good: "We have understood everything, great and small," they say.' And so the Bearer, Begetter took back their knowledge:
> 'What should we do with them now? Their vision should at least reach

nearby, they should see at least a small part of the face of the earth, but what they're saying isn't good. Aren't they merely "works" and "designs" in their very names? Yet they'll become as great as gods, unless they procreate, proliferate at the sowing, the dawning, unless they increase.'

'Let it be this way: now we'll take them apart just a little, that's what we need. What we've found out isn't good. Their deeds would become equal to ours, just because their knowledge reaches so far. They see everything.' And when they changed the nature of their works, their designs, it was enough that the eyes be marred by the Heart of Sky. They were blinded as the face of a mirror is breathed upon. Their vision flickered. Now it was only from close up that they could see what was there with any clarity.

And such was the loss of the means of understanding, along with the means of knowing everything, by the four humans.

There are perhaps some parallels here with the celebrated account of the first fall in Genesis. At the serpent's suggestion Adam and Eve eat the forbidden fruit of 'the tree of the knowledge of good and evil', which causes God to exclaim, 'Behold, the man is become as one of us' and to banish them from Eden.[20] This correlation is arguably reinforced by more details from the Gnostic texts, for example the *Apocryphon of John*, despite the usual oppressive tone:[21]

And in that moment the rest of the powers became jealous, because he [Adam] had come into being through all of them and they had given their power to the man, and his intelligence was greater than that of those who had made him, and greater than that of the chief archon. And when they recognized that he was luminous, and that he could think better than they, and that he was free from wickedness, they took him and threw him into the lowest region of all matter.

The question of whether the veil of amnesia was imposed on our earliest human ancestors from the outset or only introduced at some point later, perhaps even linked to the theme of debasement, is one to which we will return in the epilogue.

CONCLUSION

In terms of orthodox opinion Joseph Campbell comments on the Mesopotamian creation texts and their biblical derivatives at some length.[22] Of course he discusses the simple symbolism of creation from mother earth, and the gradual increase in emphasis on the role of male gods in the creation story as their society became increasingly patriarchal.[23] He also notes the marked change in attitude that results from the introduction of the idea that humankind was created as a servant of the gods.[24] These are all solid observations, but again he arguably fails to spot the deeper symbolism of the spiritual messages that almost certainly lie beneath the surface of these creation accounts.

We should be clear that there are two separate but related ideas that interest us here, and that some accounts contain both while others mainly concentrate on just one. The first is the simple idea that at some point 'successful' humans were created, and that broadly speaking their distinguishing features were their ability to 'talk' and 'see' properly, as well as to 'give thanks for their creation' and 'know who they were'. Whether this was brought about by infusions from godly essence or in other more symbolic ways, there is a strong argument that these are attempts to answer the question 'what is it that really makes us human?' Our suggested answer, based on reinterpreting these accounts from a Rational Spiritual perspective, is that it was when experienced, individualized souls were first able to incarnate en masse that the modern human race would have received the incredible catalytic boost that would start to pave the way for the development of advanced culture and, eventually, civilization as we know it today.

This interpretation is reinforced by the other, related idea found in those accounts that describe multiple, *unsuccessful* attempts to create the human race. Of course these might be purely symbolic. But again there is a strong argument that they refer to failed previous attempts by highly conscious, individuated souls to incarnate in human or protohuman forms that were insufficiently physiologically advanced to properly play host to them – and especially to house the golden race.

To close this chapter it is intriguing that potential support for just such a view comes from Michael Newton's interlife regression research, which was introduced briefly in the preface. As he reports:[25]

> A few of my more advanced clients declare that highly advanced souls who specialize in seeking out suitable hosts for young souls evaluated life on Earth for over a million years. My impression is these examiner souls found the early hominid brain cavity and restricted voice box to be inadequate for soul development earlier than some 200,000 years ago.

8

THE ORIGINS OF THE WORLD

At the end of chapter 5 we discussed the idea of the conscious metaverse that underpins a series of progressively evolving universes, and saw how this might be what the Hindu universal cycle traditions are attempting to describe. More than this, though, it seems that at some point knowledge of this was widespread, at least in terms of an understanding of how each universe emerges from its slumber at what we might call 'the dawn of Brahma'; because this is the veiled message preserved in the sacred traditions of the 'origins of the world' on every continent of the globe.

Of course in properly reinterpreting these traditions we have to see through the inevitable distortions and contextual differences regressively introduced by people who had lost sight of their original message. For example we saw the confusion between the terms *earth* and *universe* in some of the Hindu traditions, and nearly all of the origin traditions talk about the creation of the earth when, if we step back and look at the big picture from a spiritual perspective, it soon becomes clear they are echoing a universal esoteric wisdom concerning the creation of the universe as a whole out of nothing. This is why it is arguably more appropriate to refer to them as cosmogony traditions. Indeed it is here more than anywhere that the orthodox failure to appreciate the wisdom underlying supposed mythology is at its most glaringly obvious.[1]

IN THE BEGINNING

Let us first remind ourselves of the biblical narrative at the beginning of Genesis:

1. In the beginning God created the heaven and the earth.
2. And the earth was without form, and void; and darkness was upon the face of the deep. And the Spirit of God moved upon the face of the waters.

The second verse is clearly describing a time when there was a formless void that had connotations of water, depth and darkness, and which contained the spirit of God. Proof that this has as usual been condensed from more detailed sources is provided by the following wonderfully descriptive passage in the *Hermetica*:[2]

> In the deep there was boundless darkness and water and fine intelligent spirit, all existing by divine power in chaos. Then a holy light was sent forth, and elements solidified out of liquid essence. And all the gods divided the parts of germinal nature.

The same sense of awe pervades their multiple descriptions of the universal energy or consciousness that animates everything in the universe both seen and unseen, which we tend to refer to simply as 'source':[3]

> The monad, because it is the beginning and root of all things, is in them all as root and beginning... the monad contains every number, is contained by none, and generates every number without being generated by any other number.

> This is the god who is greater than any name; this is the god invisible and entirely visible. This god who is evident to the eyes may be seen in the mind. He is bodiless and many-bodied; or, rather, he is all-bodied.

> God, who is energy and power, surrounds everything and permeates everything, and understanding of god is nothing difficult, my child... If matter is apart from god, my son, what sort of place would you allot to it? If it is not energized, do you suppose it is anything but a heap? But who energizes it if it is energized? We have said that the energies are parts of god... Whether you say matter or body or essence, know that these also are energies of god... And this is god, the all.

Despite their shortcomings the Gnostic texts too provide some fascinating material. For example *On the Origin of the World* commences as follows:[4]

> How well it suits all men, on the subject of chaos, to say that it is a kind of darkness! But in fact it comes from a shadow, which has been called by the name darkness. And the shadow comes from a product that has existed since the beginning. It is, moreover, clear that it existed before chaos came into being...
> When the ruler saw his magnitude – and it was only himself that he saw:

he saw nothing else, except for water and darkness – then he supposed that it was he alone who existed. His [missing] was completed by verbal expression: it appeared as a spirit moving to and fro upon the waters.

This passage introduces us to three key ideas consistently expressed in origin traditions: that of the use of the word *chaos* being misunderstood; that of the 'power of the Word' in the creation process; and that of the ultimate creative power recognizing it is alone. In addition this power is described in the *Tripartite Tractate* as 'a spring which is not diminished by the water which abundantly flows from it', and as something that 'cannot be grasped: nor is it possible for anyone else to change him into a different form or to reduce him, or alter him or diminish him... who is the unalterable, immutable one'.[5] How closely these intriguing descriptions mirror the scientific fact that energy cannot be destroyed, it can only change its form.

MESOPOTAMIA

Unfortunately the Mesopotamian texts are again somewhat deficient in this area, revealing only the faintest traces of any original wisdom. In part this may be explained by the fact that the only real origin tradition that survives is the relatively late *Epic of Creation*; but these are its opening lines:[6]

When skies above were not yet named
Nor earth below pronounced by name,
Apsu, the first one, their begetter
And maker Tiamat, who bore them all,
Had mixed their waters together,
But had not formed pastures, nor discovered reed-beds;
When yet no gods were manifest,
Nor names pronounced, nor destinies decreed,
Then gods were born within them.

All we can really extract from this is that at one time there existed only the primeval waters of Apsu and Tiamat, and that nothing else was manifest until the gods were born from them.[7]

EGYPT

These are the earliest verses of *The Story of Re* introduced in chapter 2:[8]

In the beginning, before there was any land of Egypt, all was darkness, and there was nothing but a great waste of water called Nun. The power of Nun was such that there arose out of the darkness a great shining egg, and this was Re.

Now Re was all-powerful, and he could take many forms. His power and the secret of it lay in his hidden name; but if he spoke other names, that which he named came into being.

To flesh this out let us turn to John Baines and Geraldine Pinch, who provide an interesting summary of ancient Egyptian cosmogony in their essay in *World Mythology* – even though it is a fine example of the way modern commentators tend to concentrate on prosaic descriptions of the various guises the gods take,:[9]

Before the gods came into existence there was only a dark, watery abyss called the Nun, whose chaotic energies contained the potential forms of all living things. The spirit of the creator was present in these primeval waters but had no place in which to take shape...

The event that marked the beginning of time was the rising of the first land out of the waters of the Nun. This primeval mound provided a place in which the first deity could come into existence. He sometimes took the form of a bird, a falcon, a heron, or a yellow wagtail, which perched on the mound. An alternative image of creation was the primeval lotus, which rose out of the waters and opened to reveal an infant god. The first deity was equipped with several divine powers, such as Hu ('Authoritative Utterance'), Sia ('Perception') and Heka ('Magic'). Using these powers, he created order out of chaos. This divine order was personified by a goddess, Ma'at, the daughter of the sun god. The word Ma'at also meant justice, truth and harmony. The divine order was constantly in danger of dissolving back into the chaos from which it had been formed.

The first deity became conscious of being alone and created gods and men in his own image and a world for them to inhabit. Deities were said to come from the sweat of the sun god and human beings from his tears. The power of creation was usually linked with the sun, but various deities are also named as the creator [Ptah in the Memphite tradition, Ra-Atum in the Heliopolitan, and Amon-Ra in the Theban]. At the temple of the sun god in Heliopolis, the Benu bird... was said to be the first deity. Depicted as a heron, the shining bird was a manifestation of the creator sun god, and brought the first light into the darkness of chaos. When it landed on the primeval mound, it gave a cry that was the first sound.

As with the Near Eastern traditions we see from these two passages that the concept of darkness and waters is to the fore, with the added insight in the latter that these contain the *potential* for all forms of life. What is more we find the first deity being able to create by 'speaking names' or using the gift of 'authoritative utterance', suggesting again that their Word is sufficient to trigger the emergence and creation process. Meanwhile the symbolism of the primeval lotus clearly mirrors its use in the Indian cyclical worldview that we discussed in chapter 5.

This is also the first time we have encountered the all-pervasive theme of 'order being created out of chaos', and this allows us to better understand the confusion referred to earlier that seems likely to have pertained at least since the classical Greek era. The key is that under the Orphic system the god Chaos originally represented the 'yawning void'.[10] So, rather than representing some purely psycho-materialist concept of universal order that is mirrored in the ordered nature of these new civilizations, this theme surely conveys the idea of creation of an 'order' of energy and life forms out of a 'chasm' of nothingness. This interpretation is arguably born out by the following extract from the rarely mentioned *Book of Knowing the Genesis of the Sungod*:[11]

The Master of Everything saith after his forming:
'I am he who was formed as Khepri.
When I had formed, then only the forms were formed.
All the forms were formed after my forming.
Numerous are the forms from that which proceeded from my mouth.
The heaven had not been formed,
The earth had not been formed,
The ground had not been created
For the reptiles in that place.
I raised myself among them in the abyss, out of its inertness.
When I did not find a place where I could stand,
I thought wisely in my heart,
I founded in my soul.
I made all forms, I alone.
I had not yet ejected as Shu,
I had not spat out as Tefenet,
None else had arisen who had worked with me.
Then I founded in my own heart;
There were formed many forms,
The forms of the forms in the forms of the children,
And in the forms of their children.'

INDIA

Moving farther east, the suggestion that the Indian *Vedas* are some of the finest philosophical texts known to humankind is nowhere more clearly demonstrated than in their conception of cosmogony. This is described with great eloquence in the *Rig Veda*:[12]

1. There was neither non-existence nor existence then; there was neither the realm of space nor the sky which is beyond. What stirred? Where? In whose protection? Was there water, bottomlessly deep?

2. There was neither death nor immortality then. There was no distinguishing sign of night nor of day. That one breathed, windless, by its own impulse. Other than that there was nothing beyond.

3. Darkness was hidden by darkness in the beginning; with no distinguishing sign, all this was water. The life force that was covered with emptiness, that one arose through the power of heat.

4. Desire came upon that one in the beginning; that was the first seed of mind. Poets seeking in their heart with wisdom found the bond of existence in non-existence.

5. Their cord was extended across. Was there below? Was there above? There were seed-placers; there were powers. There was impulse beneath; there was giving-forth above.

6. Who really knows? Who will here proclaim it? Whence was it produced? Whence is this creation? The gods came afterwards, with the creation of this universe. Who then knows whence it has arisen?

7. Whence this creation has arisen – perhaps it formed itself, or perhaps it did not – the one who looks down on it, in the highest heaven, only he knows – or perhaps he does not know.

Could we ask for a finer description of the ineffable, unnamable, unknowable, infinite, immanent and transcendent life force of the universe, which slumbers in the dark, watery void that contains nothing and yet – at the same time – the potential or seed of everything?

THE ORIENT

This theme is repeated in a somewhat cryptic extract from one of the Taoist *Essays from Huai Nan Tzu*.[13]

(1) There was the 'beginning': (2) There was a beginning of an anteriority to this beginning. (3) There was a beginning of an anteriority even before the beginning of this anteriority. (4) There was 'the existence'. (5) There was 'the non-existence'. (6) There was 'not yet a beginning of non-existence'. (7) There was 'not yet a beginning of the not yet beginning of non-existence'.

This is followed by a commentary that forms part of the original text:

(1) The meaning of 'There was the beginning' is that there was a complex energy which had not yet pullulated into germinal form, nor into any visible shape of root and seed and rudiment. Even then in this vast and impalpable void there was apparent the desire to spring into life; but, as yet, the genera

of matter were not formed.

(2) At the 'beginning of anteriority before the beginning' the fluid of heaven first descended and the fluid of earth first ascended. The male and female principles interosculated, prompting and striving among the elements of the cosmos. The forces wandered hither and thither, pursuing, competing, interpenetrating. Clothed with energy, they moved, sifted, separated, impregnated the various elements as they moved in the fluid ocean, each aura desiring to ally itself with another, even when, as yet, there was no appearance of any created form.

(3) At the stage 'There must be a beginning of an anteriority even before the beginning of anteriority', Heaven contained the spirit of harmony, but had not, as yet, descended: earth cherished the vivifying fluid, but had not ascended, as yet. It was space, still, desolate, vapory – a drizzling humid state with a similitude of vacancy and form. The vitalizing fluid floated about, layer on layer.

(4) 'There was the existence' speaks of the coming of creation and the immaterial fluids assuming definite forms, implying that the different elements had become stabilized. The immaterial nuclei and embryos, generic forms as roots, stems, tissues, twigs and leaves of variegated hues appeared. Beautiful were the variegated colors. Butterflies and insects flew hither and thither: insects crawled about. We now reach the stage of movement and the breath of life on every hand. At this stage it was possible to feel, to grasp, to see and follow outward phenomena. They could be counted and distinguished both quantitatively and qualitatively.

(5) 'The non-existence' period. It was so called because when it was gazed on no form was seen: when the ear listened, there was no sound: when the hand grasped, there was nothing tangible: when gazed at, it was illimitable. It was limitless space, profound and a vast void – a quiescent, subtile [sic] mass of immeasurable translucency.

(6) In 'There was not yet a beginning of non-existence', implies that this period wrapped up heaven and earth, shaping and forging the myriad things of creation: there was an all-penetrating impalpable complexity, profoundly vast and all-extending; nothing was outside its operations. The minutest hair and sharpest point were differentiated: nothing within was left undone. There was no wall around, and the foundation of non-existence was being laid.

(7) In the period of 'There was not yet a beginning of the not yet beginning of non-existence', Heaven and Earth were not divided: the four seasons were not yet separated: the myriad things were not yet come to birth. Vast-like even and quiet, still-like, clear and limpid, forms were not visible.

Although the apparent order of these commentaries is somewhat confused, and there is perhaps a subtle suggestion that they ignore physical evolution, they do attempt to say something about the incredible complexities of the universe emerging into its various realms and forms, both physical and nonphysical. Another essay continues the theme:[14]

> The divinities Yin and Yang were separated... the hard and soft being mutually united... creation assumed form. The murky elements went to form reptiles: the finer essence went to form man. Hence, spirit belongs to Heaven and the physical belongs to Earth. When the spirit returns to the gate of Heaven and the body seeks its origin, how can I exist? The 'I' is dissolved.

The implication seems to be that during the night of Brahma the void remains completely undifferentiated and unitary, whereas at the commencement of the day of Brahma – or year, or life, the terminology really does not matter – the first thing the creative power does is split into two, in this case represented by the Yin and the Yang. These apparent dualities representing male and female, positive and negative, light and dark and so on are often misunderstood as opposites, but in fact they are better seen as complementary, unified principles that exist as contrasts on a single scale and have to be balanced. Indeed in this context it is useful to think of the night of Brahma as a state of stasis or equilibrium that has to be knocked out of equilibrium if any sort of dynamic of creation and evolution is going to occur. In many traditions this is represented somewhat prosaically as the supreme creator recognizing he is alone, and becoming so frustrated that he creates one or more companions for himself – as we saw, for example, with the Egyptian first deity in the commentary previously discussed.

Perhaps unsurprisingly Japanese cosmogony follows the same line. Their two most sacred ancient texts, the *Kojiki* or 'Record of Ancient Matters' and the *Nihongi* or 'Chronicles of Japan', were compiled in the early part of the eighth century, each having similar content; the opening lines of the latter are as follows:[15]

> Of old, Heaven and Earth were not yet separated, and the In (Yin) and Yo (Yang) not yet divided. They formed a chaotic mass like an egg which was of obscurely defined limits and contained germs.
> The purer and clearer part was thinly drawn out, and formed Heaven, while the heavier and grosser element settled down and became Earth.
> The finer element easily became a united body, but the consolidation of the heavy and gross element was accomplished with difficulty.
> Heaven was therefore formed first, and Earth was established subsequently.

GREECE

In Greek cosmogony we find that, while many accounts contain the somewhat prosaic distortions we have come to expect, traces of the original wisdom still shine through in places. For example here are the opening lines of Ovid's *Metamorphosis*:[16]

> Ere land and sea and the all-covering sky
> Were made, in the whole world the countenance
> Of nature was the same, all one, well named
> Chaos, a raw and undivided mass,
> Naught but a lifeless bulk, with warring seeds
> Of ill-joined elements compressed together.
> No sun as yet poured light upon the world,
> No waxing moon her crescent filled anew,
> Nor in the ambient air yet hung the earth,
> Self-balanced, equipoised, nor Ocean's arms
> Embraced the long far margin of the land
> Though there were land and sea and air, the land
> No foot could tread, no creature swim the sea,
> The air was lightless; nothing kept its form,
> All objects were at odds, since in one mass
> Cold essence fought with hot, and moist with dry,
> And hard with soft and light with things of weight.
> This strife a god, with nature's blessing, solved;
> Who severed land from sky and sea from land,
> And from the denser vapors set apart
> The ethereal sky; and, each from the blind heap
> Resolved and freed, he fastened in its place
> Appropriate in peace and harmony.
> The fiery weightless force of heaven's vault
> Flashed up and claimed the topmost citadel;
> Next came the air in lightness and in place;
> The thicker earth with grosser elements
> Sank burdened by its weight; lowest and last
> The girdling waters pent the solid globe.

This passage at least contains the idea of the undifferentiated nature of the void. Of course we might have expected to be able to turn to Plato for some rather better fare, as usual, but in fact cosmogony is not one of his strong points.

POLYNESIA

If we now turn to indigenous traditions from around the world, Roland Burrage Dixon provides the following entirely consistent overview of Polynesian cosmogony in *The Mythology of All Races*:[17]

> The essential elements of this form of the myth may be stated as follows. In the beginning there was nothing but Po, a void or chaos, without light, heat, or sound, without form or motion. Gradually vague stirrings began within the darkness, moanings and whisperings arose, and then at first, faint as early dawn, the light appeared and grew until full day had come. Heat and moisture next developed, and from the interaction of these elements came substance and form, ever becoming more and more concrete, until the solid earth and overarching sky took shape and were personified as Heaven Father [Rangi] and Earth Mother [Papa].

So, for example, one Maori tradition reported by Dixon begins as follows:[18]

> Io dwelt within the breathing-space of immensity.
> The Universe was in darkness, with water everywhere,
> There was no glimmer of dawn, no clearness, no light.

Another is even more esoteric:[19]

> From the conception the increase
> From the increase the swelling
> From the swelling the thought
> From the thought the remembrance
> From the remembrance the consciousness, the desire.
> The word became fruitful:
> It dwelt with the feeble glimmering
> It brought forth night;
> The great night, the long night,
> The lowest night, the loftiest night,
> The thick night, the night to be felt,
> The night touched, the night unseen.
> The night following on,
> The night ending in death.
> From the nothing, the begetting,
> From the nothing the increase
> From the nothing the abundance,
> The power of increasing, the living breath;
> It dwelt with the empty space.

Meanwhile the cosmogony of the Society Islands, for example, follows similar lines:[20]

He existed. Taaroa was his name.
In the immensity
There was no earth, there was no sky,
There was no sea, there was no man.
Taaroa calls, but nothing answers.
Existing alone, he became the universe.
Taaroa is the root, the rock's foundation.
Taaroa is the sands.
It is thus that he is named.
Taaroa is the light.
Taaroa is within.
Taaroa is the germ.
Taaroa is the support.
Taaroa is enduring.

Again we find the idea that the creative power in the void contains the potential germ or seed of all things that will eventually emerge.

AMERICA

How do the indigenous traditions of the Americas compare? First let us hear once again from the Hopi Indians of the north:[21]

The first world was Tokpela (Endless Space).

But first, they say, there was only the Creator, Taiowa. All else was endless space. There was no beginning and no end, no time, no shape, no life. Just an immeasurable void that had its beginning and end, time, shape, and life in the mind of Taiowa the Creator.

Then he, the infinite, conceived the finite. First he created Sotuknang to make it manifest, saying to him, 'I have created you, the first power and instrument as a person, to carry out my plan for life in endless space. I am your Uncle. You are my Nephew. Go now and lay out these universes in proper order so they may work harmoniously with one another according to my plan.'

Sotuknang did as he was commanded. From endless space he gathered that which was to be manifest as solid substance, moulded it into forms, and arranged them into nine universal kingdoms: one for Taiowa the Creator, one for himself, and seven universes for the life to come.

This account typifies the Amerindian approach which, unlike those of the East, tends to anthropomorphize the power in the void, personifying it as a 'supreme creator'. But we can also see quite clearly that this does not prevent it from describing the fundamental nothingness of the void, and how it then differentiated into various universes – or in our terms realms or planes. Meanwhile the similarities of Mayan cosmogony can be seen from the following extract from the *Popol Vuh*:[22]

> Now it still ripples, now it still murmurs, ripples, it still sighs, still hums, and it is empty under the sky.
>
> Here follow the first words, the first eloquence:
>
> There is not yet one person, one animal, bird, fish, crab, tree, rock, hollow, canyon, meadow, forest. Only the sky alone is there; the face of the earth is not clear. Only the sea alone is pooled under all the sky; there is nothing whatever gathered together. It is at rest; not a single thing stirs. It is held back, kept at rest under the sky.
>
> Whatever there is that might be is simply not there: only the pooled water, only the calm sea, only it alone is pooled.
>
> Whatever might be is simply not there: only murmurs, ripples, in the dark, in the night. Only the Maker, Modeler alone, Sovereign Plumed Serpent, the Bearers, Begetters are in the water, a glittering light. They are there, they are enclosed in quetzal feathers, in blue-green.
>
> Thus the name, 'Plumed Serpent'. They are great knowers, great thinkers in their very being.

This account continues by describing specifically how 'the earth arose because of them, it was simply their *word* that brought it forth'.

AFRICA

In his essay on Africa in *World Mythology,* Roy Willis points out that many of its indigenous traditions tend to contain the idea of a 'cosmic egg' as also found in, for example, Egyptian and Japanese cosmogony. But what does this egg contain? The Dogon describe it as being 'the seed of the cosmos' that 'vibrated seven times, then burst open', so this is just another way of depicting the potential or seed within the void.[23] He also suggests that their neighbors the Bambara have one of the most philosophical cosmogonies in Africa:[24]

> In the beginning emptiness, *fu,* brought forth knowing, *gla gla zo*. This knowing, full of its emptiness and its emptiness full of itself, was the prime creative force of the universe, setting in train a mystical process of releasing and retracting energy.

MISSING THE POINT

The foregoing origin traditions are only those in which at least some of the original esoteric wisdom comes through, but we have still amassed evidence from almost every part of the globe. Admittedly we have seen that some of them continue by describing how either the supreme deity – or various other deities created by him – proceed to separate heaven and earth from the waters, place the stars in their proper positions in the sky, arrange the seasons and so on. But these are the relatively prosaic or exoteric aspects that only serve to demonstrate how much the original wisdom had become lost or distorted by the time these traditions as we now have them were composed. Unfortunately these are the very aspects that most modern scholars of mythology tend to concentrate on, instead of properly examining, distilling and comparing their highly consistent underlying content and placing it in its proper metaphysical – indeed spiritual – context.

It is perhaps to be expected that modern encyclopedias and compendia of mythology should follow this route; they are, after all, aiming at a broad audience.[25] But it is somewhat surprising that the more in-depth studies of experts such as Joseph Campbell and Mircea Eliade should yet again fail to appreciate the true message of these traditions. For example in *The Masks of God* the former suggests that all except the 'most rarefied' origin myths involve a creator, and that this is a byproduct of the simple childhood response of regarding everything as being created by someone.[26] Meanwhile these more rarefied accounts are not identified but it is clear the more esoteric indigenous traditions from around the world are not included. For example the only American cosmogony that he covers in any detail is that of the Apache Indians of New Mexico, which is one of the more prosaic anyway.[27] He does not discuss the far more interesting Hopi and Mayan traditions in any of the four volumes of his masterwork, and the African and Polynesian cosmogonies that we have reviewed are similarly ignored. Not only that but, for all that he seems to respect the high philosophy of ancient India and China, discussing their general themes at some length, nowhere does he cover their origin traditions in any detail.[28]

All we are left with, then, are Campbell's deliberations on the cosmogony of the ancient Egyptians. He begins by appearing to praise the philosophical leap made by the Memphite priests of the Old Kingdom in according to the deity Ptah the power of creation by the Word – comparing this with the later, devolved Heliopolitan tradition in which the deity Atum's creative powers are more prosaically symbolized by his 'taking his phallus in his fist'.[29] But this is as far as he goes, and we are left uncertain about his real views on the degree of esoteric wisdom possessed by the ancient Egyptians and indeed other ancient cultures. Although we must clearly accept that Campbell's aim was not to concentrate on origin myths per se, these omissions are somewhat dispiriting for anyone who devotes many weeks of study to his extensive but intricate and sometimes meandering work.

Eliade's most relevant work *Myth and Reality* is considerably shorter, so perhaps he can be rather more excused for failing to appreciate the esoteric wisdom that consistently underlies global cosmogonies. In fact he does devote a whole chapter to them but concentrates entirely on their magic and prestige in tribal cultures – for example how they are used to reinforce and celebrate the birth of a new chief, or the initiation of a young adult, by reference back to the original creation.[30] In none of his various works on mythology does he seem to investigate the more esoteric aspects of these traditions, or of those of the more established ancient civilizations.

COMMON SOURCE

We have seen that in every part of the world there are origin traditions that contain a number of regularly repeated themes, even if some are heavily veiled and even if each tradition does not contain full details of every theme. They can be summarized as follows:

- During the night of Brahma the universe remains completely dormant. In the more sophisticated traditions it is conceptualized as a void, although it is often more prosaically described as a chasm, as an abyss, as the deep or as the primeval waters.

- The dormant creative power within the void is described in the more sophisticated traditions in abstract terms such as the One, the All, the Universal or the Absolute, although the more prosaic traditions anthropomorphize it into a supreme creator deity.

- This power contains the potential germ, embryo or seed of all forms that will be created in the universe when a new day of Brahma commences.

- At this point the potential is actualized by the mere will or Word of the creative power. The energization process can perhaps be conceptualized as the blow of a hammer on an anvil, which scatters sparks and energy waves in all directions. Descriptions of light emerging from darkness are attempts to convey the same concept.

- The energy that is initially dissipated by this cosmic explosion starts to coagulate into a variety of vibrational states, creating the various dimensions and the forms that inhabit them. Their vibrational state determines their level of physicality, varying from the purest energy form of the highest aspects of the ethereal realms right down to the dense physical plane exemplified, for example, by our own planet with all its myriad lifeforms. Phrases such as 'separating heaven and earth' are an attempt to convey this in simple terms.

At this point it would be useful to return to the question of how this incredible consistency across huge geographic and temporal boundaries might have come about. We briefly saw in chapter 1 that the orthodox approach to mythology allows for two possibilities: geographical diffusion from a common original source, and separate but parallel development in each location. But when we introduce a spiritual worldview we need to adopt a rather different view of the latter, because when it comes to more esoteric themes such as the origins of the world and indeed the universe itself – that is, what we might refer to as 'fundamental spiritual truths' – it has particular scope to come into play. This is because more experienced souls incarnating in separate communities are able to tap into this universal spiritual wisdom – whether spontaneously or during meditation and so on does not really matter here – and to introduce these channeled truths to their fellows. By contrast, because the consistent traditions of a highly spiritual golden race who became debased and were destroyed primarily represent a genuine human memory of former times, these would have been passed down orally by the survivors and by successive generations until they were put into written form perhaps only about 5000 years ago. This is essentially diffusion at work.

As for distortions, we have repeatedly seen that these can be introduced via this latter method, but actually the same is true of the former. Not only will some fundamental truths have been distorted by diffusion anyway, but even channeled information can be suspect, as we will find out in Part 2. In particular even genuine human mediums can be operating in a cultural or religious context that is so far removed from that of the original universal truths that any messages they receive *can* be subjectivized and distorted to a quite horrible degree. In fact this is just as true today as it has ever been, perhaps more so.

In terms of when all this knowledge transfer might have taken place, although of course the deliberate channeling and introduction of spiritual truths can occur in any community at any time, it seems reasonable to suppose that it would have happened as a minimum both in the early stages of the golden age and also after any major catastrophe, as discussed in chapter 3.

When it comes to the aftermath of the last catastrophe, if the universal truths were indeed reintroduced at this point it may be that they remained relatively pure in their oral transmission right through to the point when they were incorporated into early Vedic philosophy – because as suggested in chapter 2 this seems to display a relatively unspoiled sophistication compared to the arguably more regressive traditions of Mesopotamia and even Egypt. This is very much Campbell's view, as can be seen in the quote from *The Masks of God* reproduced in chapter 6 when he discusses the 'devolution of tradition' that must have occurred at some point in early Mesopotamian history – *before* the earliest texts we have so far found were compiled. The same argument for a regression in the intellectual quality of its worldview can surely be made about ancient Egypt too, however much that may be more controversial to some.[31] So perhaps the *Vedas* do represent some of the least distorted remnants of a great universal philosophy that predated the emergence of these first major civilizations.

But why did they take this backward step, at least in the Near rather than Far East? We have already mentioned several times that there is a strong motive to use any orthodox religious system as a mechanism of entirely political control, a development that has unfortunately persisted as a significant element of all traditional religions ever since. But what was the original underlying motive for that control? Apart from the obvious desire of some men to control their fellows, there was a far more practical issue. If the new city-states were to survive with their specialisms of labor and so on, they had to have a guaranteed source of food. So the whole process of agriculture needed to be brought under central control. Of course it could be argued that in more matriarchal societies this could be achieved in an entirely fair and cooperative way. But in the apparently power-obsessed, patriarchal environment that seems to have pervaded these first civilizations of the modern epoch from an early stage, coercion would have been required. Of course physical force would be one way, but in the long run that is hard work and a constant investment. Far better to win control of minds using sophisticated religious mechanisms.

CONCLUSION

It would appear that, while various scholars of mythology have noted certain similarities between certain origin traditions, they have nevertheless tended to concentrate on their more prosaic aspects at the expense of the esoteric. As a result they have completely failed to appreciate their true meaning and importance. In fact arguably the consistency of the profound spiritual understanding displayed in the cosmogonies found across the globe has never before been properly appreciated, and it is high time that it was.

Furthermore we would do well to remind ourselves that the theme of a forgotten race who became debased and were destroyed was in many cases recorded by the same authors in the same documents. Admittedly we know that some of the versions we now have were cobbled together from multiple sources. Yet the depth of esoteric wisdom they display, particularly in their opening sections dealing with cosmogony and the golden age, suggests that it would be simplistic and reductionist to write off their entire contents. Indeed the position adopted by most modern scholars that they all derive from a mixture of superstitious nonsense and sophisticated yet purely psychological constructs – and which is which rarely seems to matter – is surely untenable in the face of the evidence we have collated in Part 1.

Not only that but maybe there is evidence from other more concrete disciplines, such as archaeology and geology, that supports our ancestors' version of events. It is to this we will now turn in Part 2.

PART TWO

CORROBORATION

9

ARCHAEOLOGY

There are a number of ways in which we can investigate whether physical and other evidence bears out the various themes developed from the worldwide texts and traditions in Part 1. In this chapter we are interested in examining the archaeological evidence concerning when the modern human race emerged, and indeed what we mean by 'modern'. We will be looking for specific signs of two main events: first of when the initial wave of individuated souls might have successfully incarnated en masse; and second of when our golden race might have flourished. We will also allow ourselves a little speculation about the realistic level of cultural advancement they might have achieved.

CREATION VERSUS EVOLUTION

If we are to establish the rough time window in which these two main developments took place, the first issue we must tackle is the thorny one of creation versus evolution. But even before we look at this from the perspective of timescales, it will not be inappropriate for us to first consider it from the perspective of the atheism-versus-religion debate itself.

This is incredibly complex for a number of reasons, not least because there are various forms of creationist opposition to hardline, atheistic evolution. As we saw in the preface the form of traditional Christian creationism that preaches all life was simultaneously given form by God in 4004 BCE is rightly dismissed as entirely unscientific. But 'theistic evolution' or 'evolutionary creationism' merely argues that the universe itself and the original chemical cocktail that led to life did not arise by chance but by divine guidance, while accepting that its subsequent development has occurred via evolutionary mechanisms.[1] But as we saw in chapter 7 some adherents of this view even argue that this guidance is ongoing, sometimes giving evolution an 'energetic nudge' in the right direction. As to what we really mean by 'divine guidance' in Rational Spiritual terms, there can surely be little doubt that there are discarnate souls who are interested in and keep an eye on progress on our planet from the ethereal realms, helping to make sure major parts of the 'grand earth plan' come to fruition; and this almost certainly included making sure the human form evolved on earth in the first place. There is certainly evidence of such guidance on other planets in the interlife regression material collated by Michael Newton.[2] Indeed it is fascinating to speculate whether or not an energetic 'human blueprint' is in use on other planets as well.[3]

Allied to this, it may even be that there are highly experienced souls from other planetary systems who may be much less physical than us and who have a similar task, as some channeled material seems to suggest. In fact surely it would be very hard for us to tell the difference between them and genuinely discarnate souls apart from listening to whatever they told us about who they were; and one might ask what it would matter anyway. This is where the boundaries between spiritual and supposedly extraterrestrial phenomena become somewhat blurred. But in any case let us be clear that we are not talking about the sort of physical genetic experiments by extraterrestrials who still control our lives, which idea was dismissed in chapter 2 not least because the interpretations of the Mesopotamian texts that originally lie at its heart are nothing less than fabrications. Nor are we talking about mother ships carrying huge stocks of plant and animal life around the universe like some giant Noah's ark. It is just the normal process of evolution receiving a little added, energy-directed impetus at various times. Crucially this more spiritual approach allows us to remain true to the fundamental message of all the most profound communications, which is that our spiritual growth as a race, and our future path, is entirely under our own control.

In any case, whether or not divine guidance and 'the hand of God' is involved, there is every reason to suppose that the orthodox archaeological view of the broad timescales for human evolution is correct – even if they are subject to constant refinement. The main revisionist challenge to the orthodoxy has come from Hindu creationists such as Michael Cremo and Richard Thompson in their 1993 work *Forbidden Archaeology*, their prime evidence being supposedly anomalous modern human remains dating back millions of years. But in fact their material is selective and severely lacking in credibility.[4] So it is the orthodox context that we will use for our attempt to define the time windows in which our two major developments occurred.

DIVERGING FROM OUR COUSINS

Before we look at human evolution specifically we should give ourselves some overall context of the timescales for global evolution; that is, of the earth itself and of the lifeforms on it.

Yrs Ago	Era	Period	Epoch	Evolutionary Steps
4.5bn				Earth formed
4bn				Single-cell life forms
3.5bn				Multi-cell life forms
570m	Paleozoic	Primary	Cambrian	Marine invertebrates
510m			Ordovician	
440m			Silurian	Marine vertebrates
410m			Devonian	Amphibians
365m			Carboniferous	
290m			Permian	Land reptiles
250m	Mesozoic	Secondary	Triassic	Sea reptiles
210m			Jurassic	Air reptiles
145m			Cretaceous	Birds
65m	Cenozoic	Tertiary	Paleocene	Mammals
55m			Eocene	
35m			Oligocene	Primates
25m			Miocene	Hominids (c. 8m ya)
5m			Pliocene	
2.6m		Quaternary	Pleistocene	*Homo* genus (c. 2.5m ya) *Homo sapiens* (c. 200k ya)
12k			Holocene	

Figure 4: Evolution in the Geological Ages [5]

Current thinking is that, while the universe itself burst into manifestation nearly 14 billion years ago, the earth was formed around 4.5 billion years ago during the birth of our solar system. It is estimated that primitive single-cell life forms developed in the primeval chemical cocktail about 0.5 billion years later, and that the first multi-cell forms emerged about 0.5 billion years after that. It then took nearly 3 billion more years for life forms of any significant size and complexity to appear during the Cambrian explosion. At the other end of the scale the divergence of our *Homo* line from that of our primate and hominid cousins took place only around 5 million years ago. This shows that, although there can be sudden periods of 'punctuated equilibrium' during which significant changes occur rapidly, with new species evolving and old ones dying out, evolution is normally an extremely slow and laborious process. It also shows that *we* have only been around for a tiny fraction of the lifetime of our planet.

The orthodox archaeological view of human evolution is well summarized by Richard Leakey, one of the discipline's most influential modern figures who carried on the pioneering paleanthropological work of his parents Louis and Mary in East Africa, in his 1994 work *The Origin of Humankind*. But before we go further we should take heed of his general warning concerning the paucity of evidence:[6]

> My anthropological colleagues face two practical challenges in addressing these problems. The first is what Darwin called 'the extreme imperfection of the geological record'. In his *Origin of Species,* Darwin devoted an entire chapter to the frustrating gaps in the record, which result from the capricious forces of fossilization and later exposure of bones. The conditions that favor the rapid burial and possible fossilization of bones are rare. And ancient sediments may become uncovered through erosion – when a stream cuts through them, for instance – but which pages of prehistory are reopened in this way is purely a matter of chance, and many of the pages remain hidden from view. For instance, in East Africa, the most promising repository for early human fossils, there are very few fossil-bearing sediments from the period between 4 million and 8 million years ago. This is a crucial period in human prehistory, because it includes the origin of the human family. Even for the time period after 4 million years we have far fewer fossils than we would like.
>
> The second challenge stems from the fact that the majority of fossil specimens discovered are small fragments – a piece of cranium, a cheekbone, part of an arm bone, and many teeth. The identification of species from meager evidence of this nature is no easy task and is sometimes impossible. The resulting uncertainty allows for many differences of scientific opinion, both in identifying species and in discerning the interrelatedness of species. This area of anthropology, known as taxonomy and systematics, is one of the most contentious.

In fact back in 1859, when *On the Origin of Species* was first published, Charles Darwin assumed that humankind had split off from the apes at a very early stage and quickly developed all the traits we associate with human life – a view that mollified him as a committed Christian in that it allowed our species to retain a degree of special status. The three most important of these human traits were bipedalism, technology in terms of tools and weapons, and an enlarged brain; and Darwin argued that they were all linked together in a self-inflating chain reaction.

He was writing in an era when the only fossil evidence of our ancestors consisted of relatively late Neanderthal remains from Europe, but this thinking predominated even as increasing numbers of older specimens were uncovered. A part of the upper jaw of a small apelike creature labeled *Ramapithecus* was discovered in Tertiary sediments many millions of years old in India in 1932 and, although it was immediately reported to have more hominid than ape characteristics, it was left somewhat in obscurity while other far less ancient discoveries hogged the limelight. However that all changed in the early 1960s when Elwyn Simons of Yale University shocked the establishment by speculating that it was bipedal, and must therefore represent our earliest humanlike ancestor. It was estimated that these protohumans must have evolved as much as 15 or even 30 million years ago.

This view was in turn challenged in the late 1960s when two biochemists at Berkeley University, Allan Wilson and Vincent Sarich, adopted a revolutionary approach by comparing the blood proteins of modern humans and apes, arguing that the rate of mutation of their molecular structure acted as a clock. This suggested that their divergence had occurred no more than 5 million years ago. Paleanthropologists were slow to accept this new technique, but similar experiments continued to confirm its findings. Then the decisive discovery of new and more complete *Ramapithecus* remains in Pakistan and Turkey in the early 1980s indicated that it did continue to live in the trees and was *not* bipedal.

More recent genetic tests have pushed the date for the divergence of hominids from apes back to somewhere between 8 and 5 million years ago, and this figure is now broadly accepted. However the issue of what caused it remains highly contentious. Darwin's 'linkage' has been proved false, because the earliest signs of stone tools do not appear until around 2.5 million years ago, and this *did* coincide with brain expansion sufficient to differentiate the genus *Homo* for the first time, leaving a several-million-year gap back to the time when our earliest ancestors descended from the trees and became bipedal. This latter characteristic, with its associated advantage of freeing the upper limbs and allowing the hands to develop to cope with more intricate tasks, has therefore become the defining mark of the hominid–ape divergence.

There is also a broad consensus about *where* this occurred – in East Africa sometime after the formation of the Great Rift Valley, which from around 20 million years ago began to increasingly act as a natural barrier separating the east and west sides of the continent and their ape populations. As a result the climate and ecology of the eastern side dramatically changed, with dense forest being replaced by more sparse woodlands and then by grasslands and savannah.

However there are a number of schools of thought about *why* bipedalism acted as such an impetus to hominid evolution, in terms of the advantages it conferred. One suggestion is that the freeing of the arms allowed the males to collect more food for the females, who as a result of improved nutrition and diet were able to produce more offspring than their ape counterparts. But this implies monogamistic tendencies that are not borne out by the continued divergence in size between the larger males and smaller females at this stage of hominid evolution, this being a common trait of polygamistic species. Another is that this form of locomotion, although not as swift, was more energy-efficient in the hot climate and therefore required less food. Yet another is that it allowed our ancestors to operate more efficiently when standing in water – which would be advantageous either when crossing the increasingly abundant swamps of the area, or even perhaps when adapting to catch fish by hand in inland lakes and shallow coastal seas. This area continues to be one of heated ongoing debate among evolutionists themselves.

Given that *Ramapithecus* was more ape than hominid, the genus that has now been accorded the status of the first possessor of the fundamental characteristic of bipedalism is *Australopithecus*. For some time the now considerable remains uncovered in the Hadar region of Ethiopia were thought to be the earliest, and they include the almost complete skeleton of the infamous Lucy. These remains were categorized as a single species, *Australopithecus afarensis,* and date from between 3 and 3.5 million years ago. But further remains unearthed in South and East Africa have confirmed that a number of other australopith species developed, the earliest just over 4 million years ago. In fact the latest classifications include a new although similar genus, *Ardipithecus,* which is thought to be slightly older still, and one tentatively classified as *Kenyanthropus,* which dates to at least 3.5 million years ago and may or may not represent our closest hominid ancestor.

Although all australopiths and similar genera are thought to have died out by about one million years ago, another branch of the family tree had been developing. Remains first discovered by the senior Leakeys at Olduvai Gorge in East Africa show that by at least 2.5 million years ago an entirely different genus had emerged. *Homo habilis* had a significantly thinner cranium indicating a slighter overall build, although the major reason for classifying it as the first of the genus *Homo* was its significantly increased cranial capacity. This had nearly doubled from the average of 450 or so cubic centimeters of australopiths. Another contemporary species that has since been classified is *Homo rudolfensis*.

Associated with the emergence of *Homo* are the first stone tools, signifying the start of the Paleolithic or Old Stone Age. Initially these were small flints with sharp edges classified as Olduwan technology that required significant skill to produce, and may have been used not just for butchering meat but also to cut saplings and reeds for shelters. Indeed the shift from vegetarian to meat eater significantly increased this species' survival prospects. Then about 1.6 million years ago a new type of Acheulean technology emerged, involving larger flints that were shaped into hand axes, cleavers and picks – which not only required even more skill and patience to produce, but also indicated a more developed and not merely opportunistic spatial awareness of the differentiated shapes desired. These tools are associated with a species known as *Homo erectus*, which first emerged about 1.9 million years ago and had a cranial capacity of between 900 and 100 cubic centimeters; and with *Homo ergaster*, although there is some dispute about whether this really is a separate species.

Emergence (Yrs Ago)	Genus or Species	Cranial Capacity (cc)
4.4m	*Ardipithecus*	?
4.2m	*Australopithecus*	375–550
2.5m	*Homo habilis*	800
1.9m	*Homo erectus*	900–1100
0.5m	archaic *Homo*	1250–1700

Figure 5: Cranial Development

Another huge step would have been the ability to control fire, and the earliest signs of this date to around 1.3 million years ago. Then from around 0.5 million years ago several different species emerge that are closely associated with our own, for example *Homo heidelbergensis* and *rhodesiensis*, and these are sometimes loosely classified under the grouping of *archaic Homo*. Included in this is the better-known *Homo neandertalensis* that emerged about 250,000 years ago, coincident with a further expansion of the toolkit into Mousterian technology. All these species had a larger cranial capacity of anywhere between 1250 and 1700 cubic centimeters. In fact our modern human brains average less that this, but we should remember that improved neural networking, possibly as a result of more evolved thought processes and so on, mean size is not everything.

CONSCIOUSNESS AND LANGUAGE

If we broaden our search for what it is that really differentiates the human species, for some time the orthodox view persisted that it was when early humans first developed self-awareness that their consciousness started to diverge substantially from that of their ape cousins. However in 1970 psychologist Gordon Gallup came up with an ingenious test.[7] He placed a red spot on the forehead of various primates, and placed them in front of a mirror. He then waited to see whether they would investigate by touching the curious anomaly on the reflected image, thinking that they were confronted with another animal, or by touching it on their own forehead, which would indicate they recognized the image as their own. Contrary to the conventional wisdom of the time he found that chimpanzees and orangutans tended to touch themselves, although gorillas tended to touch the reflection – although in more extensive tests the latter too have now been found to pass.

Of course modern studies, often shown in popular documentaries, have also revealed that primates living in large groups have an advanced social network and awareness of group politics – which requires not only some sense of self, but also a sense of one's allies and enemies, of *their* allies and enemies, of how these alliances change over time, and even of the need to deliberately and consciously change them to one's own advantage. All of this tends to indicate a sufficient degree of self-awareness in certain other primates that it cannot be the major differentiating factor of human consciousness.

Some commentators instead suggest that the difference in humans is our ability not only to predict how others will behave, but also to empathize with how they feel. Yet primates living in groups have been seen to exhibit altruistic behavior. Anyone who is close to a domestic cat or dog will also be aware that they can sense mood changes in humans and that their empathy is, at least sometimes, more than just manipulation to gain food. More recently film footage of, for example, elephants cooperating to save one of their kin from drowning in a bog reinforces the view that this too cannot be the main distinguishing factor.

Is it possible to look for more clues in the link between consciousness and language? This is another area of great debate, but it seems that species such as *Homo heidelbergensis* and *neandertalensis* were probably the first to develop a primitive language of any consequence.[8] There is also much debate about whether a more developed consciousness would have precipitated the development of language or vice versa. Whatever the mechanism it seems likely that in protohumans they developed in a gradual and interlinked process that commenced as long as several million years ago, and went hand in hand with advances in social interaction and tool use. Then again we all know that some animals also have highly developed forms of communication, and not always of the audio variety, so maybe even this is not a clear test.

The one area that may be more definitive is our awareness of our own mortality. Admittedly there is now evidence that elephants display signs of group grief when one of the herd dies; and there is widely circulated footage of, for example, a male sparrow feeding his dying mate who had been run over by a car, and then exhibiting heart-rending signs of grief after she dies. But what certainly is clear is that we are the only species that decided long ago to ritually bury our dead. This represents a huge milestone in the development of consciousness and sophisticated thought, and we will return to the earliest evidence of it shortly.

THE EMERGENCE OF MODERN HUMANS

Homo erectus is thought to have migrated from Africa into Eurasia more or less from the outset, that is a little less than 2 million years ago. But from about 27,000 years ago the *only* remains we find anywhere in the world are those of fully modern humans – who by this time are not only distinguished by their slighter build, more upright forehead and less protruding jaw, but also by their more advanced tools and evidence of culture proper. So what happened in the intervening period, and exactly when did our species, *Homo sapiens*, emerge?

Relatively recently the age of the earliest *sapiens* remains, from the Omo river in Ethiopia, has been pushed back to around 200,000 years.[9]

This data is reasonably well supported by genetic testing, because in 1987 Wilson conducted further studies to determine when modern humans first emerged, using mitochondrial DNA that is passed on only by women. These indicated that the most recent common female ancestor, 'mitochondrial Eve', lived around 150,000 years ago in Africa – a finding that has done much to shape the now widely accepted 'out of Africa' model of modern human emergence. Peter Oefner and his colleagues at Stanford have more recently developed a technique that uses Y-chromosome DNA to attempt to date the common male ancestor as well, tentatively suggesting that 'Adam' lived only around 50,000 years ago.[10] This would imply that earlier male lineages contemporary to Eve died out for some reason, leaving one relatively recent common father.

Meanwhile another study carried out in 1998 by Stanley Ambrose at the University of Illinois suggests that a bottleneck occurred in human evolution around 71,000 years ago, coinciding with a six-year volcanic winter following the eruption of the Toba super volcano in Indonesia.[11] Indeed he suggests that this led to a '1000-year-long instant ice age', and that genetic evidence suggests the human population was reduced to as little as 10,000 at around this time. We will return to the possible significance of these findings in the epilogue.

As to where our first human ancestors evolved, the dominant theory is that this again occurred somewhere in East Africa, from where they migrated just as their *Homo erectus* ancestors had done.[12] But if we now concentrate on the first *fully* modern humans, or *Homo sapiens sapiens*, genetic evidence seems to trace an African group who crossed the mouth of the Red Sea into the Arabian Peninsula around 70,000 years ago, possibly as a result of dramatic climate change following the Toba event. From here it appears they went in different directions. One group followed the coast eastwards and by 50,000 years ago had reached southern Asia, from where they managed to cross the sea to Australia 10,000 years later. The other group moved north into the Near East and Central Asia; and by 40,000 years ago the Cro-Magnon culture had populated Europe in significant numbers.

THE DEVELOPMENT OF CULTURE

Let us now turn our attention to what the archaeological record tells us about the development of human culture. We should start by heeding another warning from Leakey:[13]

We have to remember that the vast preponderance of human behavior in technologically primitive human groups is archaeologically invisible. For instance, an initiation ritual led by a shaman would involve the telling of myths, chanting, dancing, and body decoration – and none of these activities would enter the archaeological record. Therefore we need to keep reminding ourselves, when we find stone tools and carved or painted objects, that they give us only the narrowest of windows onto the ancient world.

Nevertheless the evidence of early culture emerging in the Middle Paleolithic is expanding all the time. For example it seems that in the Twin Rivers cave in Zambia as many as six different pigments were being produced some time between 400,000 and 200,000 years ago – which would certainly suggest body painting and rituals, as well as some degree of language, at a very early stage.[14] Meanwhile the earliest definitive proof of ritual burial comes from the Qafzeh and Skhul caves in Israel, and dates back to around 95,000 years ago.[15] Here pits were dug, skeletons were deliberately laid on their side and sometimes together (see Plate 1), and animal bones were placed on the chest.

The earliest universally accepted sign of abstract or symbolic art so far comes from the Blombos cave in South Africa, where an engraved piece of ochre dated to anywhere between 100,000 and 70,000 years ago was found. It has evenly spaced, diagonal lines forming a series of diamond or lozenge shapes (see Plate 2).[16] A number of shells with worked holes that probably allowed them to be strung together as a necklace were also found in the cave. Another example dated to around 54,000 years ago comes from the Quneitra site in Israel's Golan Heights, in the form of a flat piece of stone inscribed with nested semicircles and vertical lines (see Plate 3).[17] Meanwhile a plank of wood manufactured from mulberry, discovered at Nishiyagi in Japan, has been given the same approximate date.[18]

Because of this evidence some experts argue that 'behavioral modernity' developed gradually over a long period.[19] However they do not seem to make the distinction between 'primitive culture' and 'culture proper' as defined in the preface. The use of fire, deliberate burial, and the production of simple jewelry, pigments for body painting and primitive art can all surely be classified under the former. But from about 50,000 years ago something extraordinary seems to have happened: the quantum leap forward into culture proper signaled the start of the Upper Paleolithic Revolution.[20]

Yrs Ago	Era	Culture	Developments
2,500,000	Lower Paleolithic	Olduwan	Small flints
1,800,000		Acheulean	Stone tools - c. 12 main types
700,000			Use of fire
250,000	Middle Paleolithic	Mousterian	More advanced stone tools - c. 60 main types
100,000-50,000			Isolated ritual burial, shell necklaces, first abstract art, wooden plank
50,000	Upper Paleolithic	Various	
40,000		Aurignacian	More complex tools; regular ritual burials; stylized and realistic animal/human figurines; finely drilled beads for body adornment; bone flutes
28,000		Gravettian	Firing of clay
21,000		Solutrean	Cave paintings
17,000		Magdalenian	Advanced cave art; geometric art
11,500	Neolithic		Agriculture; stone buildings; urbanization; protowriting
6,000			City-states
5,000			Pictographic writing

Figure 6: Major Cultural Advances

It was now too that humans began to engage in more elaborately ritualized burials, with a wonderful example coming from the Sungir cave in Russia (see Plate 6). Within this grave were over 13,000 small, drilled, ivory beads and over 250 perforated fox teeth, which had been used both to adorn clothing and to make fine necklaces and other jewelry. Indeed it seems that such body ornamentation was widespread and relatively standardized in Europe, Asia and Africa by at least 40,000 years ago, suggesting the existence of a shared system of communication and probably trading links over wide geographic areas.[21]

As for pottery, although it is normally only associated with the advent of the Neolithic, the subsequent but overlapping Gravettian culture that first emerged around 28,000 years ago was the first to use fired clay to make artifacts and figurines;[22] and recent discoveries in China show that by at least 18,000 years ago it was being used for pottery itself.[23] Meanwhile the magnificent sculpted artifacts and especially cave paintings with which we are most familiar tend to be associated with the Solutrean and Magdalenian cultures that emerged around 21,000 and 17,000 years ago (see Plates 7 and 8).[24] Compared to the cultures that were producing Venus figurines, these show a marked shift to a more hunter-based and male-dominated society, possibly because of the climatic upheavals associated with the last glacial maximum.[25] They also indicate engagement in what we now refer to as shamanic practices.[26]

One other development during the Upper Paleolithic is the widespread use of geometric patterns in rock art. These include dots within circles, grids, chevrons, curves, zigzags, nested curves, rectangles and, in one isolated case, a swastika.[27] This abstract form of art was clearly a progression from the earlier finds mentioned above from the Blombos cave and Quneitra sites; and it would go on to become even more conspicuous on the megaliths associated with Neolithic temples and burial mounds all over western Europe, by which time it had developed to include cups and rings, spirals, linked spirals, mazes and lozenges.[28] There is every reason to suspect these patterns had an esoteric significance, possibly connected to shamanic trance states that may or may not have been induced by the use of hallucinogens, and they reveal just how spiritually aware our Paleolithic and Neolithic ancestors were.[29]

FARMING AND URBANIZATION

For a long time the Neolithic Revolution was regarded as having begun in the Near East about 10,000 years ago, ushering in the hugely significant switch from nomadic hunter-gathering to farming and urbanization.[30] But recent discoveries have changed all that.

Evidence of earlier farming has come from, for example, the Natufian culture who were living in sizeable permanent settlements in the Levant from 14,500 years ago; not only were they hunting and fishing, but they were also cultivating wild strains of cereal crops.[31] Abundant agricultural tools have been found on these sites, including flint-bladed sickles for harvesting, grinding stones and storage pits. Similar finds have been made at various sites in the Nile Valley dating from around the same time.[32]

If we turn now to urbanization, for many years the earliest example of a true urban development was the infamous town of Jericho in Palestine, a 'walled city' with interior houses and courtyards first developed as long as 10,000 years ago.[33] But this is no longer the sole example of early urbanization. To the northwest in the Anatolian region of Turkey the settlement of Catal Hoyuk was first excavated back in 1959, and since then a number of nearby sites such as Nevali Cori and Gobekli Tepe have also been unearthed.[34] They are all contemporaneous with Jericho and contain multiple stone buildings, including not only homes but also communal and ceremonial structures, along with elaborately carved stone columns bearing animal motifs. Each site also exhibits some degree of agricultural activity.

Yet more recent discoveries in Syria not only indicate that Neolithic urbanization was relatively widespread, but also push the date of its onset back by as much as 1500 years. The oldest site so far discovered, Jerf el-Ahmar, was first excavated by a Franco-Syrian team led by Danielle Stordeur in 1995 (see Plates 9 to 12).[35] They found it was initially occupied as far back as 11,600 years ago. What is more at only slightly more recent levels they found a number of small terracotta plaquettes bearing what they speculate may be mnemonic symbols; these etchings are twice as old as the first pictographic writing developed in Sumer some 5000 years ago (see Plates 13 to 15). They also uncovered evidence of crop cultivation and of domestication of grain. But unfortunately both Jerf el-Ahmar and Nevali Cori have already been submerged by the construction of new dams, while many other sites in the area remain under threat from similar projects.

These settlements were repeatedly built upon for millennia, but in time they were abandoned. In the meantime around 6000 years ago new, even more imposing cities began to spring up, with more varied communal buildings such as temples, bakeries, breweries and potteries. What is more their emergence is no longer traced solely to Mesopotamia but also again to Syria, where excavations at the site of Tell Hamoukar since 1999 have unearthed an impressive city of similar age covering some 500 acres.[36]

MAVERICKS

The foregoing is a largely orthodox analysis of human emergence and cultural development, but we should be clear that this does not in any sense make it infallible. New evidence, techniques and theories are emerging all the time; and although the speculations of most revisionists can be dismissed because they demonstrate no proper knowledge of the orthodox evidence that invalidates them, there are some highly qualified specialists whose currently unorthodox views at least deserve an airing.

We have already seen that genetic research has led to the widespread acceptance of the out of Africa model of modern human emergence. But some still dispute this theory, and apparently with good reason. For example Robert Bednarik, an Australian specialist in early symbolism, fundamentally questions the assumptions behind the various genetic models:[37]

> Assumptions about a neutral mutation rate and a constant effective population size are completely unwarranted, and yet these variables determine the outcomes of all the calculations. For instance, if the same divergence rate as one such model assumes (2%-4% base substitutions per million years) is applied to the human-chimpanzee genetic distance, it yields a divergence point of 2.1 to 2.7 million years, which we consider to be unambiguously wrong. Nei (1987) suggests a much slower rate, 0.71% per million years, according to which the human-chimpanzee separation would have occurred 6.6 million years ago, which is close to the estimate from nuclear DNA hybridization data, of 6.3 million years. But this would produce a divergence of Moderns [modern humans] at 850,000 years ago, over four times as long ago as the favored models, and eight times as long ago as the earliest fossils of Moderns ever found... Instead of unambiguously showing that Moderns originate conclusively in one region, Africa, all the available genetic data suggest that gene flow occurred in the Old World hominids throughout recent human evolution (Templeton 1996).

As for the development of culture itself Bednarik sides heavily with the idea of a slow and lengthy development, but also argues that earlier species were far more advanced that is normally allowed. In particular he pinpoints stone tool finds at various sites on the island of Flores in southern Indonesia dating to around 800,000 years ago, although no skeletal remains of their makers have yet turned up.[38] Sea levels were much lower during the last ice age, with far greater quantities of the earth's water trapped in massive ice sheets, but it is known that Flores remained disconnected from the main Asian coast throughout this period. So, argues Bednarik, a pre-sapien species of *Homo* must have been using some sort of raft.[39] This suggests a shared and reasonably complex language allowing for sophisticated cooperative working. It also means that, as well as producing roughly appropriate lengths of tree trunk or bamboo, they were using some sort of vines, sinews or fibers to lash them together, and making knots too. Of course none of this survives in the archaeological record.

He also describes how, despite the scant and usually ignored evidence of tools and other artifacts made from wood dating to the Lower and Middle Paleolithic, microscopic wear surveys of the cutting edges of early stone tools seem to show that the majority were used to work wood. Likewise he maintains that a small number of bone and ivory artifacts from these eras are largely ignored. But he goes further. He has personally examined hundreds of artifacts purported to show evidence of early human artistic working, and has rejected the vast majority of them as resulting from natural phenomena:

> By far the most common examples are objects of bone, limestone, ivory and ostrich eggshell, which I have shown to bear mycorrhizal grooves [from fungi] that may resemble engravings... bones can be perforated by animal teeth and corrosive agents, gastropod shells are commonly bored through by parasitic organisms. Similarly, natural surface markings on rock have often been archaeologically misinterpreted, and again I have corrected numerous such instances.

Nevertheless he contends that some authentic examples of exactly this kind of manmade 'paleoart' *have* been found, and he pinpoints several isolated but very early finds: for example two drilled pendants from Austria, one a tooth and the other a piece of bone, dating back to 300,000 years ago; and three drilled ostrich-shell beads from Libya, probably used for necklaces, dating to 200,000 years ago. Indeed Bednarik has concluded from extensive personal experiments with such beads that they were deliberately manufactured in the smallest possible size that was not too fragile; that huge amounts of extra effort were put in to ensure they were perfectly spherical; and that the holes were drilled right at the center. All of this, he says, shows a desire to make something that was perfect, indeed a status symbol designed to show that the wearer – or his of her tribe – were 'pushing the available technology to its very limits'. Given all this he makes a wonderful concluding observation:

> How would an interstellar visitor interpret the carved ivory figurines of an incomplete chess set? If his anthropology were as simplistic as ours he may well explain its knights as evidence of an equine cult. It is at this level that most interpreting of Pleistocene symbolism has occurred, which I find quite unsatisfactory.

Bednarik and others often mention two of the more controversial finds to come from professional archaeological digs, both excavated in Israel by teams led by Naama Goren-Inbar. The first is a fragment of plank made from willow uncovered at a site in the northern Jordan Valley in 1989, which they reported to be highly polished on one side because no tool marks were evident, and as having one completely straight and deliberately beveled edge; the date for this is estimated at anywhere between 250,000 and 750,000 years old.[40] The second is a lump of volcanic rock found at a site in the Golan Heights that is claimed to be the world's earliest-known sculpture at 250,000 years old; although, even if it was worked by human hand, the 'Berekhat Ram figurine' is extremely primitive.[41]

For what it is worth for the last few centuries revisionists have repeatedly written about a variety of other anomalous artifacts purporting to show high levels of advanced culture dating back hundreds of thousands and even millions of years. Indeed they still do to this day. These artifacts include, for example, ancient boats, pestles and mortars, iron nails and cups, copper coins and various pieces of artwork – usually found in deep mine and well shafts. Although some of these are still available for inspection, and for most found in the last century pictures are freely available, not a single one stands out as proper evidence of advanced culture before the Upper Paleolithic.[42] In some cases this is because the evidence is centuries old and purely anecdotal; in others because the archaeological context was never properly established at the time of the find; in others because there is clear misidentification – for example of what is clearly a decorated, bell-shaped, Victorian candle-stick holder that was supposedly blasted out of a quarry; and in still others because it is a clear piece of fakery, such as the local newspaper editor whose mother reported that she found a silver necklace inside a lump of coal. Little wonder then that orthodox archaeology pays these anomalies no attention at all.

But there are other mavericks operating within the scholarly community who concentrate on more recent prehistory. For example in his 1999 work *Neanderthals, Bandits and Farmers* British biologist Colin Tudge argues that protofarming was common throughout the Upper Paleolithic; and in his *Lost Civilizations of the Stone Age*, published in the same year, compatriot anthropologist Richard Rudgley does likewise.[43] This is surely where we too must start to diverge from the orthodox view, especially when we consider that its explanations for farming's apparently sudden appearance in the Neolithic – for example changes in climate and local population pressures – involve conditions that would have been present at various times and in various places throughout the Upper Paleolithic as well.

Indeed there can surely be little question that farming would have developed in stages, and that the process would have at least commenced in the Upper Paleolithic. Although local climate in different places at different times would have had a significant impact, we can construct a typical, general scenario. It commences with nomadic hunters gathering increasing quantities of wild grasses, buries, nuts and other naturally occurring foodstuffs, and storing and carrying with them whatever would last through the winter. They would then have developed seasonal settlements, deliberately managing the wild food resources in their chosen sites in spring and summer months before following the animal herds during the winter. The major breakthrough would have come when they discovered how to deliberately plant wild seeds, and in time to cultivate and accumulate sufficient crops to get them through the winter without leaving en mass; at this point more permanent settlements would have emerged, although some of the hunters might still have to follow the migrating herds during winter. Coupled with this, dependent on where they were, would have been the possibility of developing parallel skills in animal husbandry and fishing. The final stage would have been the deliberate domestication of both animals and crops by breeding desirable strains, coupled with further skills development in areas such as irrigation and food storage.[44]

MISSING EVIDENCE

Most scientists would argue with some justification that missing evidence is no evidence at all, and it is certainly true that as yet no definitive evidence of a late Pleistocene culture of the level of advancement we are proposing has been uncovered – at least not in terms of the sort of large, permanent, stone settlements that we find at the start of the Neolithic from around 11,500 years ago.

But the wealth of textual, physical and other contextual evidence that we have collated surely demands that we make some educated guesses about our forgotten race, and indeed allow ourselves to indulge in a little conjecture about the sorts of lives they might have been leading and the materials they might have been using. Is it at all feasible that they could have been as cultured as we are suggesting and yet no broad, properly contextual evidence of this has yet been unearthed?

The first issue we might usefully address is what is technologically possible for a culture that has not mastered the use of any kind of metal – which is something we *might* have expected to find evidence of by now if it was being used. The fact is that, if they were sophisticated in their use of flint and bone blades combined with wood for handles, then almost nothing would be impossible for them, certainly in agricultural and probably in construction terms. We have already seen, for example, that multiple flint blades were being sunk into probably wooden handles to make sickles for harvesting in the Levant well before the supposed start of the Neolithic in Europe; moreover, if we forget weapons and concentrate on tools, modern flintknappers are clearly capable of making not only knives and chisels but also saws and a whole variety of other tools.[45] If they were constructing buildings from mud-brick or wood, these tools would be more than enough to build sophisticated settlements. The same goes for wooden ships and so on. What about the absence of pottery, which like metal would survive better in the archaeological record? Again if a culture was experienced in its use of wood it could turn bowls and other items of domestic furniture on a bow-lathe, while leather sacks and other materials could be employed for larger scale food and drink storage.

What about the issue of building in stone: would our forgotten race have been happy to construct their settlements using other materials? Why not? In some countries in Europe, for example, there are many wooden buildings but that does not make for a society that is any less culturally advanced. An absence of stone might tend to suggest not only that they lived in more temperate climes but also that they were unconcerned about defense, but in the golden age this would have made perfect sense, while there is no reason why their subsequent debasement should necessarily have involved warfare – especially if population levels were low enough, and food production methods efficient enough, that there was no need to compete for resources. It might also be argued that such an advanced culture would want to make bold statements in stone about their spiritual beliefs and so on, as our Neolithic ancestors clearly did with their huge, carved megaliths. But what if our golden race were so spiritually aware that they really did not feel the need to make such statements?

Turning to the issue of preservation, of course conditions would have to be incredibly favorable for any trace of wood or other perishable materials to survive in the archaeological record for more than a few thousand years at most, let alone more than 10,000 years. To reinforce the point most archaeologists would accept that wooden shafts must have been used for spears for tens of thousands of years, yet we never find them. So the only evidence of even highly cultured activity under such assumptions would still tend to be multiple flint blades. The only sizeable stone objects we might expect to find would be grinding stones for grain, but even these might have been better fashioned from hard wood that was merely weighted down with stones. The advantages would include being easier to make to size and with handles or other apparatus attached to drive their rotation, and being more easily portable. Of course we are assuming that they had all these appropriate stocks of wood, but if they were as advanced as we are suggesting they would either have deliberately settled where they had all the raw materials they needed within easy reach, or they would have imported what they needed by sea. Remember also that our scenario does not have massive worldwide populations all competing for scarce resources, but developing pockets of advanced culture in specific advantageous locations.

To make matters worse in terms of detection of evidence, the selection of archaeological sites is horribly, even though quite understandably, skewed. Permanent stone-built sites to some extent identify themselves if they are not too buried under sand, earth, forest, jungle and so on. Caves are an obvious place to excavate, but they were either home to genuinely primitive cultures, or they are only going to provide a glimpse of the level of culture of people who used them for shelter during adverse weather and winters or serious climatic changes – or for ritual purposes and therefore not as their primary dwelling. The only other sites archaeologists can obviously investigate are those open sites where strata are readily in evidence and human remains have already been found, such as the multiple sites in Africa for example, but these involve far older periods and remains than concern us here. Other than that it is surely fair to say that it is largely a matter of luck what archaeologists or for that matter members of the public turn up.

The other issue is that in the past artifacts were often discovered by amateurs, for example laborers engaged in construction, mining or agricultural work. Yet in the modern era well boring, mining, quarrying, foundation digging and plowing tends to be performed using high technology, providing far less chance for a human operator to detect artifacts. So our chances of fortuitous and random discoveries are lessening. Of course a counterbalance to this is the increasing amateur use of metal detectors in the West at least, but if our forgotten race was not using metal this is irrelevant.

So even *if* someone was looking for evidence of truly advanced Upper

Paleolithic cultures who did not use metal or pottery or erect brick or stone buildings, despite having sizeable permanent settlements – which, of course, archaeologists are *not* – arguably it would still be like looking for a needle in a haystack. Worse still what if, as suggested in chapter 3, most of our culturally advanced ancestors lived on the coast so they could travel and trade easily, at a time when sea levels were much lower? And what if these now underwater areas were also massively damaged by huge tsunamis, or submerged under a hail of volcanic debris, or ripped apart by ferocious hurricanes? We will return to which obvious settlement locations are now under the sea in chapter 10, but it is clear that the odds of finding anything worthwhile soon tend towards zero under this weight of adverse circumstances – which are, nevertheless, not only realistic but, arguably, the most likely to have pertained.

CONCLUSION

Is there anything about early human evolution that suggests more than just a mechanistic, evolutionary impetus? Certainly it would be a mistake to claim there is anything *definitive* that supports a more spiritual take on the process, but we might suggest that the orthodox arguments about how and why we diverged from our ape cousins are not entirely definitive. For example if bipedalism alone conferred such an evolutionary advantage, why did all the other bipedal species die out while other non-bipedal primate species carried on perfectly happily? Or if, for example, the use of tools expands the brain and leads to evolutionary leaps in consciousness, how come the various primates and other animals that use primitive tools – for example to crack open nuts – have not developed as serious rivals to our human dominance? Ditto with spatial awareness, which birds building nests and beavers building dams, for example, show in abundance. Meanwhile we have also seen that communication and even language is sophisticated in a number of other species, as is the ability to cooperate and play politics within a group context, and even to show empathy and mourn the dead. One could argue that all of these developments should have allowed these species to evolve much more than they have; yet only we humans have actually done so. Was there a bit of energetic nudging and guidance, as discussed at the outset?

Meanwhile we have seen that fully modern humans emerged somewhere around 200,000 years ago. So do we have any clues as to when the first individuated souls incarnated; any signs, perhaps, of the sort of evolutionary leap that would surely have been the outcome of such a significant spiritual catalyst?

It seems that in the early stages human consciousness and culture did evolve relatively gradually, progressively pulling us clear of our hominid cousins. But as we have seen one of the most significant milestones that differentiates us from other species is an awareness of our own mortality; and, in contrast to so many of the other issues under discussion, there is one very clear archaeological indicator of this awareness – deliberate, ritualized burial. We have seen that the first evidence of such activity dates back to around 95,000 years ago in Israel, and it not only shows an awareness of mortality but must also, surely, be linked to the development of attitudes toward the afterlife. No mechanism is more likely to have provided this catalyst than a newly acquired appreciation of the temporary nature of physical life, and of the eternal nature of the soul – an appreciation that would surely have arisen when individuated souls successfully incarnated in a physical body that possessed the appropriate mental capabilities.

The problem with this evidence is that it appears to be a relatively isolated incident, because as we have seen the practice does not appear again in the archaeological record for tens of thousands of years. Almost certainly this reflects a degree of incompleteness. But we are still led to the conclusion that the experiment in Israel, while it may not have been unsuccessful in terms of the quality of the physical vehicle – they were at least *Homo sapiens* even if not fully modern humans – did not usher in any widespread change in culture at that point. Of course it might have been deliberately designed as one of a series of small-scale experiments, the rest of which we have not yet discovered.

What we can say of course is that by 50,000 years ago we have a major breakthrough with the onset of the Upper Paleolithic Revolution. It is from this point on that culture *proper* at the very least seems to emerge. But we must surely allow for the fact that the successful incarnation of individuated souls would have taken some time to take hold in any widespread way, as this new kind of 'spiritual human' really learned to master the art of survival and to *fully* develop the *primitive* culture – including sophisticated language and so on – that had already been emerging for tens, even hundreds, of thousands of years. If we take these two dates as boundaries, then, we can reasonably suggest that individuated souls must have started incarnating in serious numbers some time between 100,000 and 50,000 years ago. But can we narrow this down at all? Probably the most significant event that we know about in that period, that *may* mark some significant change in *spiritual* conditions *if* the genetic theory is broadly right, is the exodus of fully modern humans out of Africa around 70,000 years ago. Again we will return to the possible significance of this date in the epilogue.

Can we say that the Upper Paleolithic Revolution marks the start of the golden age? Not necessarily. Again the cultural developments at this point may well have taken some time to really take hold. This would certainly be true of any sizeable, permanent, coastal settlements showing evidence of genuinely *advanced* culture for the first time. So the question of how long it would have taken for our forgotten race to really flourish to the point where the golden age proper commenced, and of how widely they then spread their net, remains extremely difficult. What we can say is that at some point there would have been previously unseen population growth in the settled communities that had spread to the most advantageous parts of the globe and had properly mastered the art of survival. This in turn would have allowed for the *mass* incarnations of individuated souls for the first time, which in its turn would have provided a strong impetus to the development of genuinely advanced culture.

To come at this from a different angle, we have already seen that the idea that fully modern humans were showing all the signs of culture proper for tens of thousands of years before they even thought about experimenting with farming is at least highly questionable. What is more if they were successfully farming far earlier than is normally accepted, how long was it before they started to build seriously large settlements with all their associated specialisms of labor, and time for nonessential, cultural endeavors? Tudge in particular argues that early farmers found themselves in a vicious spiral, because the more successful their farming the more their population grew and the more they needed to produce, and so on. Such a dynamic could soon lead to genuine urbanization. What is more, once they had started down this route, how long was it before they began to look further afield for trading partners, and to navigate the seas that separated them?

We have seen that the first evidence of sizeable settlements built from stone comes from the start of the Neolithic. Yet, although he is referring to far earlier artifacts, Bednarik again makes a hugely important point:

> If the earliest found representatives of a class of material evidence are among the most deterioration-resistant types of that class, then the probability of significantly older, less resistant types is very high indeed.

In other words such developments do not spring from nowhere, they normally have a series of precedents showing gradual development. So if such advanced settlements suddenly appear in the Neolithic, it is highly likely that similar settlements built from less durable materials would have been gradually developing in size and sophistication for a long time beforehand. Generally speaking the dates for all the major cultural firsts are being continually pushed further and further back, and it may even be that – despite the needle-in-a-haystack problem – proper evidence for our culturally advanced forgotten race will finally emerge over the coming decades.

In the meantime the key question remains. Is it reasonable to suggest that people who were capable of taking the time to produce stunning and sometimes intricate works of art, musical instruments, tools and weapons, and of organizing highly elaborate ritual burials, would continue to struggle to survive as nomads for tens of thousands of years? Or is it far more likely that what we see in the archaeological record from at least 40,000 years ago, which mainly comes from Europe, is only the tip of the iceberg of the level of culture, maybe even civilization, that was really present. Present, perhaps, in settlements that we have yet to uncover because we have not yet looked in the right places on the globe; or, even more likely, in settlements that we will never discover because they were catastrophically destroyed before being permanently submerged.

So, despite the lack of physical evidence, the *contextual* archaeological evidence, coupled with that of the texts and traditions, arguably means our hypothesis of a culturally and spiritually advanced golden race that flourished in the Upper Paleolithic starts to gain some serious credibility. Our next stop, then, is to search for any geological evidence of a major catastrophe that wiped them out and hid them from our view.

10

GEOLOGY

The idea that the earth has been rocked by major catastrophes has been around for a long time. Christian scholars of the seventeenth and eighteenth centuries used primitive geological studies to support the biblical notion of a global flood not long after God created the world. But by the early part of the nineteenth century a more rational view of an earth that had been repeatedly ravaged over a far more prolonged timeframe had begun to emerge. The leading exponent of this new catastrophist school was the gifted French scientist Georges Cuvier, who reached his conclusions by studying the various geological strata that had been laid down in the environs of the Paris basin.

Yet by the mid-nineteenth century this view had in turn been challenged, with Charles Lyell at the forefront of the new uniformitarian or gradualist school. They proposed that many huge boulders found all over the world had been carried to their current locations not by a worldwide flood but by gradual glacial movement over prolonged periods, and the theory of ice ages was born.

ICE AGES

We now know that here have been many ice ages during the earth's history with the most recent, the Pleistocene, thought to have started around 2.5 million years ago.[1] Analysis of ocean-floor sediments and ice cores has revealed that it was dominated by as many as 11 major cycles of glacial encroachment of the polar ice caps towards more temperate zones, followed by interglacial retreat. The extent of glaciation differed in each cycle, as it did on each continent in each cycle, but North America and the northern parts of Europe and Asia were most affected, being considerably closer to the North Pole than South America, Africa and Australasia are to their southern counterpart. This also means that any general dates given in summaries such as this are approximate guides only.

For our purposes the most important phase of the Pleistocene is the 'last glacial period' that began around 110,000 years ago, reaching its height at the 'last glacial maximum' around 20,000 years ago. Figure 7 reveals that at this point glaciation reached as far down as the 50th parallel in most parts of northern Europe and the western US, and even down to the 40th parallel and sometimes less in the eastern US; and as a result sea levels were generally 100 meters or more lower than they are now.[2] Then a significant retreat began to take us towards the current interglacial, known as the Holocene, which began around 12,000 years ago.

Figure 7: Maximum Glaciation in the Late Pleistocene [3]

So much for the effects. By contrast geologists are far less united about the causes of ice ages and their fluctuations. Probably the most widely-accepted theory is that of Milankovitch cycles, which combine the effects of various underlying cycles relating to earth's orbit and axial tilt, but this is far from providing a complete explanation for the observed variations.[4] We also know from the modern preoccupation with global warming that any models of worldwide climate have to consider huge numbers of variables that interact with each other in hugely complex ways, whether or not human factors are at work. Above all we know that the earth's climate is in fact extremely sensitive, and easy to knock out of equilibrium.

QUESTIONABLE EVIDENCE OF DESTRUCTION

Gradualism remained dominant for more than a century, but challenges to it started to emerge in the mid-twentieth century. The pioneers were left pretty much on the fringes, but in the last few decades catastrophism has made such a dramatic recovery that the two theories have to coexist and combine. The turning point came in 1980 with the publication of a landmark paper by Walter and Luis Alvarez, proposing that the impact of a huge asteroid caused the mass extinction of the dinosaurs around 65 million years ago, at the Cretaceous-Tertiary boundary.[5] When the 180-kilometer-wide Chicxulub crater was located on the seabed off the Yucatán peninsula ten years later, and dated to the same time, the theory rapidly gained acceptance; the asteroid that created it was estimated to have been around ten kilometers wide. Rather less clear is what caused the extinction of 90 percent of all species at the Permian-Triassic boundary around 250 million years ago, because the most obvious signature of an extraterrestrial body – higher levels of iridium in rock strata – are not so far associated with that timeframe. Nevertheless the fact that major extinction events have occurred a number of times in earth's history is now undisputed, even if the causes have been varied.

All this means that in contemporary academic circles the work of leading catastrophists such as Richard Huggett and Trevor Palmer is now widely respected.[6] But some real controversy remains, and it surrounds the idea that a major, relatively recent catastrophe occurred at the end of the Pleistocene, perhaps even causing it.

MASS EXTINCTIONS

Although most animal species had managed to survive the Pleistocene relatively unscathed, somewhere between 13,000 and 11,000 years ago a significant number of North American species disappeared from the archaeological record.[7] These were predominantly large mammals such as mammoths, mastodons and native cats, and there is similar evidence of megafauna extinction in northern Eurasia at much the same time. This much is not controversial, but again what is less clear is the cause. The one factor that has a major bearing on that is the timeframe over which these extinctions occurred.

Those who insist they were spread over several thousand years at least are currently in the orthodox majority, and they offer three main explanations. First, relatively rapid climate and associated habitat changes that did not suit these large mammals; second, the relatively recent arrival of 'Clovis people' in the Americas who hunted these species to extinction; and third, the introduction of lethal diseases by these people and the domesticated animals they brought with them. Because each of these explanations faces some problems in explaining the evidence, a combination of these factors is usually preferred.

But some catastrophists reference a body of physical evidence that, in their view, tells a very different story.

SIBERIAN MAMMOTHS

Perhaps the most celebrated is that of the large numbers of supposedly flash-frozen mammoths that were found in the permafrost of northern Siberia by explorers in the eighteenth and nineteenth century. Some of these were supposed to have been in such a fine state of preservation that their meat was apparently eaten with no ill effects. Cuvier was one of the first to write about these discoveries, arguing not only that the Siberian climate must have been sufficiently temperate for such animals to live there *before* the end of the last ice age, but also that they no longer live there despite the fact that the global climate has generally become warmer.

However they were really brought to the public's attention by probably the most celebrated leader of the resurgent catastrophist movement, Immanuel Velikovsky, in his 1955 work *Earth in Upheaval*. This gathered together a multitude of old and new evidence for the first time, but as far as the mammoths are concerned he suggests that some of them had surviving red blood corpuscles that seemed to indicate death by drowning or suffocation, possibly by poisonous gas.[8]

The other major catastrophist to emerge at this time was Charles Hapgood, whose *Earth's Shifting Crust* was first published in 1958 then republished under the title *The Path of the Pole* in 1970. In terms of the mammoths he adds that as many as 20,000 pairs of tusks were exported from Siberia in the last few decades of the nineteenth century alone, and emphasizes that both meat and ivory must be frozen swiftly and permanently in order to remain edible and workable.[9] He further provides a table of radiocarbon dates on a selection of mammoth and other animal remains found predominantly in the US, which place a significant proportion of their deaths in the period from 13–9,000 years ago.

Velikovsky and Hapgood, although by training a psychoanalyst and a science historian respectively, both use geological sources for their evidence. But some of these were relatively old and unreliable even in their day, and further professional studies of their supposed evidence have been undertaken more recently with far better understanding of geological layers, and far more accurate dating technology. Unfortunately for many revisionists these tend to cast serious doubt on catastrophic interpretations. With respect to the Siberian mammoths, apart from questioning the assertion that they were suddenly flash-frozen and the numbers of animals involved, modern research also indicates that the dates of the remains vary considerably, falling into two main periods from 45–30,000 and 17–10,000 years ago.[10] This of course suggests their demise was not caused by a sudden, one-off event.

ALASKAN MUCK

Velikovsky and Hapgood both cite reports that twentieth-century gold mining in Alaska revealed a similar tale of sudden destruction of mammoths and other animals, their bones well preserved but thrown about in a catastrophic melee within a layer of muck deposits that in some places reached 45 meters in depth.[11] Many of the bones were reported to be relatively recent in that they were not fossilized, and partial skeletons were apparently jumbled together, dismembered and disarticulated; nor were there any teeth marks or other signs of them having been the victims of predators. To cap it all the muck was reported to contain masses of twisted and splintered trees to bear witness to the ferocity of the catastrophe that had affected a huge area.

Hapgood reproduces an extensive quote from popular contemporary archaeologist Frank C Hibben of the University of New Mexico, who visited the sites himself. It is full of dramatic descriptions of 'earthshaking volcanic eruptions of catastrophic violence', 'toxic clouds of gas from volcanic upheavals' and vivid descriptions of the remains themselves:[12]

> Mammoth and bison alike were torn and twisted as though by a cosmic hand in Godly rage. In one place, we can find the foreleg and shoulder of a mammoth with portions of the flesh and the toenails and the hair still clinging to the blackened bones. Close by is the neck and skull of a bison with the vertebrae clinging together with tendons and ligaments and the chitinous covering of the horns intact. There is no mark of a knife or cutting instrument. The animals were simply torn apart and scattered over the landscape like things of straw and string, even though some of them weighed several tons. Mixed with the piles of bones are trees, also twisted and torn and piled in tangled groups; and the whole is covered with fine sifting muck, then frozen solid.

But, again, more modern studies cast doubt on catastrophic interpretations of this evidence.[13] Apparently they reveal not a jumbled, chaotic mass but rather a series of seven well-defined geological layers dating back as far as 3 million years ago. What is more the tree remains are limited to three specific layers only, and the dislocated state of the animal remains has been somewhat exaggerated. In particular it would appear that landslides and mudflows created by the melting of the permafrost have created a confused picture in places, which the original investigators failed to appreciate or to place in the clearly stratified broader context.

ANOMALOUS ANIMAL REMAINS

Velikovsky chronicles similar evidence of jumbled animal remains from other countries. First from various caves in Britain and France explored by geologist William Buckland in the early nineteenth century.[14] He continues by discussing various British, European, American and even Asian sites investigated in the late nineteenth century, where rock fissures and other crevices and pits were apparently filled with similar debris.[15] As usual, though, there are problems with this evidence. Buckland himself changed his mind about what he had found in, for example, Kirkdale cave, deciding instead that it was used by hyenas who dragged in the carcasses of various other animals and devoured them; indeed by 1840 he had completely forsaken catastrophism for the gradualist approach of glaciation.[16] Meanwhile much of the other evidence is questionable at best.[17]

Velikovsky's final body of evidence involves anomalous marine remains.[18] He describes how the relatively recent skeletons of whales and other large sea animals have been discovered north of Lake Ontario, in Michigan, in Vermont and near Montreal. There is little modern material available about these discoveries, but what there is indicates that dating is problematic.[19] Not only that but sperm whales are a well-known attraction in the fresh waters of Lake Michigan today, so perhaps this is not the enigma that Velikovsky suggests.[20]

Overall then we can see that pretty much all of the material cited by Velikovsky and Hapgood contains substantial flaws, even though it continues to be unquestioningly peddled by some revisionists. So is there any other evidence of a major catastrophe at the end of the Pleistocene?

EXTRATERRESTRIAL BODIES

We have seen that one of the most obvious causes of major catastrophes in earth's history is the impact of some sort of extraterrestrial body, typically a comet or asteroid. Velikovsky firmly believed in this idea before it was generally accepted;[21] and now there is plenty of evidence that bodies smaller than the ten-kilometer object that ended the dinosaurs' reign have regularly impacted with devastating consequences for life on earth. For example evidence suggests that bodies of between two and five kilometers in diameter impacted in the Southern Ocean southwest of Chile, and somewhere in Indochina, some 2 million and 800,000 years ago respectively.[22]

What are the effects? Of course these depend heavily on the location and size of the impact, but generally speaking if it occurs on land it causes general tectonic upheaval, activates volcanoes and has two competing knock-on effects: the mass emission of carbon dioxide from volcanoes tends to produce global warming via the greenhouse effect, but at the same time the blanket of dust and debris thrown into the atmosphere tends to blank out sunlight for considerable periods and acts to reduce global temperatures. By contrast an impact in the ocean causes massive tidal waves, and while the immediate consequences for the quality of the atmosphere are less, the knock-on effects of ocean warming and both initial and longer-term evaporation of sea water are still quite profound. In addition there is a third option, which is the explosion of such a body in the air – that is, after it has entered the earth's atmosphere but before it can hit land or sea.

The first notable research into evidence for an impact at the end of the Pleistocene is arguably that of astronomers Victor Clube and Bill Napier. In their 1990 work *The Cosmic Winter* they suggest that the modern orbits of the Comet Encke, the asteroid Oljato and the Taurid meteors derive from the disintegration of a giant comet some 9500 years ago. In particular they report on ice-core studies indicating that a significant quantity of dust was deposited in the last years of the Pleistocene, which has been found to have the same chemical content as that deposited in the Tunguska region of Russia by another extraterrestrial body in 1908. Napier has separately pointed out that even a 200-meter-diameter body would produce devastating tidal waves if it hit the ocean.[23]

Clube and Napier are sometimes ridiculed for attempting to trace the memory of this supposed impact in the texts, art and architecture of our ancient civilizations, but their work is generally accepted as scientific in nature. The same cannot be said, unfortunately, of Derek Allan and Bernard Delair's 1995 work *When the Earth Nearly Died*. They follow a similar line, although they suggest that the catastrophe was caused by the close passage of a large extraterrestrial body, possibly even a runaway planet, at the earlier date of 11,500 years ago. Their linking of this to the Greek tradition of Phaethon is one thing. But their highly literal translation of the Mesopotamian *Epic of Creation*, which we encountered several times in Part 1, is completely contextually inappropriate; yet they use it to determine the supposed path of the extraterrestrial body in question.[24] Not only that but they appear to borrow significantly from Zecharia Sitchin's much earlier and equally misguided work on the subject without crediting him in their voluminous footnotes.[25]

An even more serious criticism of Allan and Delair is their suggestion that all supposed evidence of glaciation – boulder deposition, underlying rock striation and so forth – was in fact caused by cascades of water from the massive flooding induced by this one catastrophic event.[26] This denial of ice age theory is simply not tenable, and is compounded by their following Velikovsky and Hapgood in questioning the age of various mountain ranges – another fringe theory that receives little or no orthodox support. So despite the highly detailed and well-referenced appearance of their work, it is questionable to say the least.

THE CAROLINA BAYS

Probably the best-known physical evidence put forward in support of extraterrestrial disruption at the end of the Pleistocene are the Carolina Bays. These were described by Velikovsky as 'oval craters thickly scattered over the Carolina coast of the United States and more sparsely over the entire Atlantic coastal plain from southern New Jersey to northeastern Florida'.[27] In fact they had been discovered in aerial photographs taken over South Carolina in the 1930s, but they are now thought to number as many as half a million, the largest being 14 miles in length. They also display some remarkably consistent features in that most are to some extent oval, have their longest axes more or less oriented northwest to southeast, and have an elevated rim of earth at the southeastern end.[28]

In Velikovsky's day it was commonly accepted that some form of extraterrestrial agent must have been involved in their creation. The first major study by Frank Melton and William Shriever in 1932 concentrated on the evidence in Carolina itself, and concluded that the bays had resulted from the impact of a meteorite shower anywhere from 50,000 to a million years ago.[29] Then in 1952 William Prouty proposed not only a much more recent date of about 11,000 years ago, but also the idea that they were created by shock waves resulting from the aerial explosion of an extraterrestrial body before it hit the ground.[30] At about the same time evidence began to emerge of supposedly similar elliptical bays as far afield as Alaska and the Yukon down to the Beni region of northeast Bolivia.[31]

As always a key issue is the age of these bays. In the 1950s a team from Duke University found a layer of bluish clay that appeared to have been deposited in some of the Carolina examples shortly after their formation, and the sediments immediately above and below this yielded radiocarbon dates in the range of 11–10,000 years ago.[32] However more recent surveys provide a wide range of dates stretching back tens of thousands of years, suggesting they were not formed simultaneously by one major catastrophic event.[33] The supposed similarity of other formations away from the eastern seaboard is also called into question, as is the supposedly uniform orientation. Indeed it is now commonly accepted amongst geologists that all these formations were created by purely terrestrial processes, although there remains plenty of debate about what these might have been – with wind and subsurface water erosion the preferred candidates.[34]

All this appears to leave us with precious little reliable evidence for a late-Pleistocene catastrophe. But that is not the end of the story.

THE YOUNGER-DRYAS EVENT

Most of the pro-catastrophe research considered so far in this chapter is relatively old and obsolete, but there have been some more recent developments that are worthy of scrutiny at the minimum. Although various more academic papers provide the support, their focal point is a work called *The Cycle of Cosmic Catastrophes*, published in 2006. Its main author is Richard Firestone, a nuclear physicist from the Lawrence Berkeley National Laboratory, and there are two key areas of heated archaeological and geological debate that the book sets out to explain.

The first is the sudden disappearance of the Clovis culture from North America around 13,000 years ago, after only 500 years or so of existence.[35] After this point virtually nothing appears in the archaeological record until the apparently much sparser Folsom and other similar cultures emerge around 11,000 years ago.[36] So there appears to be a gap of at much as two millennia in which there is precious little human activity of any consequence across the whole of North America. The second curiosity is the so-called Younger-Dryas stadial.[37] Generally the global climate had been entering a warmer interglacial phase after the last glacial maximum around 20,000 years ago, and yet from around 13,000 years ago there is evidence of a rapid reversal, at least across most parts of the northern hemisphere. This 'Big Freeze' lasted until 11,500 years ago. One theory is that it was caused by a change in the thermal currents in the North Atlantic, possibly as a result of a sudden influx of fresh water from a glacial melt or dam-burst in Northeast America. But experts are hardly in conclusive agreement as to what triggered it and nor it seems has such a reversal been a common feature of previous glacial terminations.

Firestone argues that the alignment of the two sets of dates is no coincidence, and that the Clovis culture was virtually wiped out by a bombardment of extraterrestrial debris – now commonly referred to as the 'Younger-Dryas Event' – which also caused the mass extinctions of megafauna mentioned previously. Of course the lives of any large animals not caught up in the immediate conflagration associated with such a catastrophe would soon be proportionately more threatened by their greater dependence on scarce food supplies, whether vegetarian or carnivore.

Firestone first became involved in this research via Bill Topping, an archaeologist from Michigan who had stumbled upon an unusual feature of the chert flints from various Clovis sites: many of them had multiple microscopic particles of iron embedded beneath the surface, although always on one side only, and experiments proved they must have been traveling in excess of 1000 miles an hour. The depth of the tiny craters decreased progressively the further away from the Great Lakes the site was, suggesting that this area was near the center of the event.[38]

Firestone then visited various Clovis sites himself, collecting and analyzing various samples.[39] He found:

- The same tiny craters with buried magnetic grains, not just in chert but also in mammoth tusks from Siberia as well as Alaska – suggesting the event had impacted the whole northern hemisphere. Again these would only ever be on one side.

- Abundant tiny magnetic grains and spherules just at the end of the Clovis-layer sediment at the Younger-Dryas boundary, but not above or below.

- Markedly increased levels of radioactivity in sediment at the same boundary, and in chert and tusk samples.

- A widespread 'black mat' of dense, dark, organic material right on the boundary, thought to have been formed by the decomposition of algae. No Clovis or megafauna remains are ever found above it, only below. This mat corresponds to a similar layer called the

Usselo horizon found at a number of sites in Northern Europe.

- Tiny pieces of molten black glass with holes in it like 'foam' that were not of the normal silica glass composition.[40]

In addition he devotes a chapter to drumlins.[41] These are whale-shaped hills whose formation is known to be associated with glaciation because they are commonly found at the edges of glacial spread in North America and northern Europe. Although the exact mechanism by which they were formed is unclear, the most widely accepted theory involves a '*catastrophic flooding release of highly pressurized water flowing underneath the glacial ice*'.[42] He contends that drumlins have been generally carbon-dated to the end of the Pleistocene, and he also found a high concentration of magnetic particles in the original top level of several examples in Alberta.

Firestone also attempts a thorough reappraisal of the Carolina Bays, noting the following:[43]

- The pure white sand on many of their rims is not found elsewhere in the region, and is indicative of superheating.

- Ten of them contained concentrations of magnetic particles in their rims.

- The wind and subsurface water theories cannot explain why so many bays actually overlap each other, and why wind and water have conspicuously failed to create any more of them in the last 10,000 years.

- The often non-sequential dating of bay layers is due to the blasting of sediment into the air and its jumbled redeposition, rendering most dating attempts flawed.

- There is evidence of more eroded bays across Nebraska, Kansas and Texas.

- The bays generally show a marked similarity to the shallow craters that litter the surface of the moon and of Mars.

- There are not more of them on earth purely because we have more wind and surface water action to *erase* them, while those that survive must be relatively recent.

- They are shallow and elliptical, just as on the other planets, because they were created by the low-angle impacts of secondary debris.

- They have several groups of alignments, pointing to several main impact sites. One of these is Lake Michigan, which is itself a main crater because there is no sediment within it dating to before the Younger-Dryas Event.

- Even main craters such as Lake Michigan are relatively shallow because they were caused by comet rather than asteroid explosions in mid-air, comets being much less dense.

- All of this represents a significant body of argument for a sudden, extraterrestrial cause of widespread bay formation.

Firestone places all this considerable quantity of evidence within the broader context of an original supernova explosion 41.000 years ago. But whether or not that is appropriate his basic evidence is not without its critics. In particular a separate team from the Universities of Wyoming and Arizona have attempted to replicate his findings in a number of Clovis sites, several of which were part of his original research, and as far as magnetic grains and spherules in sediments are concerned they report no evidence whatsoever of a higher concentration at the Younger-Dryas boundary.[44] Yet Firestone reports that his test with a supermagnet was so simple and effective that the chief archaeologist at one of the sites both teams visited, Topper in South Carolina, accepted that it could be used to locate the Clovis layer when this is problematic.[45] In addition the Wyoming-Arizona team do not address, for example, the issue of radioactivity or, perhaps most important, of the grains buried deep within chert and ivory. On top of that there are plenty of other specialists who were either involved in the original research, or who have entered the fray since with new evidence, who support the idea of a catastrophic Younger-Dryas Event.[46]

The debates about this event and about, for example, drumlin and bay formation, are by no means over; undoubtedly further research will shed more light on all these issues. But for the moment at least it does look as if substantial evidence of a late-Pleistocene catastrophe is finally available. To be more precise this evidence seems to suggest that it was caused by one or more comets or fragments thereof exploding in mid-air at the very least above what are now the Great Lakes, and that all this happened some time around 13,000 years ago.

POLE SHIFTS AND REVERSALS

Before we move on there are a couple of catastrophe-related topics that have received widespread attention in the revisionist world, especially in recent decades, and that might usefully be clarified. The first is the idea of the *physical* poles that mark the axis around which the earth rotates changing their position, and the second is of the *magnetic* poles doing likewise and even reversing. These are quite different issues because magnetic north and true north are not the same.

AXIS SHIFTS VERSUS CRUSTAL DISPLACEMENT

If we commence with physical pole shifts, it is the offset of the plane of the equator from that of our ecliptic orbit around the sun – currently about 23.5 degrees – that not only creates the seasons but also, if it changed, would alter the configuration of the tropical, temperate and arctic zones of the earth. Cuvier certainly supported the concept of pole shifts, and felt that one must have occurred suddenly in a relatively recent epoch in order to account for the apparently flash-frozen mammoths of Siberia and Alaska.[47] Then both Velikovsky and Hapgood argued that an explanation was required for the inconsistent glaciation across the globe whereby certain northerly regions remained free of ice even at the height of the Pleistocene.[48] They also suggested there are various enigmas in arctic and even antarctic regions – for example, fossilized trees, forests and coral reefs – indicating that these may once have been temperate zones.[49] These ideas were picked up in the mid-1990s by revisionists such as Rand Flem-Ath and Graham Hancock.[50]

There are two main mechanisms by which a pole shift could occur. Either the entire earth could shift its position relative to the sun in a genuine axis shift, or the hard outer crust or lithosphere could move relative to the semimolten mantle underneath in a crustal displacement. The latter would have the same effect in terms of climate change at a particular location on the landmass, albeit that the angle of the ecliptic would actually remain unchanged. Both mechanisms, however, require a huge amount of force.

Hapgood favored the latter theory, arguing that crustal displacement would be caused by an asymmetrical build-up of ice at the poles. However he admitted that any significant shifting of the crust would take several thousand years at least, because there would be great resistance to the crust trying to move over the mantle. So his use of it to support the idea of a late-Pleistocene catastrophe is somewhat self-defeating. So if there were any need to invoke some special mechanism to explain apparently anomalous climatic evidence, a genuine axis shift would seem to be the more likely candidate.

But what catalyst would provide enough energy to cause such a sudden shift of the whole planet that it produced massive, rapid and permanent climate change? Velikovsky argued that there is only one, and that is the impact of an extraterrestrial body.[51] More recently mathematician Flavio Barbiero has backed up this view with detailed research that 'analyses the behavior of a gyroscope subjected to a disturbing force, and shows that the torque generated by the impact of a relatively small asteroid is capable of causing almost instantaneous changes of the axis of rotation and therefore instantaneous shifts of the poles in any direction and of any amplitude'.[52]

The problem with all this, however, is that the supposedly anomalous climatic evidence that triggered these theories has more recently been proven to be perfectly explainable via existing, non-catastrophic mechanisms. For example the supposed fossil enigmas in arctic regions date to remote epochs when there was almost no glaciation at all, while inconsistent glaciation is perfectly well understood.[53]

There is no credible, physical evidence of crustal displacement having occurred at the end of the Pleistocene or at any other time.[54] As for an axis shift, even though science may not yet have all the answers to the vagaries of ice ages, it would have to be well down the list of possible explanations for them. Having said that, if there had ever been an axis shift at some time in the past it is hard to see how we would definitively know.

MAGNETIC POLE REVERSALS AND SOLAR FLARES

Particles of molten rock with any iron content align themselves with the magnetic poles as they solidify, thereby keeping a permanent record of their position at the time.[55] But in the early twentieth century geologists found that some rocks were magnetized in a completely different direction to what they expected, and in time further research revealed that the magnetic poles have completely switched tens of thousands of times in earth's history. Contrary to many popular reports such geomagnetic reversals are almost certainly not cyclic but entirely sporadic; for example, at some times in earth's history the field has remained unchanged for tens of millions of years, while at the opposite end of the scale two reversals have been known to occur within as little as 50,000 years.

It is also highly unlikely that such reversals are indicative of crustal displacement or axis shifts in the past, although this is what Hapgood suggests. The most commonly held theory about the source of earth's magnetic field is that convection currents in the molten core act as a dynamo, so that changes in the field would be the result of changes in that flow. What would be the effects of a complete reversal if one were to occur? We cannot say because no one has lived through such an event in recorded history, the last one having occurred around 780,000 years ago. But as far as we know it did not cause mass extinctions of our distant ancestors or any other species, and there is certainly no time correlation between reversals and mass extinctions. There would, however, be a significant impact on animal species that use the earth's magnetic field to navigate, such as migrating birds. Related to all this is the question of how rapidly such reversals occur and, although it is clear that the rate of change of the field's strength and direction can vary considerably, it seems highly unlikely that they can happen literally 'overnight'.

Popular reports also suggest that we are due for another reversal shortly, but again there is no solid evidence for this. The field has been weakening over the last century and a half and recently this has accelerated, as has the change in direction of polarity, but the latter is still relatively slow at tens of kilometers per year. Above all expert opinion is united that these changes are well within historical parameters, and that fluctuations over time are so unpredictable that to attempt to extrapolate them – especially in any sort of linear fashion – is entirely inappropriate.

A rather different issue is the fact that earth's magnetic field interacts with that of the sun and other planets, all of which determines the extent and shape of the magnetosphere.[56] Indeed it is our magnetic field, combined with our atmosphere, that normally protects us from the winds or flares that emanate from the sun. However related research into 'sun spots' – areas of intense magnetic activity on the sun's surface – suggests these operate on an 11-year cycle, and that at the high points 'coronal mass ejections' cause geomagnetic storms that can cause serious disruption on earth.[57] These cycles have presumably been going on for a very long time, and there is no evidence that they have ever produced worldwide catastrophes. Nevertheless with our increasing dependence on all things electrical it is clear that the potential for widespread disruption is now far greater than it used to be; the most recent example of just such a storm knocking out electrical power supplies over a wide area of Quebec in 1989 should perhaps serve as a warning to us all.

MEMORIES

So much for the physical evidence that there was a major catastrophe towards the end of the Pleistocene. But did memories of these terrible events manage to survive in oral form for thousands of years before being incorporated, sometimes in somewhat distorted form, into the written traditions of the earliest civilizations of the modern epoch?

We have already mentioned the abundance of generalized flood traditions from around the world, but some of them appear to contain particularly detailed descriptions of just the sort of ancillary events that would support the idea of an extraterrestrial event, possibly even including an axis shift. For example we saw in chapter 2 how in the Ethiopian *Book of Enoch* 'the earth became inclined' as 'destruction approached', 'the earth labored, and was violently shaken', 'the moon changed its laws' and 'many chiefs among the stars... perverted their ways'; and how in the Mesopotamian *Erra and Ishum* Marduk-Enlil made 'the positions of the stars of heaven change' and 'did not return them to their places'. In chapter 4 we saw how in the Taoist *Essays from Huai Nan Tzu* 'the four seasons failed', 'thunder-bolts wrought havoc', 'hailstones fell with violence' and 'noxious miasma and untimely hoarfrosts fell unceasingly'. Then in chapter 5 we saw how in Plato's *Timaeus* Phaethon was described as the child of the sun who 'harnessed his father's chariot but was unable to guide it along his father's course', as a result of which there was 'a widespread destruction by fire of things on the earth'; and how during one destruction in the Hopi traditions 'the world teetered off balance', 'mountains plunged into seas', 'seas and lakes sloshed over the land' and 'the world froze into solid ice', while during another 'waves higher than mountains rolled in upon the land' and 'continents broke asunder and sank beneath the seas'. This is all in addition to the more general descriptions of multiple destructions by flood, fire, volcano, hurricane and earthquake preserved in the various South American world age traditions we reviewed.

There are many similar and detailed descriptions of apparently catastrophic events in the traditions of indigenous cultures around the world, not only from the Americas but from Africa, Australasia and Oceania too.[58] Meanwhile Mesopotamian texts include numerous references to fierce battles conducted by the gods, especially those associated with atmospheric phenomena. They include Ninurta, who is not only the god of war but also of floods, and is further identified with the 'thunderbird' known as Imdugud; and Ishkur, the storm god.[59] Furthermore they have weapons with similar associations, such as the *abubu* or flood weapon, and the *kasusu* or wind weapon.[60]

One of the finest examples is the Sumerian *Ninurta Myth* that dates to the beginning of the second millennium BCE and is a composite of three original parts. In the first Ninurta is accompanied by his trusty friend and weapon Sharur, described as 'the one who lays low multitudes' and 'the flood storm of battle', while engaging in a fierce battle with the enigmatic Azag, an object or creature whose main weapon is its 'dreadful aura'. The translator, Thorkild Jacobsen, suggests that Azag is a tree of some sort on the basis that it is described as being the product of 'heaven copulating with verdant earth', but arguably this is just as likely to represent an impacting extraterrestrial body. This possibility is strengthened when we find Jacobsen admitting that Azag's description at the end of this part changes enigmatically to *zalag* stone, no translation of which is even attempted.[61] Meanwhile Ninurta's march into battle is described thus:[62]

> The evil wind and the south storm were tethered to him, the flood storm strode at their flanks, and before the warrior went a huge irresistible tempest, it was tearing up the dust, depositing it again, evening out hill and dale, filling in hollows; live coals it rained down, fire burned, flames scorched, tall trees it toppled from their roots, denuding the forests. Earth wrung her hands against the heart, emitting cries of pain... the desert was burnt off as if denuded by locusts, the wave rising in its path was shattering the mountains.

We then find that when Ninurta attacks Azag 'the sun marched no longer, it had turned into a moon... the day was made black like pitch';[63] and when Azag retaliates:[64]

> It screamed wrathfully, like a formidable serpent it hissed from among its people, it wiped up the waters in the highland, swept away the tamarisks, it gashed the earth's body, made painful wounds, gave the canebrake over to fire, and bathed the sky in blood, the interior it knocked over, scattered its people, and till today black cinders are in the fields, and ever heaven's base becomes to the observer like red wool – thus verily it is.

Finally, once the battle is over, we are given the following description of the aftermath:[65]

> In those days the waters of the ground coming from below did not flow out over the fields. As ice long accumulating they rose in the mountains on the far side... in dire famine nothing was produced.

If any literal rather than symbolic interpretation of this text is appropriate then it is certainly possible to argue that it describes a catastrophe of some sort, which is unlikely to have been merely local given that Mesopotamia itself has not been icebound for many millions of years.[66]

If we now turn to the world age traditions of the classical Greek writers, although we have seen they are somewhat unreliable, they do in general follow up on the Mesopotamian themes of violent gods associated with severe atmospheric phenomena. For example in his relatively short *Theogony* Hesiod does not mention the flood specifically, but his descriptions of Zeus' wars with the giant Titans and with Thyphoeus – the forerunner for the later Phaethon – are highly comparable to those of Ninurta.[67] Nor is it any surprise that Scandinavian traditions continue in the same vein. For example at the end of the first part of Snorri's *Edda* we find the passage that describes Ragnarok, the 'twilight of the gods'. On the face of it this is presented as a forecast of a time to come, but arguably it is much more likely to be a distorted description of events that took place long ago – especially given its two survivors at the end who go on to 'people the world':[68]

> Snow will drive from all quarters, there will be hard frosts and biting winds; the sun will be no use. There will be three such winters on end with no summer between... the wolf will swallow the sun and that will seem a great disaster to men. Then another wolf will seize the moon and that one too will do great harm. The stars will disappear from heaven. Then this will come to pass, the whole surface of the earth and the mountains will tremble so violently that trees will be uprooted from the ground, mountains will crash down, and all fetters and bonds will be snapped and severed... The sea will lash against the land... Surt will fling fire over the earth and burn up the whole world... The sun will go black, earth sink in the sea, heaven be stripped of its bright stars; smoke will rage and fire, leaping the flame, lick heaven itself... While the world is being burned by Surt, in a place called Hoddmimir's Wood, will be concealed two human beings called Lif and Lifthrasir. Their food will be the morning dews, and from these men will come so great a stock that the whole world will be peopled.

Of course we must be ever vigilant for the symbolism in these accounts, particularly those describing battles involving gods and their weapons. Nevertheless it seems reasonable to suggest that the detailed body of textual and traditional evidence of catastrophe from all around the world is underpinned by some genuine memories of a terrible worldwide destruction, whose survivors were keen to preserve the knowledge of what had happened.

LIKELY LOCALES

We have already seen that our modern human ancestors had moved out of Africa and across Asia to reach Australia by 40,000 years ago. So our forgotten race would clearly have had a great deal of freedom to travel to any climate that suited them across a wide geographic area.

So what was the climate like during the late Pleistocene, in particular from around 50,000 years ago? Global temperatures were anything from five to ten degrees Celsius colder at different times, so it would be obvious for them to focus on what are now the tropical zones on either side of the equator. Even the temperate zones just outside the tropics of Cancer and Capricorn, which lie on the 23rd parallel north and south respectively, might have been perfectly habitable because, as we can see from Figure 7, even at the height of the Pleistocene the ice sheet only reached down to the 50th parallel in northern Europe and far less in northern Asia. But generally it is probably sensible to limit our search to the tropical zones, as shown between the two lines in Figure 8.

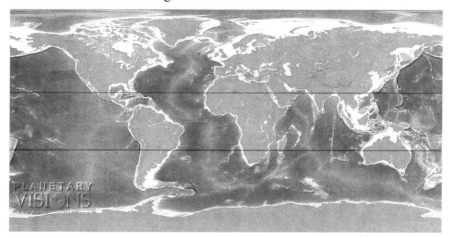

Figure 8: The Continents in the Late Pleistocene [69]

But we must also factor in our fundamental assumption that our forgotten race would have wanted to live on the coast for ease of trading – that is, for ease of carrying heavy and bulky quantities of goods by boat instead of dragging them by land. This immediately imposes some logistical limitations. The coastlines of the American continent in the tropical zone are abundant, including those of much of Mexico, Columbia, Venezuela, Peru and Brazil, not to mention the islands of the Greater and Lesser Antilles. The same is true of the West African coast from Senegal down to Angola. However, even if our forgotten race were expert sailors, each of these destinations would have represented an extremely long voyage both from each other and from anywhere else. By contrast anywhere on a huge stretch of equatorial coastline from northern Mozambique up across Arabia and India and on into Southeast Asia and Indonesia could easily have been traversed just by hugging it and keeping land in sight.

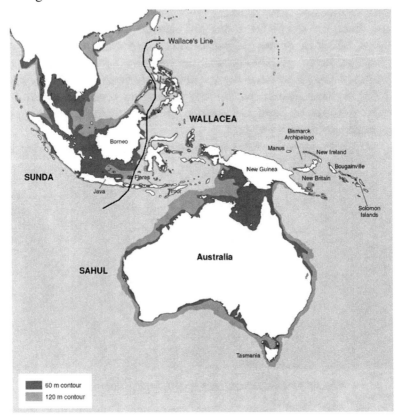

Figure 9: The Sunda and Sahul Shelves

If we now turn to sea levels, around 50,000 years ago they were 75 meters lower while during the last glacial maximum around 20,000 years ago they were a full 120 meters lower.[70] So, except in those areas where there is little in the way of continental shelf, *all* coastlines have been pushed inwards to a greater or lesser extent. Not only that but if we look at Figure 8, in which the white underwater areas are less than 200 meters in depth, we can see that in the tropical zone the greatest area of now sunken landmass that was above water during the late Pleistocene is in Southeast Asia. Closer inspection of this area in Figure 9 shows that the bulk of the islands that now make up Indonesia were connected to each other and to the main Asian continent, forming a landmass extension known as the Sunda Shelf or 'Sundaland'. Similarly the Sahul Shelf connected Australia and New Guinea, although there was a deepwater divide between these two even then.[71]

But for us to pinpoint our forgotten race still further we need to appreciate that the ice age climate varied considerably even at any given latitude.[72] For example if we refer back to Figure 7 we can see that some parts of northeast Asia and Alaska were never glaciated despite being extremely cold, because weather patterns in these areas remained particularly dry so snow could not fall. Similarly the climate and vegetation in different parts of the tropical zone varied considerably, as today. Some areas were mainly desert, others tropical rainforest or woodland. But the ones we are most interested in were the areas of tropical grassland, where rainfall and other conditions would have been most conducive to the cultivation of crops.

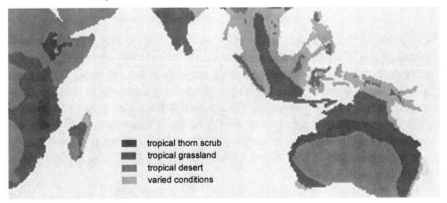

Figure 10: Vegetation at the Last Glacial Maximum

Figure 10 shows the vegetation in the key coastal areas previously discussed at the last glacial maximum. The very darkest grey areas represent tropical thorn scrub, but the next darkest are those representing tropical grassland. We can see that these conditions persisted in south and central East Africa, but as we head north along the coast we reach a considerable area of extreme tropical desert – represented by the medium grey shading – that continues all along the northeast African and Arabian coastline until we reach India. Here we return to grassland across the entire country, conditions also found in central Southeast Asia and northern

Australasia. The lightest shade of grey that surrounds much of this represents a variety of other conditions. Of course all these conditions would have varied at other times during the late Pleistocene but, generally speaking, if we are looking for locations conducive to both settled agriculture and trading by sea over reasonable distances, then the now submerged coastal areas of India and Southeast Asia are arguably the strongest contenders.

In this context it is useful to consider the scholarly contribution of British geneticist Stephen Oppenheimer. In his 1999 work *Eden in the East* he uses oceanography, archaeology, linguistics, genetics and what he quaintly refers to as folklore to propose that the world's most ancient known civilizations in China, India, Mesopotamia and Egypt all originated from a highly cultured population living in Southeast Asia in the late Pleistocene – which was forced to disperse when their homeland was submerged as sea levels rose.[73]

CONCLUSION

Despite the fact that much of the older evidence for a major catastrophe at the end of the Pleistocene has now been comprehensibly rebutted, the more recent research of Firestone et al still presents a strong case. If they are right it most likely involved some sort of interaction with one or more comets around 13,000 years ago. Wherever our forgotten race had spread to at the time – and our best guess would be the former coasts of India and Southeast Asia – their settlements could easily have been wiped out by huge tsunamis; and if that did not destroy them, subsequent rapidly rising sea levels would have.

This must surely have been followed by a transitional period of great hardship and difficult climatic conditions, during which they may have had to return to a more hunter-gatherer lifestyle and survive as best they could, all the time waiting for the climate to re-stabilize and to see where it might be best to settle down again. Over a period of as much as 1500 years they probably spread out from equatorial regions and into what were becoming the new temperate zones that would now be best suited for the reestablishment of agriculture and permanent settlements, and the Neolithic sites uncovered in the Near East may represent the earliest phase of this rebuilding process. Building in stone in more remote inland areas might now have become a necessity to protect themselves from marauding nomads still struggling to survive – one that neatly dovetailed with their understandable desire to avoid repeating the fate of their submerged, coast-based ancestors.

Not only that but it seems these generations of survivors preserved the memory of what had befallen their forebears in the more vivid catastrophe traditions that survive all around the globe.

11

LOST CONTINENTS

Legends of the lost continents of Atlantis and Lemuria have proliferated massively in the last few centuries, and they show little sign of abating. But do they have any sort of solid foundations, and if so do they have anything of value to offer us in our search for our forgotten race?

PLATO'S ATLANTIS

The oldest account of Atlantis is provided by Plato in his *Timaeus* and *Critias*. We have already noted in chapter 4 that, although he provides a remarkable description of the original spirituality and subsequent debasement of the inhabitants that is completely consistent with our main theme, the aspect that has tended to captivate revisionists ever since is the tantalizing but far more prosaic one of its original location.[1]

Their search has usually involved trying to match a variety of sites to his lengthy descriptions not only of its general whereabouts – that is beyond the 'Pillars of Hercules' or Straits of Gibraltar – but also of its layout.[2] The main acropolis apparently comprised a vast palace with several temples surrounded by concentric rings of land and water, forming a complex network of bridges, canals and docks encircled by a huge outer wall with dense adjacent housing. All this lay on a large flat plain surrounded by mountains, but the entire island was much larger and split into ten districts, each ruled by a separate governor. The buildings were constructed from stone as well as timber, their walls covered with metals such as gold, silver, bronze, tin and 'orichalc'.[3] The temples were full of gold statues, there were public baths and gardens and an elaborate water system, the docks contained large trireme ships and were a hive of activity, and there was even a horseracing track. Plato concludes by providing details of the military and political organization of the island. It is of course all this that sowed the seeds of the idea that the Atlanteans had a relatively high level of technology, at least equivalent to anything that existed in his own time.

Although much of this is consistent with the general idea of a culturally but not technologically advanced civilization, suggestions of the widespread use of stone and metal in art and architecture may owe more to Plato's vivid imagination than to ancient records of what is now prehistory. We also saw previously that his whole account is placed within the artificial political context of the supremacy of the antediluvian Athenians. But this does not have to mean that it is entirely fictitious, because we already know how common it is for old traditions to be expediently edited to suit the political needs of the time.

Yet even if we limit ourselves to the general location, it is clear that most contenders for Plato's Atlantis are seriously flawed. The Greek island of Santorini or Thera is one of the favorites because it is a volcanic caldera that suffered a massive eruption around 1500 BCE, which had disastrous consequences for both itself and Minoan Crete.[4] Yet not only is it within the Mediterranean rather than beyond its entrance but it does not fit with his 9500 BCE timescale for the destruction either. The suggestion that a landmass named Atland or Aldland in the North Sea disappeared under the waves around 2200 BCE suffers from similar shortcomings.[5] Meanwhile the idea that the continent of Antarctica was in what is now the southern Atlantic, and therefore largely free of ice until it was moved to its present location by a crustal shift at the end of the Pleistocene, is not borne out by geological evidence.[6] A more recent suggestion is a submerged landmass in the Caribbean Sea in the vicinity of Cuba, but as we will see in the next chapter the physical evidence for this is less than convincing.[7]

Of course a large, submerged continent within the Atlantic Ocean itself is the best known of all the suggestions – and the two names are very close, although conventional thinking is that the ocean is named after the Greek god Atlas.[8] What is more, as we will shortly see this idea has tended to be accompanied by the similar suggestion that the earlier Lemurian civilization inhabited a former continent in the Indian or Pacific Oceans. However the relatively modern confirmation of the theory of continental drift via the understanding of plate tectonics has tended to leave both these ideas very much on the fringes.[9] That is not to say that the idea of sunken landmasses is entirely rejected by professional geologists, it is just that the major ones they do accept – such as the Kerguelen Plateau in the far south of the Indian Ocean, and the Zealandian Continent that surrounds New Zealand – were submerged tens of millions of years ago.[10] The only conventionally accepted submerged continent that fits into reasonable timescales for human evolution is Sundaland, which we have already pinpointed as one of the most likely locales for our forgotten race. In this context at least one other researcher has recently placed Atlantis in what is now Indonesia, and that is Arysio Santos in his 2005 work *Atlantis: The Lost Continent Finally Found.*[11]

In any case what is arguably more interesting than the locations of Atlantis and for that matter Lemuria, and has been less well documented in recent decades, is the body of work that follows up on the nature of their inhabitants and of their destruction. Much of this material is not only old but has also supposedly been channeled from ethereal sources, and in the epilogue we will discuss this method of gaining information in more detail. But for the moment suffice to say that, although there is an argument that channeled material should not *necessarily* be rejected on a priori grounds, its reliability can vary considerably from source to source and from channel to channel. Nevertheless it will be instructive to see whether it sheds any interesting light on our central theme.

FOUNDING FATHERS

In his excellent 1954 compilation of Atlantis traditions, *Lost Continents*, Lyon Sprague de Camp chronicles the various references to Plato's account in the work of his mainly Greek and Roman successors. Then as now they were clearly split between believers and skeptics, but they added nothing new from any other ancient source.[12]

Then from about the sixth century all discussion of Atlantis seems to have disappeared, until it began to be resurrected after the Spanish conquest of South America in the sixteenth century. Initially the favored suggestion was that the Americas themselves were Plato's target, but it became increasingly clear that in many indigenous American traditions their ancestors were reported as having arrived from the East after their home continent sank, so the focus shifted to the Atlantic Ocean. These traditions were first recorded by Diego de Landa, a Spanish priest who became bishop of Yucatán after the conquest. Although on one side his religious fervor led him to seek out and burn as many original Mayan books and codices as he could find he also, almost schizophrenically, spent a great deal of time learning and recording as much as he could about Mayan customs and religion, leaving an invaluable legacy. However he seems to have frightened two Mayan assistants into furnishing him with a completely false alphabet for supposedly translating each Mayan glyph into its equivalent in the Roman alphabet, and it was not until the twentieth century that scholars realized each glyph is a whole syllable.[13]

In fact de Landa's false alphabet remained lost until the 1860s anyway, but then French historian Charles-Etienne Brasseur de Bourbourg rediscovered it and attempted to use it to translate the *Troano Codex*.[14] He coupled this with a hugely fertile imagination to produce a mangled tale of a lost continent from a work that, as we saw in chapter 5, is now known to be largely divinatory. Far worse, according to Sprague de Camp he found there were two glyphs he could not translate that vaguely resembled de Landa's *m* and *u* and, with a massive leap of logic, concluded they spelled out the name of said continent. This is how the name *Mu* entered modern folklore, but we should be clear that it has no sound basis. It was also around this time that the name Lemuria was coined by the zoologist Philip L. Sclater. Contemporary geologists believed there had once been a landmass connecting India and Madagascar, and he proposed that this accounted for lemurs being found in those two countries but not in Africa. The name has stuck ever since, even though it is now more often associated with the Pacific.[15]

Not long after this the Jersey-born antiquarian Augustus Le Plongeon entered the fray. But he compounded Brasseur de Bourbourg's errors in translating the *Troano Codex* and, with the assistance of various other inscriptions from the ruined city of Chichen-Itza, conjured up a tale of Queen Moo of Atlantis or Mu who fled from the devastation to Egypt where she had the Great Sphinx built as a memorial.[16] He also quoted the work of various contemporary 'pyramidiots' who insisted that these monuments too had been erected when Atlantis sank. We saw briefly in chapter 3 that all this flies in the face of the sound archaeological evidence that these monuments are only around 4500 years old but, because these ideas retain a significant degree of popular support, we will return to them in the next chapter.

But from an exoteric perspective at least it was former US politician Ignatius Donnelly who really resurrected the Atlantis tradition in the modern era with the publication of *Atlantis: The Antediluvian World* in 1882. He follows the line that it was a lost continent in the Atlantic, and asserts that the survivors of its civilization went on to found the earliest historically known ones on each side of that ocean after their homeland was destroyed. Yet we have already seen that this location is suspect. What is more he discusses the supposedly sudden emergence of the ancient

Egyptian civilization, and the supposed similarity between its pyramids and hieroglyphs and those in South America.[17] These observations too are highly suspect, but again because modern revisionists continue to repeat them we will return to them in the next chapter.

HPB

By contrast it was the infamous Russian-born Madame Helena Petrovna Blavatsky who fired up the more occult or esoteric side of the Atlantis legends at around the same time.[18] She traveled extensively in India and the Far East, although in her later years she split her time between England and America. She founded the Theosophical Society in 1875, and not long afterwards released her two best-known works, *Isis Unveiled* in 1877 and *The Secret Doctrine* in 1888. Both of these are massive, two-volume compilations stretching to more than fifteen hundred pages that are well referenced, but with a grammatical style that makes them particularly hard going. She has often been accused of plagiarism, not without some cause; indeed she herself admitted in later life that some of her channeling, including the apparent mid-air materialization of letters from the 'masters' who were its main source, was faked. Nevertheless it would be somewhat simplistic to reject the entirety of her huge and massively influential corpus on these grounds alone.

In particular some of the most interesting aspects of her work from our perspective are the stanzas reproduced from an 'archaic manuscript' to which she claims to have had access called the *Book of Dzyan*. Needless to say some argue that these are just fakes too, but recent research by theosophical scholar David Reigle reveals the possibility that they formed part of a closely guarded commentary on the *Books of Kiu-te*, the more common form of which is the *Kala Chakra*, the first tantra of a portion of the Tibetan Sacred Canon known as the *Kanjur*.[19] If so they *may* be relatively untainted by Blavatsky's own extensive commentaries on them, which as we will shortly see contain clear faults. It is therefore worth reproducing in full those stanzas that describe the five 'root races' of humanity:[20]

Stanza 5

18. The First were the sons of Yoga. Their sons the children of the Yellow Father and the White Mother.
19. The Second Race was the product by budding and expansion, the asexual from the sexless. Thus was, O Lanoo, the Second Race produced.

174

20. Their fathers were the Self-born. The Self-born, the Chhaya from the brilliant bodies of the Lords, the Fathers, the Sons of Twilight.

21. When the Race became old, the old waters mixed with the fresher waters. When its drops became turbid, they vanished and disappeared in the new stream, in the hot stream of life. The outer of the First became the inner of the Second. The old Wing became the new Shadow, and the Shadow of the Wing.

From the stanzas themselves it appears that these first and second races, described as 'self-born' and 'sweat-born' respectively, were only energetic beings with no physical body.[21] The third 'egg-born' race was then the first to become fully physically manifest:

Stanzas 6 to 8

22. Then the Second evolved the Egg-born, the Third. The sweat grew, its drops grew, and the drops became hard and round. The Sun warmed it; the Moon cooled and shaped it; the wind fed it until its ripeness. The white swan from the starry vault overshadowed the big drop. The egg of the future race, the Man-swan of the later third. First male-female, then man and woman.

23. The self-born were the Chhayas: the Shadows from the bodies of the Sons of Twilight.

24. The Sons of Wisdom, the Sons of Night, ready for rebirth, came down, they saw the vile forms of the First Third. 'We can choose', said the Lords, 'we have wisdom.' Some entered the Chhaya. Some projected the Spark. Some deferred til the Fourth. From their own Rupa they filled the Kama. Those who entered became Arhats. Those who received but a spark, remained destitute of knowledge; the spark burned low. The third remained mind-less. Their Jivas were not ready. These were set apart among the Seven. They became narrow-headed. The Third were ready. 'In these shall we dwell', said the Lords of the Flame.

25. How did the Manasa, the Sons of Wisdom, act? They rejected the Self-born. They are not ready. They spurned the Sweat-born. They are not quite ready. They would not enter the first Egg-born.

26. When the Sweat-born produced the Egg-born, the twofold and the mighty, the powerful with bones, the Lords of Wisdom said: 'Now shall we create.'

27. The Third Race became the Vahan of the Lords of Wisdom. It created 'Sons of Will and Yoga', by Kriyasakti it created them, the Holy Fathers, Ancestors of the Arhats.

28. From the drops of sweat; from the residue of the substance; matter from dead bodies of men and animals of the wheel before; and from cast-off dust, the first animals were produced.

29. Animals with bones, dragons of the deep, and flying Sarpas were added to the creeping things. They that creep on the ground got wings. They of the long necks in the water became the progenitors of the fowls of the air.

30. During the Third Race the boneless animals grew and changed: they became animals with bones, their Chhayas became solid.

31. The animals separated the first. They began to breed. The two-fold man separated also. He said: 'Let us as they; let us unite and make creatures.' They did.

32. And those which had no spark took huge she-animals unto them. They begat upon them dumb Races. Dumb they were themselves. But their tongues untied. The tongues of their progeny remained still. Monsters they bred. A race of crooked red-hair-covered monsters going on all fours. A dumb race to keep the shame untold.

These stanzas are confusing at best and self-contradictory at worst, but in general they seem to be describing a race with different strains or 'subraces', some good, some not so good. What is more they seem to bear out the theory, proposed in chapter 7, of multiple and initially unsuccessful incarnation attempts by individuated souls. In particular there seems to be uncertainty about whether the available forms are 'ready' for experienced souls to incarnate into, and a decision by some souls to 'defer til the fourth'; and a description of some of the race as 'dumb', reminding us of the traditions in which unsuccessful humans are 'silent' or 'cannot speak to praise their creators'.

Stanza 9

33. Seeing which, the Lhas who had not built men, wept, saying: –

34. 'The Amanasa have defiled our future abodes. This is karma. Let us dwell in the others. Let us teach them better, lest worse should happen.' They did.

35. Then all men became endowed with Manas. They saw the sin of the mindless.

36. The Fourth Race developed speech.

37. The One became Two; also all the living and creeping things that were still one, giant fish-birds and serpents with shell-heads.

This fourth race must surely be the golden race, not least because the theme of their subsequent debasement rings out loud and clear:

Stanzas 10 to 11

38. Thus two by two on the seven zones, the Third Race gave birth to the Fourth-Race men; the gods became no-gods; the sura became a-sura.

39. The first, on every zone, was moon-colored; the second yellow like

gold; the third red; the fourth brown, which became black with sin.[22] The first seven human shoots were all of one complexion. The next seven began mixing.

40. Then the Fourth became tall with pride. We are the kings, it was said; we are the gods.

41. They took wives fair to look upon. Wives from the mindless, the narrow-headed. They bred monsters. Wicked demons, male and female, also Khado (dakini), with little minds.

42. They built temples for the human body. Male and female they worshipped. Then the Third Eye acted no longer.

43. They built huge cities. Of rare earths and metals they built, and out of the fires vomited, out of the white stone of the mountains and of the black stone, they cut their own images in their size and likeness, and worshipped them.

44. They built great images nine yatis high, the size of their bodies. Inner fires had destroyed the land of their fathers. The water threatened the Fourth.

45. The first great waters came. They swallowed the seven great islands.

46. All Holy saved, the Unholy destroyed. With them most of the huge animals, produced from the sweat of the earth.

Despite the likely distortion that this race bred with inferiors to produce monsters, and the debatable suggestion that they were erecting huge cities containing huge stone statues, these stanzas contain all the traditions with which we are already familiar: the preoccupation with the material, the loss of the third eye of spirituality, and the eventual destruction by flood, which also eliminates most large animals.

Stanza 12

47. Few men remained: some yellow, some brown and black, and some red remained. The moon-colored were gone forever.

48. The Fifth produced from the holy stock remained; it was ruled over by the first divine Kings...

49 ...who re-descended, who made peace with the Fifth, who taught and instructed it.

And so we come to the fifth race, the survivors of the catastrophe who went on to found our current race. We even find the first 'divine kings' reincarnating to instruct their fellows, which has clear echoes of the more spiritual form of knowledge transfer we discussed in chapters 3 and 8.

If we now turn to the current topic of lost continents, there is no explicit mention of them in these stanzas. But Blavatsky's commentaries place them in the following context:[23]

- *The First Race,* although ethereal, inhabited the 'Imperishable Sacred Land' of which 'little can be said', although 'the pole star has its watchful eye upon it'.

- *The Second Race* resided in Hyperborea, named after the Greek traditions of a continent in the north, which at one time 'stretched out its promontories southward and westward from the North Pole' and 'comprised the whole of what is now known as Northern Asia'.

- *The Third Race* inhabited Lemuria, following Sclater's terminology, although Blavatsky identifies the continent with the entirety of the present Indian Ocean, right across to Indonesia and on down to Australia.

- *The Fourth Race* then migrated to *Atlantis,* which is implied to have been somewhere in the Atlantic and originally, somehow, an extension of Lemuria.

Blavatsky provides plenty more detail on these lost civilizations, but much of it confusing and contradictory. Fundamentally this aspect of her work is undermined not only by her proposed location for the Lemurian and Atlantean continents but even more by her dates for when they flourished. She asserts that the former emerged sometime before 18 million years ago and sank about 5 million years ago, while the bulk of the latter was submerged in stages between 2 and 1 million years ago, although the last remnants did not disappear until 9564 BCE. All of this is, of course, totally at odds with modern archaeology and geology.

To make matters worse she insists that various ancient monuments should be redated, and that the Lemuro-Atlanteans were highly technologically advanced – a stance that, as we will see in the next chapter, continues to be maintained by many modern revisionists despite substantial evidence to the contrary. For example she too commits the now-so-obviously-fatal mistake of proposing that the Great Pyramid was built by the last remnants of the Atlantean civilization around 78,000 years ago.[24] She suggests they may have been responsible for the pyramids at Angkor Wat in Cambodia and in Central and South America too, whereas we now know that all these structures are only a few thousand years old at most.[25] But she is at her most imaginative when she is one of the first to suggest, even in the 1880s, that the Indian epics contain descriptions of aeronautics – a skill supposedly taught to their ancestors by the Lemuro-Atlanteans.[26] Meanwhile there are obvious references to giants and semi-human chimeric monsters in the stanzas of the *Book of Dzyan,* and in the Hindu and other traditions to which she refers in her commentaries; but instead of recognizing them as already distorted, she compounds the problem in her detailed descriptions of some regressive Lemuro-Atlantean subraces.[27] Finally we might note that she places the root races within the overall context of the Hindu world cycles of manvantaras and so on that we discussed in chapter 5.[28]

So much for Blavatsky's distortions. As to her sources for the Atlantean and Lemurian material, it is clear that she drew extensively on a number of contemporary works. From a prosaic perspective these include Donnelly's *Atlantis*, and Louis Jacolliot's interpretations of Hindu traditions that posit a former continent in the Pacific rather than Indian Ocean called Rutas.[29] From an esoteric perspective one of the major sources she openly and repeatedly references is her fellow theosophist Alfred P Sinnett's *Esoteric Buddhism*, published in 1883, even though her ego cannot help but proclaim that she taught him everything he knew.[30] As to the extent to which her more occult speculations about Lemuria and Atlantis may have been genuinely channeled, this is almost impossible to determine. In fact arguably it is even harder to establish the real provenance of this material than it is that of the stanzas of the *Book of Dzyan*.

THEOSOPHICAL EVOLUTION

The next major player in the development of occult Atlantism was the theosophist William Scott-Elliot, who broadly follows Blavatsky's narrative in *The Story of Atlantis* and *The Lost Lemuria*, published in 1896 and 1904 respectively. However he manages to exaggerate a few of her distortions still further. If we commence with the most obvious he suggests, for example, that the two large Giza pyramids were erected by Atlantean evacuees just before a catastrophe that occurred as long as 200,000 years ago, 'partly to provide permanent Halls of Initiation, but also to act as treasure house and shrine for some great talisman of power during the submergence which the Initiates knew to be impending'.[31] He also adds considerable detail about the construction and power sources of the 'aerial boats' used by more important Atlanteans for transport.[32]

We are also told that he was 'allowed access to some maps and other records physically preserved from the remote periods concerned'; and that the Atlantean maps consisted of 'a globe, a good bas-relief in terracotta, and a well-preserved map on parchment, or skin of some sort', while those of Lemuria consisted of 'a broken terracotta model and a very badly preserved and crumpled map'.[33] Six reproductions of these maps are included in his work, two purporting to show the positioning of the major continents of the world at the time when Lemuria was 'at its greatest extent and then somewhat smaller in a later epoch', and four the continent of Atlantis as it was progressively destroyed by supposed catastrophes 800, 200, 80 and 11.5 thousand years ago.[34] The detailed contours of these landmasses and islands are superimposed on the current world map for comparison, but this only helps to emphasize that their positioning is totally at odds with modern geology. Not only that but his timescales too are totally unrealistic, especially with respect to his report that Lemuria was wiped out before the start of the Eocene, which we now date to 55 million years ago.

In the preface to *The Story of Atlantis* Sinnett explicitly reveals the method by which much of it was supposed to have been composed:

> There is no limit really to the resources of astral clairvoyance in investigations concerning the past history of the earth, whether we are concerned with the events that have befallen the human race in prehistoric epochs, or with the growth of the planet through geological periods which antedated the advent of man... Meanwhile the present volume is the first that has been put forward as the pioneer essay of the new method of historical research... Every fact stated in the present volume has been picked up bit by bit with watchful and attentive care, in the course of an investigation on which more than one qualified person has been engaged, in the intervals of other activity, for some years past.

It is interesting that on the face of it this suggests that 'astral clairvoyance' – channeling in modern parlance – had not been used by Sinnett himself or by Blavatsky in preparing their previous volumes. Meanwhile it has been suggested that Scott-Elliot's theosophical colleague Charles W Leadbeater was a major channel for much of this work but, if that is true, one might argue that this is a fine example of just how unreliable such material can sometimes be.[35]

Yet is that all? It just might be worth recording what Scott-Elliot has to say about the broader context of world cycles and human development because, for all that his timescales and geology appear to be hopelessly flawed, there just may be some gems mixed in – and the advantage is that his work is far shorter and easier to analyze than Blavatsky's.[36] Like her he places everything in the context of Hindu cycles, but the encouraging thing about Scott-Elliot's interpretation of these cycles is that each manvantara is regarded not as a *repetition* of the last one, with the same cycle of increasing decadence leading to destruction, but as an *evolution* of it. If there is any validity to any of this then such an underlying assumption fits the evolution-by-experience model of universal cycles, as expounded in chapter 5, far better than the Hindu original.

Also when referring to the ape lifeform he reports that 'it was an improvement on this type which was required, and this was most easily achieved by the Manu, through working out on the astral plane in the first instance, the archetype originally formed in the mind of the Logos'. In other words he seems to be suggesting there is some sort of universal, energetic blueprint for the human form, a fascinating subject raised in chapter 9.[37] As for the root races he describes the first as 'ethereal' and the second as 'astral', presumably denoting a lowering or densening of the vibrations between the two, although he indicates that neither would be visible to us. Then he comes to the third or Lemurian race:

> Lemurian man, during at least the first half of the race, must be regarded rather as an animal destined to reach humanity than as human according to our understanding of the term; for though the second and third groups of Pitris, who constituted the inhabitants of Lemuria during its first four subraces, had achieved sufficient self-consciousness in the Lunar Manvantara to differentiate them from the animal kingdom, they had not yet received the Divine Spark which should endow them with mind and individuality – in other words, make them truly human.

This latter is surely an explicit reference to the transition from group to individuated soul consciousness discussed in chapter 7. But by contrast Scott-Elliot's subsequent reports on the traits of the various Lemurian subraces enter into the world of complete fantasy – with the earliest, for example, being giants with no bone structure, while others domesticated dinosaurs. To make matters much more complex and bewildering the development of the various subraces is intertwined with the same evolutionary patterns on other planets and star systems. So, in summary, his work seems to be broadly unreliable but with a few possible nuggets thrown in.

The channeling approach was also adopted by Rudolf Steiner in his *Atlantis and Lemuria*, first published by the Theosophical Society in 1911 then republished in broadly similar form in 1923 by the Anthroposophical Society – a breakaway movement that Steiner formed after various disagreements. In the introduction he discloses that 'such history as this is written in very different letters from those which record the everyday events of past times, for this is Gnosis – known in anthroposophical speech as the Akashic Records'.[38] But however impressively esoteric this may sound, in this work at least he broadly follows the lead of his predecessors. Yet a few comments about the mental capacities of the various races are probably worth mentioning briefly. He suggests the Lemurians had no reasoning or memory faculties, but used something akin to telekinesis to control nature; while the Atlanteans did develop memory but not reasoning, and also the ability to control the forces of nature by occult means – including mastering the magical power of words.[39]

In summary these reflections of the early theosophists continue to exert great influence in occult circles, for all that they appear to contain manifest and multiple distortions. Moreover it would appear they have exerted a strong influence on a number of other lost-continent theorists who have no direct connection with theosophy – as we will now see as we review arguably the most influential contributions to the lost-continent debate in subsequent years.

THE COLONEL

James Churchward, who designated himself 'Colonel' in later years, left it until he was in his seventies before producing a number of now well-known works, including *The Lost Continent of Mu* in 1926 and *The Sacred Symbols of Mu* in 1933. The latter appears to be a well-intentioned treatise on the common origin and universal meaning of a number of symbols that function as archetypes via the universal consciousness. Meanwhile in the earlier work he describes the pre-Atlantean lost continent of Mu, which he not only shifts away from le Plongeon's Atlantic location into the Pacific, but also dates to between 50,000 and 12,000 years ago – a far more sensible timeframe than those adopted by various theosophists.[40] But that is, unfortunately, the end of the good news.

Churchward provides no source references but his works are apparently based on two sets of ancient tablets. The 'Naacal' set were supposedly composed in Burma or even in Mu itself, and were shown to him by a temple priest in India after which the two of them proceeded to decipher them together – Churchward having studied the 'dead language' with the priest for two years before. From his interpretations they appear to contain little more than a basic esoteric view of world origins that is common to most Eastern and Western traditions, as we saw in chapter 8, and they certainly contain no obvious references to Mu itself.[41] The other set of tablets, which he came across subsequently and incorporated into a second edition of *The Lost Continent* in 1931, are described as having been discovered not long before by William Niven in Mexico. These were lost at sea towards the end of Niven's life, but from Churchward's selected reproductions they appear to contain relatively standard Mayan glyphs, which would not date to more than 12,000 years ago as he suggests.[42] In any case he appears to use these only as vague support for his far heavier reliance on Le Plongeon's distorted interpretations of the *Troano Codex* and other Mayan inscriptions as discussed previously.[43]

THE ARCANE TRADITION

Lewis Spence's work on Atlantis is in many ways more sensible than that of most other commentators in that his timescales are practically short, he does not question evolution, and he attempts to pay at least some attention to the realities of orthodox archaeology. In his 1926 work *History of Atlantis* he proposes the gradual destruction of two landmasses in the Atlantic, Antillia in the east and Atlantis in the west.[44] He also suggests that the Aurignacian and Azilian cultures, which ushered in the Upper Paleolithic and Neolithic eras respectively, were two successive strains of Atlantean refugees who colonized Europe – the first wave being more advanced than its degenerate successor.[45] This latter is an interesting proposition, but we have already seen that the Atlantic is an unlikely location, while his suggestion that there is no evidence they emerged from the East is also highly suspect. Then in his 1932 work *The Problem of Lemuria* Spence moved the earlier civilization away from the Indian Ocean and into the Pacific. But again, although his timescales are more reasonable, modern geology does not support his theory that two former landmasses existed there – supposedly inhabited by a blond-haired, white-skinned race that built the various monuments that survive to this day.[46]

In fact it is in his 1943 work *The Occult Sciences in Atlantis* that Spence makes his most useful contributions to the debate. His sources for this too are not ethereal, but reported to be a combination of ancient texts and traditions and, more especially, a set of manuscripts belonging to what he refers to as the Arcane Tradition of an anonymous secret fraternity of which he was a member.[47] Indeed he suggests such records are kept by all such fraternities and all initiates are allowed to inspect them, although they cannot make notes or copies. The most interesting aspect of this work is his description of Atlantean occult practices that are said to have included astrology, alchemy, prophecy, necromancy and divination – this information coming from what appear to be medieval French and Spanish manuscripts.[48] He also describes how these practices were primarily restricted to the higher priestly and indeed royal class, although the lower castes at some point began to practice their own degenerate 'black magic', which is what led to the downfall of the civilization.

What then are we to make of Spence's work? He certainly does not appear to take everything he reads in his sources at face value; and he shows discernment when he discusses what he regards as clear distortions introduced every time the material was recompiled or translated – from what he believes to be, originally, Egyptian sources. So, despite the fact that his most interesting material cannot be referenced or checked by outsiders, his suggestion that it was the misuse of occult practices that led to the downfall of the Atlanteans just may have some relevance to our understanding of the fate that befell our forgotten race. As such we will return to it in the epilogue.

THE AUTOMATIC AUTHOR

H C Randall-Stevens supposedly had no previous history of channeling and 'little interest in occult matters' when he received his first communication from two ancient Egyptian initiates who called themselves Osiraes and Oneferu in 1925.[49] According to eyewitnesses he recorded these communications using a sort of 'automatic writing and drawing' that was likened to the operation of a modern facsimile machine. They were published in a number of works known as the *Osirian Scripts,* the first of which appeared in 1928; these were then bundled together along with some new material and commentary in *From Atlantis to the Latter Days,* published by his own 'Knights Templars of Aquarius' in Jersey in 1954.

His supposed sources provide detailed reports of Atlantis, and even a genealogical tree of humankind's earliest ancestors.[50] But whatever its source his material does not pass the 'Giza test', because like various theosophists before him he suggests all three pyramids were erected in great antiquity after the destruction of Atlantis.[51] He even describes a network of underground passages and chambers under the Sphinx that, as we saw in chapter 3, is almost certainly a complete fabrication.[52] Not only that but there is a possibility that his detailed drawings of the underground temples in the vicinity of the Sphinx were plagiarized from a Rosicrucian source.[53] Accordingly, although his work is still occasionally quoted, it is surely insufficiently reliable to merit further consideration here.

THE SLEEPING PROPHET

In the early twentieth century Joseph Benja Leslie supposedly interviewed a variety of 'Atlantean spirits' via a medium, and collated this material into his two-volume work *Submerged Atlantis Restored*, published in 1911. This includes copious details of 'its mountain ranges, valleys, seas, lakes, bays, rivers, sections or states, cities, convulsions, submergence, geographic, geologic, ethnographic and ethnologic conditions, languages, alphabets, figures, cardinal and ordinal numbers, punctuation marks, calendar, money, the six flags of the nation, religion, enterprises, government, and much, much more'.[54] This work is now hardly ever mentioned, however, whereas that of Leslie's contemporary Edgar Cayce – the American seer often referred to as the 'sleeping prophet' – forged for him a worldwide reputation as a psychic, healer and prophet.

While in a meditative trance he performed thousands of readings for his subjects and, although he was himself unaware of the contents at the time, they were invariably transcribed. These readings spanned five decades until his death in 1945, and much of his reputation was gained as a result of his holistic medical diagnoses, which subsequent developments have proved to be soundly based.[55] But around 20 percent came in the form of 'life readings' that repeatedly suggested his subjects had enjoyed previous incarnations in Atlantis. These were collated by his son Edgar Evans Cayce in *Edgar Cayce on Atlantis,* published in 1968.

The information divulged in this way has much in common with the theosophical material, although the timescales are to some extent more realistic.[56] It can be summarized as follows. The earth was first populated 10.5 million years ago by spiritual entities who only gradually took physical form and then split into males and females. The Atlantean civilization, which emerged at least 50,000 years ago, was repeatedly destroyed. Its history was forged by conflicts between the 'Sons of the Law of One' who attempted to remain true to the righteous path, and the 'Sons of Belial' who indulged themselves in the material world and abused their power and technology. The latter gradually gained the upper hand until, aware of their imminent destruction, a number of the more enlightened Atlanteans made their escape to all parts of the globe. It was these refugees who brought civilization to, for example, Egypt – where, it will come as no surprise, they built the Great Pyramid and Sphinx in about 10,500 BCE.[57] They also set up a number of Halls of Records around the world to preserve their ancient wisdom and to warn humankind of the fate that had befallen

Atlantis. Indeed Cayce himself was supposed to be the reincarnation of one of the more important of these, a priest by the name of Ra-Ta. His readings are also replete with advanced technology, including reports of aerial and submarine craft, and the 'terrible mighty crystal' or 'firestone' whose misuse led to the last destruction.

Cayce's timescales for the emergence and destruction of Atlantis, and his clear message of debasement, fit well with our main theme. However we can also see that his readings contain all the distortions we have, unfortunately, come to expect of the genre, as well as a few additions. Many of his supporters have tended to stress the objectivity of his messages, suggesting that he had no interest in or exposure to theosophical material; indeed that as a devout Christian he was often troubled by the way they tended to revolve around the concepts of reincarnation and karma. But here we should bring in Kenneth Paul Johnson, a former theosophist and also member of the organization founded to preserve and promote Cayce's work, the Association for Research and Enlightenment. In his 1998 work *Edgar Cayce in Context* he reveals that the Atlantean material only started to emerge in 1923, when a prosperous printer by the name of Arthur Lammers who was well versed in theosophy visited Cayce for a reading.[58] Indeed one of the Association's own biographers, Thomas Sugrue, reports that Cayce then stayed with Lammers for several weeks, during which time the two of them almost certainly discussed this and similar topics at length:[59]

> He mentioned such things as the cabala, the mystery religions of Egypt and Greece, the medieval alchemists, the mystics of Tibet, yoga, Madame Blavatsky and theosophy, the Great White Brotherhood, the Etheric World.

The association with Lammers was apparently short-lived, but at about this time Cayce also struck up a close friendship with a financier by the name of Morton Blumenthal who, according to Johnson, was also an avid theosophist.[60] This collaboration lasted for seven years, and Blumenthal was closely involved in both the running and financing of various Cayce projects. Johnson even reveals that Cayce had given a lecture to the Birmingham Theosophical Society in 1922, the year *before* he met Lammers, although admittedly on medical rather than Atlantean matters. If we also consider that his readings were not monologues but were prompted by questions from his subjects, some of whom may themselves have had theosophical and similar leanings, we have the very real possibility that Cayce was merely regurgitating from his subconscious information that had already entered his conscious mind, with the few additions and distortions that would inevitably arise.

This is not to suggest in any way that Cayce was a fraud. Indeed he tirelessly devoted the bulk of his life to trying to help the thousands of men and women who came to him, probably at severe cost to his own health. But it is important to recognize the *probability* that his readings on the topic of Atlantis were almost certainly influenced by information received by perfectly normal means.

CONCLUSION

Many, many writers have followed in the footsteps of these Lemuro-Atlantean trailblazers, indeed far too many to mention. But once we get past the early part of the twentieth century it is impossible to accurately determine the value of any channeled information about these lost civilizations, simply because any channel with the slightest interest in the subject will almost certainly have been exposed to a whole plethora of books or discussions on it already. That is not to say they their messages will be completely without value, indeed there may be hugely important nuggets therein. But it is nearly always impossible to argue that their messages are 'clear', or untainted by the copious previous distortions that are still widely peddled.

One major objective of this work is to bring these distortions to light in the hope that future revisionists may work from a rather more grounded platform. Indeed in the interests of raising the levels of discernment amongst the alternative community generally let us recap the key distortions that really ought to ring alarm bells whenever they are encountered. They include, amongst other things, the idea that humans were created rather than evolved; that human evolution in physical form stretches back many millions of years, and includes giants and even part-human, part-animal hybrids; that our more recent ancestors possessed advanced technology such as aerial machines; and that the Giza pyramids and Sphinx were built in a remote epoch by Atlantean survivors.

So are we left with anything of use? If there is any value to the especially theosophical material that supports the idea of human civilizations stretching back millions of years then it must be placed in an entirely different context. One option is the idea of multiple *concurrent* versions of earth mooted previously in chapter 5, meaning these might be other civilizations that somehow coexist in another dimension. Another option relies on our acknowledgement of the fact that there are almost certainly other planets housing intelligent lifeforms both more and less advanced than us, and sometimes less physical than us. Indeed regression therapists are sometimes confronted by their clients leading apparently animal lives, or lives that are hard to recognize as earth-based.[61] This too may explain some of the channeled material we have reviewed in this chapter, especially that related to Lemuria.

But there is yet another explanation for all this that sticks to the context of earth only. It seems reasonable to accept that soul energy can gain some degree of experience without having to incarnate in physical form. So the idea of early, entirely nonphysical root races operating in earth's astral plane is not one we should dismiss out of hand. The problem comes when we try to understand the transition from this state of affairs to incarnation in physical form. Of course individuated soul energies might have attempted to incarnate in any kind of animal form at any time of their choosing; this would merely represent an extension of our theme of unsuccessful early experiments. If this then continued into the pre-hominid and hominid forms previously discussed then we start to have a half-sensible narrative: that is, a possible overlap between the nonphysical soul energies that might still have been operating from the astral plane, and the proper incarnation of individuated souls into increasingly human-like physical forms. Perhaps then the descriptions of Lemurians taking increasingly physical form start to make some sense.

Indeed perhaps we can sensibly view the Lemurian, third-race experience as an experiment in physical incarnation that acted as a stepping stone – from the purely nonphysical existence of the first two-and-a-half races, via incarnation in various animal, hominid and human forms, to the entirely modern-human form of the fourth race of Atlantis.[62] But to attribute any kind of seriously advanced culture to the third race, at least prior to say 50,000 years ago, would surely be a huge mistake; as it would to place them or their fourth-race successors on lost continents in the middle of the Pacific, Indian or Atlantic Oceans.

A question that naturally follows on from discussion of the stanzas in the *Book of Dzyan*, and of Arcane Traditions and Halls of Records, is whether we are ever likely to find a hidden cache of records of what currently remains human *pre*history; or whether any hitherto closely guarded ancient texts will ever be made public? A relatively sober assumption would be that our forgotten race, though culturally advanced, did not develop writing or feel the need to draw up historical records. If that were true then, even if the answer to either of the above questions was yes, we would only be working from much later written versions that had survived millennia of oral transmission and geographical diffusion. So the possibility of significant distortions already having crept in is high. Having said that, at least anything of genuine antiquity would probably be devoid of speculations about advanced technology and, for that matter, detailed dates.

Before we leave the subject of lost continents, it is fascinating that many of the tribal traditions in the Pacific Islands seem to retain a strong memory of a time when the sea submerged their ancestors. For example on Samoa they say:[63] 'The sea... arose, and in a stupendous catastrophe of nature the land sank into the sea... The new earth arose out of the womb of the last earth.' While on Tahiti they say:[64] 'In ancient times Taaroa... being angry with men on account of their disobedience to his will, overturned the world into the sea, when the earth sank into the water, excepting a few projecting islands which remained above its surface.' Of course it could be that these are just relatively recent memories of other islands becoming submerged. But what if they are memories of the submergence of the Sunda and Sahul shelves at the end of the Pleistocene?

In this context, Churchward records details of a number of impressive megalithic stone structures still standing on various Pacific Islands, including the Gilbert and Marshall, Kingsmill, Navigator, Cook and Marquesas Islands and the Caroline and Mariana Groups; and although it is not clear how many of these he visited he does include a number of photographs and drawings.[65] More recently the explorer David Hatcher Childress has also chronicled them in his *Lost Cities* series.[66] Their assumption that the complexity and distribution of these monuments indicates they must have been erected when all the islands were part of one huge landmass is entirely without foundation – both in its own right, and because most of them are known to be volcanic atolls created millions of years ago. Moreover the monuments themselves are almost certainly Neolithic at the earliest. Nevertheless it is surely reasonable to suggest that they might add to our understanding of what happened to the survivors of the submersion of Sundaland, and possibly of Sahul too. Although some headed northwest to start the rebuilding process some time later in the Near East, others may have chosen to take their chances on the sea, heading east to islands that would be less likely to be found and invaded by nomadic desperados.

12

LET'S GET REAL

Many revisionists both ancient and modern have tended to place the emphasis on advanced technology. Others concentrate less on technology and more on redating ancient monuments to more distant epochs, and various related issues. We have only summarily dismissed these ideas so far, but now it is time to examine the supposed evidence properly to show exactly why it collapses under any sort of real scrutiny.[1] We will consider the technological and dating 'non-mysteries' in order, before turning to the more realistic evidence for the a selection of the sort of skills our forgotten ancestors may have genuinely possessed.

TECHNOLOGICAL NON-MYSTERIES

Even the theosophists of the late nineteenth and early twentieth centuries were discussing how the Atlanteans had aeronautic vehicles, and their ideas of technological advancement were then reinforced by Edgar Cayce. Since then the preoccupation has grown, fuelled in part by the massive interest in UFOs and ETs.

In fact the British journalist Harold Wilkins was arguably the founder of the Ancient Astronaut school in the 1950s, but in the 1960s a number of contemporary writers followed a similar line to that of Erich von Däniken and Zecharia Sitchin, which we discussed in chapter 2. For example in his 1968 work *Gods and Spacemen in the Ancient East* W Raymond Drake reinterpreted a great deal of the ancient textual material that Sitchin subsequently used, and in fact his work is better referenced; but his disclosure of sources is still woefully inadequate, and on close inspection much of his material too appears to have been somewhat manipulated and distorted. Meanwhile the early 1970s saw a plethora of similar books emerging, for example from Peter Kolosimo with *Not of this World* and

Timeless Earth, and from Andrew Tomas with *We Are Not the First* and *On the Shores of Ancient Worlds.* But both showed a similar lack of scholarship by failing to provide proper references for much of their material, and an excellent flavor of these books is provided by chapter headings from Thomas' first offering: 'Electricity in the remote past', 'Did the ancients master gravitation', 'Prehistoric aircraft', 'They conquered space long before we did' and 'First robots, computers, radio, television and time viewing machines'. Not long afterwards in *Worlds Before Our Own* Brad Steiger wrote about the supposed textual and physical evidence of ancient aviation, nuclear holocausts and other advanced technology, although at least he did not follow the extraterrestrial route of his contemporaries, preferring instead to postulate a forgotten race of indigenous giants who developed this technology.

More recently Alan Alford followed Sitchin's lead in *Gods of the New Millennium* in 1996, but to his credit has since abandoned the Intervention hypothesis; while Laurence Gardner's 1999 work *Genesis of the Grail Kings* also partly followed Sitchin's interpretation of the Mesopotamian texts. This material will clearly not disappear without a fight.

ANCIENT WEAPONS AND AIRCRAFT

Many revisionist authors have attempted to interpret passages in ancient texts as descriptions of aerial and other advanced warfare, even of extraterrestrial craft. They particularly cite Mesopotamian texts such as the *Ninurta Myth* that we reviewed in chapter 10, and the *Epic of Anzu;*[2] certain biblical passages;[3] and above all the Indian epics such as the *Mahabharata* and *Ramayana*. Indeed this is the main topic of David Hatcher Childress' 1991 work *Vimana Aircraft of Ancient India and Atlantis*. Although this topic does not merit the reproduction of detailed quotes, suffice to say that as usual there is no contextual support for these interpretations, and it is far more appropriate to look at such passages from the perspective of symbolism and literary creativity. The only exception may be those cases that, as suggested earlier, just *might* represent memories of the natural catastrophe at the end of the Pleistocene.

Nevertheless these interpretations have been backed up by supposed physical evidence as well. For example a small wooden model in the Cairo Museum, which was found in a tomb at Saqqara and dates to around 300 BCE, is often purported to represent a glider.[4] It has a wingspan of 18 centimeters and has supposedly proved to be aerodynamically sound, but contextually it is far more likely to represent a stylized bird – indeed its head is very much that of a falcon, a guise used by both Ra and Horus. The only real enigma is that unlike any bird it does have a vertical tail but, if it was a scale model of a glider, why have we found no evidence of a full-size, fully operative version? As for other suggestions that certain models from South America represent powered aircraft, these too are clearly symbolic representations of birds.[5] On the face of it the most fascinating find is an Egyptian relief in the Temple of Seti I at Abydos, which does appear to show the clear profile of a modern helicopter.[6] But in fact the picture circulating on the internet was almost certainly doctored by the removal of a cartouche at the supposed craft's nose, whereas in fact the whole relief was built up in stages by recarving, a common practice in Ancient Egypt. In any case even if these doubts did not exist we can surely rule out the helicopter interpretation on the grounds that, again, no hint of such technology has turned up in the ante or postdiluvian archaeological record; and let us nor forget that even if a glider can be made of perishable materials, a powered helicopter or other aircraft certainly cannot. Nor is such an artifact small and easily overlooked.

THE DOGON

In his popular 1976 work *The Sirius Mystery* Robert Temple suggested that we were visited by beings from the Sirius star system around 5000 years ago. The major foundations of this theory were the supposed traditions of the Dogon tribe of West Africa, revealed to French anthropologist Marcel Griaule in the mid-twentieth century, suggesting that they knew Sirius had an invisible companion star that was only discovered by telescope some time later.[7] But not only had the existence of Sirius B been mathematically postulated a century earlier, but more recent interviews with the Dogon cast doubts that they were talking about Sirius at all.

To make matters worse Temple too discusses the Great Sphinx of Giza, and in particular the erosion of the walls of the limestone bedrock enclosure from which it has been sculpted. This is the feature that recent revisionists have used to suggest that it should be redated, as we will shortly see. But he goes as far as to suggest that the erosion occurred when the enclosure was originally filled with water by these beings, because they were amphibious.[8] Some of Temple's more recent work is rightly praised as we will also see shortly, but not only does this earlier work show a woeful ignorance of the commonplace symbolism of composite, hybrid beings and especially of fish, but it also defies logic when viewed in the context of the layout of the Sphinx enclosure and the Giza Plateau in general.[9]

COMPUTERS, BATTERIES AND SPARK PLUGS

In 1958 Derek de Solla Price became the first person to properly investigate the 'Antikythera computer' in the Athens museum.[10] It was found in the wreck of a Greek ship off Crete, and its inscriptions date it to the first century BCE. He estimated that when complete it consisted of between 20 and 40 interlocking bronze gears; those that survive are only 2 millimeters thick, while the largest has 240 teeth each only just over a millimeter high. Moreover, he established beyond doubt that it was an astrolabe that would have been used to predict the positions of the planets – although, somewhat ironically given its wonderfully technical nature, it was designed based on the Ptolemaic system whereby they all revolved around the earth not the sun. This device is fascinating for its uniqueness, with nothing of comparable complexity having yet been found. But we know that in the Classical period they did understand the use of gears, and above all it is relatively recent and proves nothing about earlier civilizations.

The 'Baghdad batteries' are a similar enigma. The first, discovered in 1938, consisted of a clay vase about fifteen centimeters high into which a copper tube and an iron rod had been inserted.[11] Archaeologists came to the conclusion that it was a simple battery and one, Arne Eggebrecht, built a replica containing nothing more than an acidic grape-juice solution that produced half a volt of electricity. He even went as far as to suggest that a number of ancient Egyptian statuettes have such a thin layer of gold plating that it could not have been administered by hand, but more recently this has been questioned. Indeed, although this collection of vases was looted from the Baghdad Museum in 2003 and their whereabouts is now unknown, apparently the tops of the originals were completely sealed with asphalt, so it is hard to see how any electric current could have been extracted.

It is quite stunning to think that the Parthians *might* have developed a rudimentary electrical device some 2000 years ago. But even if they *had*, what would this really mean? Just as the Antikythera device was dubbed a 'computer' to enhance the effect for the general public, revisionists discussing these 'batteries' give the impression that our forebears were running around with power tools and goodness knows what else. But they were clearly not, because yet again no such contextual evidence has been found. What is far more interesting is that, *if* these artifacts were being used to produce a small electrical current, their inventors failed to see the broader applications – and it would be another two millennia before the phenomenon was *re*discovered.

By contrast a supposedly anomalous artifact that has led many people a merry dance, and still does despite having been proved to be totally erroneous, is the 'Coso artifact'.[12] Three mineral hunters discovered an apparently ancient geode near Olancha, California in 1961, and when they cut the specimen in half the interior revealed what appeared to be a replica of a spark plug. But subsequent investigation has proved this to be no great surprise because this was no ancient geode but a recently formed conglomerate, and its enigmatic contents have now been matched perfectly to a plug made by the Champion Company in the 1920s.

MAPS AND PORTOLANS

Our final evidence in this section is less about advanced technology, and more about attempts to prove that our ancient forebears were sufficiently advanced to have sailed to and mapped the continent of Antarctica *before* it was icebound. This suggestion was originally made in 1956 by Captain Arlington H Mallory after he had investigated the infamous Piri Re'is map of 1513. It was then expanded upon by Charles Hapgood in his 1966 work *Maps of the Ancient Sea Kings,* in which he examined a number of other medieval maps and portolans, including the Oronteus Finaeus map of 1531.[13]

In chapter 11 we briefly mentioned that Hapgood's suggestion that Atlantis was the ice-free continent of Antarctica before it was shifted southward by a crustal displacement at the end of the Pleistocene is not born out by geological evidence. Boston geologist Robert Schoch is more normally associated with the age-of-the-Sphinx debate but, as he points out in his 1999 work *Voices of the Rocks*, the estimated dates for when it was last free of ice range from a minimum of 3 to a maximum of 23 million years ago;[14] so any pole shifts or other disturbances can only have tampered at the edges. Indeed it is almost certain that for the most part it became *less* glaciated at the end of the Pleistocene, not more.

But does Hapgood nevertheless have a strong basic case about the maps? Unfortunately the answer is again a resounding no, because as Schoch rightly points out the relevant portions do not match the antarctic coastline, glaciated or unglaciated, to anything like the degree Hapgood proposes. In addition it is often overlooked that classical Greek scholars theorized there must be a landmass in the southern seas to act as a counterbalance to the known ones that lay predominantly in the northern hemisphere. Aristotle was the first to coin the term Antarctica for it, but Ptolemy referred to it as Terra Australis Incognito or the 'unknown southern land', which is highly similar to the label we find on some of these medieval maps.[15]

So although our forgotten race may well have been fine seafarers and possibly even cartographers, as we will shortly see, it is clear that the evidence provided by Hapgood and his followers in support of this claim is seriously flawed.

DATING AND OTHER NON-MYSTERIES

We have seen that the early theosophists were not averse to ascribing very early dates to ancient monuments such as the Great Pyramid and Sphinx, and that trend continued right through the twentieth century with many of the Ancient Astronaut and other revisionist authors who were also somewhat obsessed with ancient technology. But as briefly mentioned in chapter 2 revisionists such as Graham Hancock, Robert Bauval and John Anthony West have more recently come to the forefront of the modern Redating movement. Not only have they done a great deal to raise public awareness of ancient civilizations and their accomplishments, but they have also moved away from the more outlandish high technology and other claims of their predecessors – for all of which they deserve full credit. Modern revisionists have also learned to give their research a fine veneer of scholarly respectability, with copious endnotes and so on, but despite this their underlying scholarship unfortunately remains questionable. So let us look more closely at their arguments to see why this is.

NO OVERNIGHT DEVELOPMENT

West's best-known work remains *Serpent in the Sky*, first published in 1979. In general it represents a fine attempt to follow up on the work of radical Egyptologist René Schwaller de Lubicz, who explored the esoteric symbolism of the ancient Egyptians in his 1961 work *Sacred Science*. West suggests in his introduction that he regards their 'science, medicine, mathematics and astronomy' as being of 'an exponentially higher order of refinement and sophistication than modern scholars will acknowledge'.

It is a moot point whether this statement was true even in its day, as is whether West and others like him have had any significant influence on the course of more orthodox Egyptology over the least few decades. But one thing that stands out is his view that such sophistication had no real development period, indeed that 'Egyptian civilization was not a development, it was a legacy' that 'proves Atlantis'.[16] This is, of course, the 'no overnight development' theory that continues to form part of the bedrock for the work of many revisionists. But, as already suggested in the preface, this idea is invalidated in a number of ways. First by a simple look at the technological progress made in the modern world in just a handful of centuries. Second by its failure to acknowledge the period of gradual development that clearly does exist in the archaeological record; for example the 80 years or so of pyramid building that preceded the work at Giza, which produced among others Djoser's Step Pyramid at Saqqara and Sneferu's Bent and Red Pyramids at Dashur.[17] Third by the fact that West is actually proposing a thoroughly punctuated development with an original Atlantean stage, then a hiatus of many thousands of years, and then its reemergence; although they might have had to wait for the climate to settle and so on after the catastrophe, would survivors who retained this advanced knowledge not have put it to good use again rather sooner?

THE AGE OF THE GIZA MONUMENTS

Arguably the most stubborn and enduring element of West's work, which forms another part of the bedrock for the entire Redating school, is his attempt to ascribe a far earlier date to the Great Sphinx than the roughly 2500 BCE suggested by Egyptologists. The main evidence at the center of this debate is the water weathering on the walls of the bedrock enclosure out of which this great monument was carved, and West relied heavily on Schoch's work in this area. The full evidence is presented in a 1993 update of *Serpents* and in a number of more recent papers by both men. Suffice to say that this issue is considered in detail in *Giza: The Truth*, in which our conclusion was that even if the Sphinx is older than the orthodox date it is by no more than one or two millennia at the very most.[18] Indeed this is Schoch's view as well, and he certainly parted company with West when the latter originally argued that it dates back as far as 10,500 BCE.[19]

This date seems to have been arrived at in conjunction with Hancock and Bauval who supported it in their hugely popular 1996 work *Keeper of Genesis*, the choice being heavily influenced by Cayce's readings on the subject. They then bolstered it with a highly dubious astronomical argument involving precession and the position of Orion's belt stars and of the star Regulus in the constellation of Leo at the time – which they refer to as the 'first time', their over-reliance on which we have already discussed in chapter 4. To make matters worse West has more recently suggested that, given the supposedly inhospitable climate in Egypt at the end of the last ice age, the Sphinx should actually be dated to the *previous* precessional age of Leo around 36,000 BCE.[20]

If we turn now to the age of the Great Pyramid itself, and if we ignore the horribly exaggerated distortions of the early theosophists and others that we discussed in the previous chapter, it was Sitchin who really set the modern redating agenda with his totally groundless accusation that Colonel Richard Howard Vyse faked the 'quarry marks' in the relieving chambers of the edifice. In fact the evidence is overwhelming that these are genuine, and they prove beyond all reasonable doubt that it was built by the Fourth Dynasty king Khufu, again around 2500 BCE.[21] In fact Hancock and Bauval do accept this date, despite their somewhat confusing argument that the *ground plan* of the three Giza pyramids was laid out to reflect the position of Orion's belt stars in 10,500 BCE, at the same time as the Sphinx was built.[22] This confusion is made worse by their apparent support for Sitchin's assertions, which seems to have been incorporated – with scant regard for the logical flow of their arguments – merely to bolster their regrettable hostility towards orthodox Egyptologists.[23] Whether this attitude itself was genuine or merely adopted for commercial reasons, it was extremely unhelpful and in any case largely unwarranted.

In fact one of the only modern Redaters who is not working from channeled material and has continued to argue for an earlier date for the Great Pyramid on more prosaic grounds is Alford; and he is, quite rightly, somewhat out on a limb on this issue.

PYRAMID AND TEMPLE CONSTRUCTION

Although less outlandish in their views, all these members of the Redating school do ascribe a *relatively* high level of technological advancement to their lost civilization, and nowhere is this better demonstrated than in their attitude toward the construction of the Egyptian and Mesoamerican pyramids and various other megalithic structures around the world.

If we take the Great Pyramid as the prime example, Hancock and Bauval suggest that it would have been impossible for the ancient Egyptians to have constructed the edifice with nothing more than simple stone and copper tools and a plentiful supply of labor; the inference being of course that they used a technology handed down by the survivors of a lost civilization.[24] But we spent considerable time examining the logistics of the Great Pyramid's construction in *Giza: The Truth*, and we reached the same conclusion as professionals who have examined the evidence properly. Although it represents an incredible piece of engineering, and its project management was comparable with anything attempted today, it was nevertheless achievable with the relatively simple tools and labor, and even more the dedication and mindset, that the ancient Egyptians possessed.[25] All pyramid building represented a national project to which virtually everyone was fully committed, probably not as slaves even though there may well have been some press-ganging, but because they were all successfully brainwashed by the idea that it was essential for the very survival of their religion and even their civilization itself.

One apparent puzzle that did perplex us at the time of our original investigations was the occasional use of incredibly large blocks of stone. For example in the Great Pyramid the largest, used to construct the floors and ceilings of the previously mentioned relieving chambers, weigh 70 tons. But even these are dwarfed by the blocks used to construct all levels of the walls of many of the ancillary temples at Giza, which weigh as much as 200 tons. But more recent research into the mechanics of their construction suggests that even these could have been dragged up and into position using sand ramps. As to the question of *why* the blocks should be so large if this made the builders' task much more difficult, a perfectly sensible suggestion is that their size would reduce the likelihood of serious earthquake damage.

Another often-touted example of 'impossible' construction is that of the Trilithon, the three massive 800-ton blocks in the walls of the Roman Temple of Jupiter at Baalbek in the Lebanon. But again the fact that this looks impossible to a layperson with no proper knowledge of ancient construction techniques does not make it the work of a lost civilization with forgotten technology, or especially of extraterrestrial invaders. In fact this was one of the easier projects undertaken by the Romans because they only had to drag the blocks downhill from the quarry, whereas on other more difficult projects they still used similar size blocks and the same system of winches and sleds that is depicted in paintings and reliefs.[26]

It would be wrong not to admit that some enigmas remain. Modern researchers from all walks of life are increasingly drawn to ever more ingenious explanations of exactly how the Great Pyramid was constructed, even using just the known technology of the time.[27] Indeed their ongoing efforts increasingly prove just how much can be achieved in terms of architecture and construction with simple tools yet incredible daring and imagination. In the meantime we may never know the purpose of the narrow so-called 'air' or 'star shafts', which run off from behind the walls of the Queen's chamber and up through the edifice's mainly solid masonry, although they do not run right through to its outer casing. But again one enigma such as this does not require us to completely abandon all the mass of contextual knowledge about ancient Egyptian civilization that has been so painstakingly amassed by orthodox scholars.

While we are on this topic Bauval and Hancock were delighted to support the findings of American engineer Chris Dunn in his 1998 work *The Giza Power Plant*. If we stick to his speciality in the first instance, he uses the evidence of the striations on one particular drill core in the Petrie Museum in London to argue that the ancient Egyptians used ultrasonics to drill hard stone like granite. Yet subsequent experiments by Denys Stocks of Manchester University have indicated that identical drill cores can be produced using nothing more than a hand-turned bow drill incorporating a copper tube, with a sand slurry acting as the cutting agent.[28]

As for the even more outlandish power plant theory that provides the provocative title for his book, unfortunately this is just the latest in a long line of ill-informed theories about the purpose of this amazing edifice.[29] If it had been built in glorious isolation in a long distant epoch then it might be perfectly reasonable to question, and wax lyrical about, its true purpose. But even Dunn accepts that it is contemporary with the other Fourth Dynasty pyramids and associated temples, tombs and other structures at Giza and elsewhere, all of which show beyond any shadow of a doubt that these complexes had a ritual and indeed funerary context. What is more this fact stands irrespective of the debate about whether or not kings like Khufu ever allowed their bodies to be actually buried inside their pyramid for fear of looting – which is known to have taken place even though increasingly sophisticated security precautions were built into pyramid designs. Indeed, although during the Fourth Dynasty the fashion was to leave internal pyramid walls free of reliefs, hieroglyphic texts or other decoration, nowhere is this context more clearly demonstrated than in the *Pyramid Texts* found inscribed on the burial chamber walls of the kings from the Fifth Dynasty onward.

COMMON ORIGINS

Moving farther afield Hancock in particular has always had a broader scope than just ancient Egypt; and the book that launched him into the spotlight of revisionist history in 1995, *Fingerprints of the Gods,* contains a great deal of discussion about, for example, Mesoamerican pyramids and other ruins. It will come as no surprise that he suggests some of these are far older than the orthodoxy allows and were built by an advanced antediluvian civilization. However American archaeologists are as insistent about their dates of between 500 and 2000 years old for these structures as their

Egyptologist counterparts, and there is every reason to trust the professionals in this instance as well.

Indeed because the weight of evidence is so strong Hancock is also forced to accept that many of these structures may *not* have been built in a remote epoch. So in one of his typically fleet-footed but not entirely logical moves he changes tack and resurrects Ignatius Donnelly's 'common origins' argument from more than a century ago, which runs that the pyramidal shape of the edifices on both sides of the Atlantic indicates their builders must have learned their skills from a common source: the survivors, of course, from a prior civilization. But this argument is just as flawed as its counterpart of no overnight development, the two usually being used in tandem. The square-based pyramidal shape is an obvious choice for a large and imposing structure, but that is where the similarity ends. Whereas the Mesoamerican pyramids are all 'stepped', the only Egyptian pyramid that corresponds to this design is the first, Djoser's at Saqqara; all its successors had smooth, shiny sides formed from high-quality casing stones that have in most cases been looted – although, for example, they are still visible at the top of the second pyramid at Giza, erected by Khafre. Hancock attempts to reinforce this suggestion with the fact that the Maya too had a hieroglyphic form of script, but again this is totally unlike any Egyptian script, while the use of pictorial symbols in early writing is hardly unusual or a great surprise that requires a common-origin explanation.

OTHER PYRAMIDS

Before we leave the subject of pyramids, their previously little-known existence in a number of other countries has been widely reported in recent decades. For example German visitor Hartwig Hausdorf stumbled upon a number of them in the Qin Chuan plains on a trip to central China in 1994; and in his widely referenced reports suggested they were of great antiquity and, of course, built by alien visitors.[30] But in fact we know that professional research into the 38 that have so far been documented dates them to the second or third millennium BCE at the earliest.[31] That is not to say they are not imposing, despite being constructed using clay and earth rather than stone. Indeed the largest is 350 meters square at the base compared to the 230 meters of the Great Pyramid of Giza, although with an original height of 75 meters it is only around half the height of its Egyptian counterpart. But there is no great mystery to them.

Even less mysterious were the reports of the largest pyramid ever discovered, first released by metalworker Semir Osmanagić in 2005.[32] These detailed what he supposedly found when excavating certain structures clustered around the Bosnian town of Visoko, but it appears that most if not all of their contents were pure fabrication; and amid subsequent outrage at the widespread worldwide publicity given to such ridiculous claims local geologists revealed that they are perfectly natural features of the landscape.

UNDERWATER STRUCTURES

Before we examine some of the more realistic skills our forgotten race might have possessed, we should discuss various underwater structures that have been located around the world in the modern era. The most celebrated is the 'Bimini Road' first reported as lying in shallow waters off the island of the same name by J Manson Valentine in 1968 – although it may or may not be a coincidence that this was exactly when and where Cayce said Atlantis would first 'rise again'.[33] Yet none of the revisionists who claim to have visited or even dived on the site have produced any sort of credible evidence of human working of what is universally agreed by geologists to be a perfectly natural formation.[34]

Then in 1987 large structures supposedly resembling temples with platforms and giant stairs were located in the waters off Yonaguni, the most southerly of the Japanese Ryukyu island chain. But Schoch, who has dived on the site himself, describes the bedrock as 'criss-crossed by many joints and fractures running vertical to the bedding planes', which is what has allowed it to form the right-angled and apparently regular shapes that have so stunned the uninitiated.[35] But however fascinating the geological processes that shaped such sites into simulacra of man-made structures might be, the acid test is that they clearly involve large areas of natural, sculpted bedrock rather than fabricated structures assembled from separate stone slabs.

The most recent discovery occurred in 2001 when oceanographers carrying out pollution checks for India's National Institute of Ocean Technology reported they had found a 'grid of geometric structures thought to be the foundations of two cities, each more than five miles wide' lying at a depth of around 40 meters in the Gulf of Cambay, some 20 miles off the coast of Gujarat.[36] But Indian officials went public with sensational claims of the earliest-known civilization without the site ever having been properly investigated by marine archaeologists because the waters are so cloudy, and with the dating of 7500 BCE based on a single fragment of wood retrieved by dredging.[37] Not only is this method extremely unreliable from an archaeological perspective, but in fact very few artifacts were recovered; and the pottery fragments were so small that some question whether they are man-made at all. Worse still the supposed structures were only revealed by side-scan sonar, which for various reasons gives only the vaguest of outlines of what is going on under the water and can easily be misinterpreted.

These latter sites were given widespread prominence by the publication in 2002 of Hancock's *Underworld*, which was accompanied by a three-part documentary shown on Channel 4. But in a detailed rebuttal the chair of Southampton's Oceanography Centre in the UK, Nic Fleming, emphasizes the poor levels of scholarship in this research and reinforces the point that all these structures are almost certainly natural geological formations.[38]

REALISTIC SKILLS

A number of orthodox and revisionist authors are now concentrating on revealing the less fanciful but previously underrated skills developed by our earliest-known civilizations, and this approach has undoubtedly led to a more balanced view of their significant cultural achievements. This just might shed useful light on the realistic skills that could conceivably have been possessed by their antediluvian forebears.

ASTRONOMY AND NAVIGATION

We are increasingly aware of just how astronomically sophisticated the early civilizations of the postcatastrophe epoch were. For this we can be thankful to pioneers like Sir Norman Lockyer, who set the tone in his 1894 work *The Dawn of Astronomy*. He suggested that the layout of a variety of ancient monuments around the world indicated they had been deliberately aligned to the sun or to certain stars at one of the equinoxes or solstices, thereby acting as extremely accurate calendars. Furthermore he realized that these alignments could be used to date the monuments, particularly using the phenomenon of precession discussed in chapter 5. His conclusive proof came when he established that changes to the layout of many ancient monuments were clearly introduced to allow for changes in the position of heavenly bodies over time.[39]

Although in itself Lockyer's work did not prove that ancient astronomers completely understood the full precessional cycle, subsequent pioneering work based primarily on a symbolic interpretation of various ancient texts and reliefs has provided strong support for this argument. Carl Jung and Schwaller de Lubicz were pioneers of this approach, but it was brought to full fruition by Giorgio de Santillana and Hertha von Dechend in their 1964 work *Hamlet's Mill*.

However as usual a health warning is needed. Nowhere is this more apparent than in Hancock's attempts in his 1998 work *Heaven's Mirror* to apply knowledge of precession, and in particular the 'marker' of the first time date of 10,500 BCE, to the layout of every monument he encounters; this includes, for example, the many temples at Angkor Wat in Cambodia that were actually constructed around the twelfth century.[40] Meanwhile Rand Flem-Ath and Colin Wilson's suggestion in their 2000 work *The Atlantis Blueprint* that all the major sacred sites of the ancient world were laid out to a global geometric blueprint, indicating advanced geodesic and other knowledge, is also probably a step too far.

Nevertheless we can say with some certainty that the astronomer-priests of our historical ancient civilizations in the Near and Far East and the Americas did have an advanced knowledge of astronomy – as did their Celtic counterparts, even though their monuments at first sight appear less sophisticated. The ancient megalithic site of Stonehenge clearly has a combined ritual and calendrical function, while much recent attention has been focused on sites such as Maes Howe in the Orkneys and New Grange in Ireland. For example in their 1999 work *Uriel's Machine* Christopher Knight and Robert Lomas suggest that these too were developed by the Grooved Ware people of the fifth to third millennia BCE as sophisticated calendars that used Venus' highly accurate eight-year cycle.[41]

All of this indicates that these ancient astronomers knew the earth was round and orbited the sun. Yet this knowledge apparently became lost to the Christianized Western world, in which the primitive idea predominated that the earth was flat and physically as well as symbolically at the center of the universe – with everything else revolving around it. Indeed the truth was only *re*discovered in the West by Nicolas Copernicus at the beginning of the sixteenth century, nearly one and a half millennia later, and even then he only agreed to publish his work on his deathbed. Meanwhile his successor Galileo was put under house arrest for the last years of his life. This amply proves, as if we did not have enough evidence already, just how distortive and destructive an influence dogmatic religion can be.

All of this also suggests that our forgotten ancestors may well have had a good understanding of astronomy, although whether precession would have been included in that is a moot point. But we can conjecture that this would have been developed not only to aid the planning of seasons for agriculture and so on, but also because it would have been extremely useful for ocean navigation.

This argument is strengthened by Crichton Miller in his 2001 work *The Golden Thread of Time*. He provides persuasive arguments that our forgotten race mastered the use of a simple bob-weighted angle-measuring dial attached to a right-angled cross for determining their position from the stars and sun with astonishing accuracy (see Plates 16 and 17). This device would of course confer great power on anyone who knew how to use it both on land and at sea; and his argument continues that our postcatastrophe ancestors commemorated this hugely important device in the archetypal symbol of the Celtic cross, even though they no longer understood its original purpose. He further suggests that anyone out at sea at the time of the catastrophe would have been least affected by any tsunamis, which cause only a swell in deep ocean rather than the breaking, destructive waves experienced on the shore; and that the most advanced astronomers of our forgotten race may even have predicted the impact of an extraterrestrial body and set sail accordingly, which gives a whole new slant to the traditions of the flood. Was Noah less of a farmer and more of an expert navigator?

Indeed early seafaring is increasingly posited by orthodox archaeologists. Robert Bednarik's suggestion in chapter 9, that *Homo erectus* managed to cross significant seas to reach Flores, will probably remain controversial for some time to come. But we have seen that the idea that some sort of rafts or simple craft were used to reach Australia by 40,000 years ago at the latest is now entirely accepted.[42] This is backed up by the 'Solutrean Hypothesis', first put forward by Smithsonian archaeologist Dennis Stanford in 1998. Based on the similarity of Clovis and Solutrean technology he proposes that Atlantic crossings were made some time after 20,000 years ago by following the edge of the ice pack in the north Atlantic.[43] So, while the idea would certainly remain anathema to most conventional archaeologists, it is not a huge leap of logic to posit that our forgotten ancestors *could have been* expert boat builders, seafarers and navigators.

CRYSTAL AND MAGNIFICATION TECHNOLOGY

Channeled material regularly suggests that the Atlanteans were using sophisticated crystal technology for a variety of purposes. Sometimes this idea is associated with energy generation and travel, and with information storage. In this latter context enigmatic 'crystal skulls' are often mentioned. A number of these are already known to exist, all supposedly of Mesoamerican origin, but some at least have been proved to be of relatively recent manufacture using powered tools – effectively, therefore, fakes.[44] This is perhaps unsurprising when we consider the money that can be made by displaying and even conducting live channeling sessions with them, especially amidst a plethora of reports of how they were created and programmed by extraterrestrials to tell us our secret history when the time is right – which it apparently is in the run-up to 2012.

But one skull in particular is perhaps not so easily dismissed, and it was brought to widespread attention in 1997 by Chris Morton and Ceri Louise Thomas in *The Mystery of the Crystal Skulls*.[45] It is the enigmatic Mitchell-Hedges skull, reputedly discovered in a Mayan temple at Lubaantun in Belize in 1924 by Anna Mitchell-Hedges, the stepdaughter of the famous explorer Frederick. It is life-sized, anatomically detailed, visibly far superior to all the others and, unique among all the skulls known to exist, has a detachable jaw (see Plates 18 to 20). Even the crystal experts from Hewlett-Packard's Santa Clara laboratories, who spent two days testing it in 1970, were not a little bemused by its quality.[46] Not only did they confirm that it had been manufactured by hand because there was no evidence of machine-tool marks, but the jaw was found to have been carved from the same block of quartz as the main skull – which would make the separation of the two pieces an incredibly complex and potentially disastrous procedure. They even suggested that hand carving it using a sand-and-water paste would require some 300 man-years of effort. Intriguingly the attempts of skeptics to debunk this artifact are almost uniquely selective and biased, with no attempts whatsoever to properly rebut the 'supposed' Hewlett-Packard tests and their conclusions.[47]

On a more prosaic note a number of optical lenses, precision ground from rock crystal, have now been located in museums all over the world. Although a few of these were being discussed at least in von Däniken's time, Temple has exhaustively tracked down a large number over several decades, presenting the results in 2000 in *The Crystal Sun* – which is a considerable improvement on his earlier work mentioned previously. Although the oldest only dates to the Old Kingdom in Egypt, it is highly unlikely that the soft metals in use at the time would have played a part in its manufacture. So is it unreasonable to suggest that our forgotten race may have been able to master magnification technology and use it in a variety of applications – maybe even to produce rudimentary telescopes to assist both astronomical observations generally and ocean navigation in particular?

It may also be relevant at this point to consider the research of geoscience professor Ivan Watkins, who like many others has studied the stonemasonry of the Incas.[48] Not only did they use large granite blocks that were often fitted together using intricate shapes, but also the joints are so accurate that even a slip of paper cannot be inserted into them. In the 1980s Watkins considered all the methods that had been proposed to date – for example hammering, grinding and polishing, wedging and chemical processes – and concluded that none properly explained these remarkable feats. But he did notice a glazing on the surface of some of the Incan stones, and further research revealed that this is exactly the effect achieved when modern producers of granite tiles finish them using a high temperature flame; indeed a simultaneous jet of water is needed to remove the spalls of quartz that appear on the surface before they melt to form the glaze. He also knew about descriptions of a 'great golden dish two men across' that was reported to have been melted down by Conquistadores; and about the research of David Lindroth of the US Bureau of Mines, who had found that 100 watts of light focused to a point about two millimeters in diameter will cut any rock to the same depth, so that accurate repeated passes would produce a much deeper cut. Putting all this together he proposed that the Inca stonemasons had used large, concave gold dishes to concentrate the rays of the sun to cut and shape rock.

This is a fascinating theory that again does not postulate high technology as such. Admittedly if our forgotten ancestors were not building in stone or using metal then it is not directly relevant to our current study, but it is conceivable that they may have been able to use smaller crystal lenses to concentrate the sun's rays for other purposes.

CONCLUSION

In the course of this chapter we have seen that the physical evidence normally presented in support of claims of advanced technology in any ancient epoch crumbles under the slightest of scrutiny. It is important to reemphasize that the main yardstick that should be used when evaluating this evidence is that of *context*. If the Great Pyramid stood alone without an accompanying complex laid out for clearly ritual and funerary purposes, and without other pyramids inscribed with ritual and funerary texts, it might be reasonable to suggest that it had some other function. But it does not. Similarly if all the ancient paintings, reliefs and other objects that are interpreted by some revisionists as indicative of a variety of advanced aerial, electrical and other technology were backed up by proper physical evidence that such advanced technology really existed, then we should perhaps be prepared to consider a literal rather than a ritual, stylistic or symbolic interpretation of them. But they are not.

Of course our forgotten race *could* have been using advanced technology handed to them by extraterrestrial visitors, for example, and it is *possible* that all such evidence was destroyed in the catastrophe. But there is really nothing substantive that points us in that direction, apart from some channeled messages that may in any case be subjectively influenced by conscious knowledge of what are in fact erroneous interpretations of ancient texts, artifacts and so on. So as long as that remains the case we should surely keep our conjectures about the forgotten race discussed in the ancient texts and traditions as grounded and realistic as possible. On that basis we do have some pointers to realistic, low-technology skills they *might* have possessed – in astronomy and navigation, and crystal and magnification technology, for example. But even then we should be clear that there is no definitive argument that, just because these skills are evident in the postcatastrophe epoch, they *must* have been present beforehand too.

The corollary to this approach is, as always, a requirement for discernment. We need to be able to stand back from any evidence and assess it and its implications calmly, without diving in and resorting to massive and ill-founded leaps of faith and logic. Of course if we are to be realistic we cannot escape the fact that, unfortunately, some such leaps may owe more to a desire to commercially exploit the understandable yearning for mystery that dwells within many of us, rather than to pure ignorance and poor scholarship. But whatever the cause we have surely been bombarded with enough materialistically oriented pseudo-archaeology over the last century and a half to satiate the hungriest of sensationalist appetites.

Some modern revisionists have led the way in reining in the more outlandish claims and materialistic obsessions of their predecessors, and in focusing more on the importance of symbolism and on the more metaphysical preoccupations of our ancient ancestors; and it is worth reemphasizing that for all this they are to be applauded. But there is also no escaping that their attempts to redate a variety of ancient monuments, along with theories of no overnight development and common origins, suffer from obvious defects. So perhaps now we can at last concentrate on what are arguably even more grounded scenarios, whose true *spiritual* message will be seen as far more exciting and relevant to us today than anything that has gone before. Indeed it is precisely this contemporary spiritual relevance that we should now explore on the final leg of our journey.

EPILOGUE: IMPLICATIONS FOR TODAY

The original message of *Genesis Unveiled* was that in repeating the mistake of becoming obsessed with the material at the expense of the spiritual we are risking the same fate as our forgotten ancestors. In the early years of the noughties when the bulk of it was written global warming was already a huge topic, but the whole issue of 2012 was only just rearing its head for a relative minority; it was not something in which I had taken much interest.

In the intervening years speculation about 2012 has massively increased, and my earliest thoughts on the matter were that suggestions of the end of the world and of something hugely negative did not resonate at all, despite my earlier warnings in *Genesis*. Then in 2009 I made the decision to start training as a regression therapist with the Past Life Regression Academy run by my old friend and collaborator on *The Wisdom of the Soul*, Andy Tomlinson. Not only has this balanced my more theoretical spiritual research with the practice of helping people with one-on-one therapy, but as a byproduct I also made some wonderful new friends.

This and other developments generally put me much more in touch with spiritual people on a regular basis, and of course the subject of 2012 would often come up. For some time I had had an increasing intuition that this would be a subject I would have to tackle in a book, one of the reasons being that so much of the material on it seemed to veer to one of two extremes. On the one hand we had the apocalyptic visions of Hollywood, and on the other the positive yet somehow sugarcoated messages from many alternative and spiritual authors that resonated no better. Many of us felt that what we needed was something positive, yet more real and grounded.

The background to how the channeled messages in *The Future of the Soul* came about is in that book and does not need to be repeated here. Suffice to say that one of the assistant trainers at the Academy, Janet Treloar, turned out to be a wonderful 'clear channel'; and over the course of two main sessions spanning over five hours she somewhat unexpectedly provided us with messages about 2012 from a diverse group calling themselves 'the council'.[1] These seemed to exactly fit the bill, and all of us who heard them resonated strongly with their combination of hardheaded realism and unbridled excitement about what lies in store.

Most important for our current purposes was the council's assertion that the current 'energy shift' is a high point in an energy cycle of approximately 26,000 years duration. This is not a new idea in itself, but given my interest in the spiritual history of the human race I was keen to know just how long these shifts have had an impact on modern humanity. It was at this point that the council's credibility could have been blown wide apart, in my eyes at least, if they had come up with a theosophy-style answer such as millions of years. But they did not. In fact they went quite the other way. Whereas in *Genesis Unveiled* I had used 100,000 years ago as a significant cultural marker because of what I now realize was the *isolated* incident of ritual burial in Israel, the council indicated that things only really began to get interesting for the modern human race about 75,000 years – that is three shifts – ago. Interest piqued I was determined to find out about what happened in these last three shifts, and especially about their underlying spiritual dynamics.

The council did not disappoint. They came up with information that I at least have never come across elsewhere and, even when some of it at first seemed counter-intuitive, it would almost immediately make perfect sense. I also questioned Janet closely about the extent of her knowledge of human evolution and early human history and prehistory and was delighted to hear that, apart from a reasonable grasp of the last few thousand years, she knew very little about anything before this. All this increased our confidence in what was coming through.

So we will now look at the underlying causes of the 26,000 year cycle itself, followed by the details of the last three shifts in turn and the new research I have conducted since the sessions to establish whether the council's information is backed up by hard evidence. We will then turn to the underlying spiritual dynamics that have shaped the history of the human soul, before finishing with the unique nature of the current shift and exactly what the future might hold for us all.

THE 26,000 YEAR ENERGY CYCLE

This is what the council had to say about the cause of the energy cycle in the original sessions:[2]

> The universe is set up in such a way that variations within it will prevent it from becoming stagnant, there will always be scope for change to varying degrees. The universe is a masterpiece of design, architecturally complex even when viewed from the perspective of the dimension you reside in. Through science and mathematics you've discovered some of the rudimentary forces governing your solar system, and indeed the universe, and you begin to understand its nature. It is architecturally perfect for its purpose, which is to constantly change and evolve. The constant and infinite alignments being made throughout direct energy, which then propels and activates change, so everything is constantly moving forward.
>
> Of these infinite alignments the one that affects the earth every 26,000 years has a specific purpose. It was set up to influence more than just your planet, but due to its magnetic nature the earth isn't just part of the alignment, it's central to it. Its movement to a slightly different position ensures it is in direct alignment to receive energy from many other parts of the universe, and indeed dimensions too. And it is magnetically weak enough that it has a greater capacity for change to take place.

The only cycle lasting of the order of 26,000 years that I was aware of is that of precession. So did this have an influence?

> Nothing on this scale happens by chance, and this apparent 'imperfection' was deliberately created and designed so that earth's alignments with other parts of the universe would constantly change. This technique is used elsewhere too.

Of all the topics covered this was clearly the most difficult for the council to convey in ways that Janet would understand, and we had so much other ground to cover that it was not explored further in the original sessions. But afterwards I decided to try to find out more about it in a brief third session that was not covered in *The Future of the Soul*.[3] Although the extra information that came through is still not definitively clear it does shed some useful extra light. The council began by talking more about the earth's magnetic field:

> Your planet is quite unique. The magnetism that surrounds it pulls and pushes in ways that you do not see, it changes its shape around earth in different directions with the ebb and flow. This field is pulled in certain directions because of the precessional alignment, it is even described as 'tipping'... It opens certain areas of the planet up, much more than at any other time it weakens the magnetic field that surrounds the earth. It is not so much the shape changing as it is a stretching, and when you stretch

something it has more opportunity to be penetrated... You can liken the magnetic field around the earth to a human body's aura.

From this it appeared they were suggesting that the process of precession, which slowly changes the angular position of earth with respect to the rest of the cosmos, creates alignments every 26,000 years that position her to be ready to receive a huge influx of energy from elsewhere. At the same time it seems the process stretches her 'magnetic aura' in such a way that the energy is able to get through far more than usual. So are changes in the magnetic poles as discussed in chapter 10 one aspect of this?

> This is why we described it as a tipping. If you imagine anything that is tipping it becomes precarious, and at some point it can go too far as the energy around the earth is stretched. It is instantaneous, and as you would say a shifting of the poles from one to the other... But this time it is unlikely to happen. There are too many living organisms on your planet that have evolved using magnetism for their survival, and the intention is not to obliterate but to add with this energy. It will feel quite close but the intention behind the energy is to come in waves so that the tipping point is not reached in one full blast... This is not an exact science. We will try to prevent the tipping but we cannot say that it will definitely not happen.

So what would be the effect of such a reversal if it were to happen?

> It is purely the energies. You would not see anything physical initially. However it is like a ripple on a pond but in reverse. The ripples get stronger inwards, and weather patterns would change dramatically. But there would be far more changes for the animal kingdom. Your instruments might fail but it would not be a threat to your life. And remember this is not our intention at this time anyway.

This seemed to confirm the research outlined in chapter 10. Turning to the extra energy directed at earth I wanted to know where it comes from:

> Energy is everywhere, it is the intention behind it that pushes it towards areas of the universe that need it at specific times. There are others in what you would call other galaxies that are using this specific time to push the energy forward when your planet is most susceptible to it and will make the most use of it... Whenever the timing is right the densest parts of the universe, the planets and the stars with mass, receive this energy so they can evolve. Just as the human body can receive energy healing, the earth is doing something very similar. In some respects you are a living, breathing blueprint of your planet... For earth the opportunities for this energy to get through are increased every 26,000 years because it is unique in terms of its polarities.

If we now look for external corroboration of this information it will come as no surprise that a number of theories about these cycles have sprung up in the buildup to 2012, although Janet and I were both ignorant of them even at the time of this third session. The first is an attempt to tie together the numbers in the precessional and yuga cycles that we discussed in chapter 5; and it originates from a different version of the Hindu tradition in *The Laws of Manu*, a text that seems to stir up controversy because of its debatable authority.[4] It dates to around the same time as the *Mahabharata* in which the traditional theory of world cycles is expounded, but the concept of divine years making up 360 normal years is clearly omitted:[5]

68. But hear now the brief (description of) the duration of a night and a day of Brahman and of the several ages according to their order.

69. They declare that the Krita age (consists of) four thousand years; the twilight preceding it consists of as many hundreds, and the twilight following it of the same number.

70. In the other three ages with their twilights preceding and following, the thousands and hundreds are diminished by one (in each).

71. These twelve thousand (years) which thus have been just mentioned as the total of four (human) ages, are called one age of the gods.

72. But know that the sum of one thousand ages of the gods (makes) one day of Brahman, and that his night has the same length.

So the total duration of the four yugas is 12,000 years, just as in Figure 3, but now instead of these being divine years they are normal years. Remember too that we saw this in the Vana Parva, one of the earlier books in the *Mahabharata*, and that the concept of divine years is only introduced implicitly in the numerically later Santi Parva, and explicitly in the completely separate and chronologically later *Vishnu Purana*.

At this point we need to bring in Sri Yukteswar, the guru whose pupil Paramhansa Yogananda became even more celebrated in the West. In *The Holy Science*, published in 1894, he was arguably the first Hindu scholar to argue that the introduction of the concept of divine years was a fabrication.[6] But he further argues that the four yuga cycles should be seen in the context of a descending cycle followed by an ascending cycle, making for a total of 24,000 years. This seems to have much more of the Jain flavor we discussed in chapter 5, but it does bring the length of the yuga cycle closer to that of precession.

Although modern commentators make much if this supposed correspondence the numbers are still significantly different; and, even more important, Yukteswar himself seems to have a very different concept in mind when he states that the 'sun revolves round a grand center called Vishnunabhi, which is the seat of the creative power, Brahma, the universal magnetism'. Elsewhere he states that 'the sun, with its planets and their moons, takes some star for its dual and revolves round it in about 24,000 years'. In fact his context even for this is rather different from ours in that he is attempting to show that 'when the sun in its revolution round its dual comes to the place nearest to this grand center... the mental virtue becomes so much developed that man can easily comprehend all, even the mysteries of Spirit'. This is all related to the supposedly different moral and other qualities of the four yugas, especially the golden krita yuga. Nevertheless his suggestion that there is an important energy center of some sort that we rotate around, and that our magnetic field may be influenced by it, has some clear similarities with the council's messages.

We briefly saw in chapter 6 that Joseph Campbell attempted to correlate the numbers in the precessional and yuga cycles too, and there are arguably more obvious links if the traditional numbers are used.[7] For example the historic estimate for a full precessional cycle is not 25,765 years – the most recent estimate as discussed in chapter 5 – but 25,920 years, a twelfth of which is 2160. When this is multiplied by 800, 600, 400 and 200 it gives the length of each traditional yuga in normal years as per Figure 3. That these numbers are symbolic and demonstrate knowledge of precession may not, therefore, be in doubt. But at the same time they are clearly *not* measuring precessional periods pure and simple, otherwise we would not have to engage in mathematical shenanigans to establish the linkages. So quite what else this tells us, if anything, is more open to debate.

If we turn now to the Maya, in his *Maya Cosmogenesis 2012* and *Galactic Alignment*, published in 1998 and 2002 respectively, John Major Jenkins argues that their long-count calendar can also be tied into the precessional cycle because five 13-baktun cycles of 5125 years produce a total of 25,625.[8] However we should remember that there is no great Mayan tradition of world ages to go with their calendar. We saw in chapter 7 that if anything there are only four ages including our own in their most sacred text the *Popol Vuh*, but in any case the whole context is more one of multiple-creation-of-man experiments than of world ages. Perhaps worse still for Jenkins we saw in chapter 5 that, in the genuine world age traditions of other Amerindian cultures, the numbers of ages and their lengths vary wildly not only from culture to culture but even sometimes within one culture. So, unlike with the yuga cycles, to propose a mathematical link between precession and Amerindian world age traditions generally is almost certainly a mistake. More specifically the supposed link between the Mayan calendar and precession is almost certainly false too.

The one link between these cyclical energy shifts and an ancient text that we might make is with Plato's composite theme of cyclical world ages possibly based on precession, as hinted at in chapter 5. However apart from anything else the council's cycles do not *always* end in catastrophe.

If we turn now to the key date of 21 December 2012, we also saw in chapter 5 that it is regarded as an end-point of a 13-baktun cycle of 5125 years in the Mayan long-count calendar. Although it had been recognized by scholars for far longer, it began to make inroads into the public consciousness when Jose Arguelles published *The Mayan Factor* in 1987. Then in their 1995 work *The Mayan Prophecies* Adrian Gilbert and Maurice Cotterell argued that the calendar was based on a highly scientific understanding of sun spot cycles and their effects on earth's magnetic field, leading to the potential conclusion that catastrophe is on its way. But since then the focus has switched steadily towards the more positive 'new era' possibilities represented by this date, aided in so small part by the proclamations of many indigenous Mayan scholars.

Jenkins uses this date in another way.[9] Not only does he identify our galactic center with Yukteswar's 'Vishnunabhi' but he describes how, because of precession, the galactic equator – the line that runs down the center of the Milky Way – will align with the rising sun at the winter solstice in 2012; that is, on 21 December. However he also reports that, because the sun is half a degree wide on our horizon, this alignment actually spans the 36 years from 1980 to 2016 – its central point having been reached back in 1998. He has therefore coined the phrase 'era-2012'.

Unfortunately, for all that Jenkins insists his alignments are accurate, there is a strong argument that the exact position of the galactic equator and the galactic center are impossible to determine with any sort of accuracy.[10] How do you define a center point or line for an ill-defined streak of densely clustered stars that meander across the night sky like a river? It is similar to the problem of deciding where one precessional age finishes and another begins: from an astronomical observation perspective there is no definitive date but rather a transitional period of tens if not hundreds of years. In any case while specific alignments may be useful from a calendrical perspective, from the perspective of earth receiving bursts of energy from other parts of the universe – which is surely the real issue here – it is hard to see how they are hugely relevant. The angular alignment of earth in relation to the rest of the cosmos may be important to this process, but this changes incredibly slowly. So even if this energy comes from a single source like the center of our galaxy and is directed straight at earth alone, which is by no means certain, it would still almost certainly be able to get through to us in the right way over, again, decades if not centuries spanning the high point of the 26,000 year cycle.

One researcher who discusses the idea of high levels of energy coming from the center of our galaxy at 26,000 year intervals without concerning himself unduly with alignments is astrophysicist Paul LaViolette. But in his 1997 work *Earth Under Fire* he postulates that these are 'galactic core explosions' that send out a massive and devastating burst of cosmic rays – the most recent one having ended the last ice age 12,850 years ago.[11] This is interesting in terms of our catastrophe theory but it does not seem to fit with the context of energies that have a positive impact; and in any case he also seems to posit what is in effect a 13,000 year cycle. By contrast in his 2006 work *The Cygnus Mystery* Andrew Collins proposes that the ancients revered the swan as symbolic of the constellation of Cygnus, which lies near the center of the galactic plane, and that the bursts of cosmic rays periodically emitted by Cygnus X-3 may have been responsible for influencing human development.[12] However the key periods he quotes do not coincide with a 26,000 year cycle.[13]

Apart from arguably useful theories concerning powerful energies coming from outside our solar system, these are only a select few of a multitude of attempts to tie ancient traditions into a precessional cycle that has a key date in 2012, and to make various other even more dubious links – as a swift perusal of Geoff Stray's comprehensive compilation *Beyond 2012* shows. One important maxim to bear in mind here is that 'you can prove anything with numbers if you try hard enough', but the broader context nearly always defeats the ingenuity of the various researchers who claim to have cracked the 2012 code. For what it is worth there is no special alignment of the planets in our solar system on 21 December 2012 either.[14]

This is arguably where the strength of the communications from the council lies, albeit that they too are hardly conclusive, especially in respect of the underlying dynamics of the energy cycle. But in refusing to confirm precise dates or alignments, or to be specific about the exact source of the energy that is culminating at this time, they certainly do not fall into the obvious traps that are present in many other channeled communications about 2012 – which, unfortunately, appear to suffer from a high degree of conscious interference. Indeed in another context they emphasize that is it not the alignments with other parts of the cosmos per se that matter at this time, it is more the *gaps* that are created.[15]

THE LAST THREE SHIFTS

All the material that we will cover from now on comes from the two original sessions. The dates used for the last three shifts are approximated to 25 rather than 26 thousand year intervals because at these remote distances in time approximations to the nearest few thousand years are arguably fine – coupled with the fact that, as we have seen, the high points of the energy cycle are more likely to be time spans rather than exact dates.

75,000 YEARS AGO

This is what the council had to say about the events of three shifts ago:[16]

> Around this time there was a major upheaval that caused a bottleneck in human evolution. So souls from elsewhere decided to use that energy shift to introduce some major changes. They chose one strain of surviving human, and they continued to influence the evolution of their physical bodies to improve their chances of survival, although by influence we mean energetically and not by physical, genetic experiments as some of you seem to believe. From that point on all the other strains, including the Neanderthals, started to die out, even if it took some time for them to become completely extinct. It is no coincidence that the evidence of these extinct human forms has been unearthed in the last hundred and fifty years, in order that in the run-up to the current shift we would be able to reveal what was really going on from a soul perspective.

Although I had forgotten it at the time of the session, I soon remembered having written about the eruption of the Toba super volcano in *Genesis Unveiled*. As we saw in chapter 9 this created exactly the sort of population bottleneck described by the council. Not only that but according to many scholars it was not long afterwards that modern humans emerged from northeast Africa and headed both north and east to colonize new lands. Were these groups the 'strain' the council says were chosen for special energetic influence and attention at that time?

50,000 YEARS AGO

The council carried on by describing the next shift:[17]

> This time there was no major upheaval. But because by then humans had properly mastered basic survival, the emphasis switched from influencing

physical development to influencing emotional development. Then culture could progress much faster and people could come together to live in larger, more settled communities.

All I knew about from around this time was what I had written in *Genesis Unveiled* about the Upper Paleolithic explosion, which is exactly when the shift from pure survival to more cultural activities seems to occur in the archaeological record. But at that point scholars dated this to around 40,000 years ago, so I was delighted when researching for this work to find this date has now been pushed back by 10,000 years, as we also saw in chapter 9. This seemed to be further confirmation of the accuracy of the council's messages.

At this point it is important to reveal that, according to the council, the major catastrophe that ended the golden age occurred not around 13,000 years ago but during the most recent shift around 25,000 years ago – although as we will see they confirmed that major upheavals occurred on both dates. So when they then began to talk about what happened *between* the last two shifts they were clearly describing our golden race, and what their lives were like before debasement set in.

One area that required clarification was whether any of the channeled material about some Lemuro-Atlanteans being only semi-physical had any foundation:[18]

Some were denser than others. Those that could lead lives away from other souls could remain quite fluid in form, but the more they encountered other souls the more solid their form needed to be to remain separate. As long as they remained apart from the rest of society, even in groups that were on the same level, they knew how to keep themselves separate from each other.

The issue of where our golden race lived was also of major interest:[19]

Near the equator. The way the earth was then the climate had more extremes, and human life was most comfortable nearer the equator. Nearer to the poles there was very little life at all. The most evolved souls were right on top of the equator.

We then moved on to their level of culture and technology:

Their technology utilized the power of their minds. Some created purely with their minds, but almost had to dedicate their whole lives to doing this, and to separating themselves off. But more and more these people used what the earth had given them to create, and they involved their minds more, a skill which has since been forgotten... They could find sources of water, for example, and they knew how to adapt them to their bodies just by thinking. So if there was an impurity within the water they would be able to find out and remove it with their minds. And the same with food. They could help their crops grow, but they still used the land. There were those that could, as you would think, create something out of thin air, but a lot of energy was put into that. So other methods were used, crystals especially... By linking with a crystal they would find its special purpose and adapt to the world around them rather than trying to get the world to adapt to their will. This is how they had progressed up until the shift, by understanding this.

It came as no surprise to hear that the golden race lived in harmony with the earth and with nature rather than trying to bend them to their will, nor that they used their understanding of the natural power of crystals. But the council also stressed how important education was to them:

Many came together with the idea that they would learn. Their schools taught them how to harness the power of their thoughts, and those highest in the field of technology went out trying to find different ways to apply it.

From the context of the rest of their messages the council's use of the term *technology* here does not mean 'advanced' in the modern sense, but again applies to harnessing the powers of the mind.

25,000 YEARS AGO

The council's messages about the golden race carry on from above by describing what happened in the run-up to the last shift:[20]

As more people came together the more they also realized how they could use the power of each others' minds. There was a new surge of energy coming through from the earth, and as energy doesn't have a consciousness itself people could use it for whatever they wanted, including for their own ends. With their minds they could send others mad. There was physical violence. But the worst were those who understood and were adept at what they could do, and who harnessed their energies together like a battery. They got into other people's minds, and would use their energy too. This was a complete mutation of their abilities, and not what was meant at all. It wasn't right, it wasn't the way that minds should work, but once made it was hard to break their contact with others' minds.

This is where we perhaps find a degree of resonance with Lewis Spence's reports of how the Atlanteans misused their occult powers, which we discussed in chapter 11. In any case the council then made it clear that a deliberate decision was made at a collective soul level to discontinue this part of the human experiment that was going awry.[21]

219

We discussed with those that oversee the earth how best to stop this. The earth was aware that it had its own power whereby it could grant great fertility, but it could also wreak much havoc. A contract was struck... The earth shook and shook, and eventually the water took what it needed to and cleansed it. Everything came from water first, so everything went back. It was right of the earth to do it this way.

Although we gained few other details about the nature of this catastrophe, they did indicate that it was an entirely natural, earth-generated event that did not involve extraterrestrial bodies. It wiped out around 40 percent of the population, although at that time this was only a tiny proportion – 'not even one percent' – of what it is now.[22] Is there any physical evidence of a major catastrophe around this time? Certainly there does not appear to be genetic evidence for a global population bottleneck as at 75,000 years ago. But whereas we know that there were very few modern human survivors of the Toba super eruption, the sixty percent of survivors from this shift would have represented a far larger population that had spread far and wide. Arguably we do not see a genetic bottleneck in human population 13,000 years ago for exactly the same reason.

Of course I was fascinated to know whether there was evidence for major volcanic activity at the time of this shift too, especially in the region of Southeast Asia where I had by now surmised our golden race were most likely living, as we saw in chapter 10. It turns out that there have only been two genuine super eruptions in the last 250,000 years.[23] The first is Toba, which we already know about, and which coincides with the catastrophe the council say occurred three shifts ago. Remembering that they report there was no major catastrophe two shifts ago, surely it would be expecting too much to find that the other one coincided with the earth-generated catastrophe they say occurred during the last shift – and that it happened in that region of the world? It is not. In fact that is exactly what we find. The only other super eruption in the last quarter of a million years occurred at Lake Taupo on New Zealand's North Island... around 26,500 years ago. The council's messages are looking stronger all the time.

Is there any evidence of other significant volcanic activity at around this time, even if it would be much lower impact than a super eruption? The answer is yes. In Bali the eruption that turned Mount Batur into a massive caldera is estimated to have taken place around 25,000 years ago.[24] We saw in chapter 11 that a significant eruption of the volcanic Greek island of Santorini was responsible for destroying the Minoan civilization on Crete, but its most significant eruption before that is also dated to around 25,000 years ago.[25] Finally Mount Popocatepetl in Mexico is thought to have had a significant eruption around 23,000 years ago.[26] If these dates are accurate they cannot all have been part of one event, but they might signal a general wave of earth-generated activity over the whole period of the high point of the last shift. On the other hand these might be regarded as just a selection of eruptions in a particular time window that are not unusual because they occur all around the world all the time. If that is so then the Taupo super eruption is still more than enough evidence on its own.

If we turn to the survivors of this catastrophe, the council reported that they 'were in places where the land was not so fertile, but also the energy was not so strong and they had not been so corrupted'.[27] So is it possible that, just as we surmised in chapter 3 and Plato confirmed in chapter 5, nearly all the human survivors from this event were the less settled, nomadic peoples who continued with a more hunter-gatherer lifestyle; and that virtually all traces of the former glories of the Southeast Asian golden civilization were soon forgotten, apart from the tales handed down by a few long-distance travelers? Indeed even though Sundaland, for example, was not permanently submerged at this time as it would be by the most recent catastrophe at the end of the Pleistocene, we cannot be sure that advanced cultural civilization got going again in the same way between the two.

One clue to this came when the council confirmed that an extraterrestrial impact had caused the most recent catastrophe, even though they were clear this was an independent event that had nothing to do with the energy cycles per se.[28] They indicated that the population had already 'dwindled anyway because we knew this was going to happen'. In other words not only were far fewer people wiped out in the most recent catastrophe, but there may not have been a great deal of rebuilding after the earlier one. This view is perhaps corroborated by the fact that in Europe at least, as we saw in chapter 9, the artwork shows a marked shift back to a more male-dominated, hunter-gatherer culture coincident with the harsher climate of the last glacial maximum around 20,000 years ago.

THE HISTORY OF THE SOUL

Arguably some of the most fascinating messages that came through from the council involve the underlying dynamics of the 'human' soul, and the changes in the way it operates when incarnate that have been introduced at various times. The first is their assertion that it was only three shifts or around 75,000 years ago that our soul energy became 'what we would recognize as human', whereas before this 'they brought with them the group memories of the human race, much as most animals still do now; this was the only way they could survive and still evolve'.[29] To me at least this was an unexpectedly late date for the transition from an animal-style group soul energy to the first successful incarnations of individuated souls.

The next major revelation was that the most significant reason for the degeneration that overtook the golden race was their decision to change the rules of incarnation, and to introduce amnesia about their true spiritual nature for the first time:[30]

> Towards the end of the Golden Age, shortly before the last shift, humans were progressing well. The bodies of those who are your ancestors today had evolved fully into the now recognizable human form, and life was thriving. Initially amnesia was just an experiment, not all chose it. Those who felt they would learn more with amnesia were the pioneers, but their fate was to be an unknown without their memories from before. They would either succeed in integrating and learning from society, or they would become outcasts due to their 'baseness'. When souls returned home they found they had learned much from this, especially the difficult experiences, so it wasn't long before all souls chose this route. But then many of them started to take the wrong path, and instead of creating they became destructive.

In other words one of the major factors underlying the original spirituality of the golden race was that they did *not* suffer from amnesia, a possibility we considered in chapter 7. But if this is correct it might require us to amend our previous suggestion in chapters 3 and 8 that only more experienced souls could tap into the universal spiritual truths to bring them to their fellows; because if the council are right then at least for the majority of the golden age everyone may have understood them.

All this raises another question. How is it that we have amnesia now, just like the later more degenerate members of our forgotten race, and yet – arguably – we do not all fly off the rails in the same way? The council's answer to this was just as revealing:[31]

> They didn't have a soul plan as you do now. Their life purpose was left up to them to decide during their incarnation. This was also changed after this time. We learned that within an incarnate body it is very hard even for a very evolved soul [with amnesia] to truly remember about spirit and so on if beforehand they don't have a plan set in place to do so. There is a baseness associated with the earth, and that baseness can draw souls who are power-crazed.

So, rather than discontinuing the amnesia experiment and returning to the old way of doing things, a further refinement was made and life plans were introduced after the last shift. This is of course how we have operated ever since, and still do now. But are there any plans afoot to lessen the degree of amnesia? To answer this we need to see what the council had to say about the current shift, and the future that awaits us.

THE FUTURE OF THE SOUL

At this point it is time for us to leave our forgotten, golden race and their descendants behind. We have learned much about them, much that helps us to understand who we are, and how we got to where we are. Indeed from a soul perspective we *are* them in all sorts of ways. But now we need to concentrate on the present and the future.

The messages from the council about the current shift were profoundly uplifting.[32] Although there are more grounded elements that we will come to shortly, they described how a new, more energetically charged earth has already been emerging for some decades. Allied to this children are being born with subtly different energy bodies that are more closely aligned to their physical bodies, so they will have far better health and longer lives. They will remember to welcome death and choose their time of departure, rather than hanging on to the physical world at all costs. They will also be able to communicate more telepathically, move out of body more easily and influence the reality they experience with their thoughts far more – much as the original golden race could. It may even be that many of us who have already been here for some years will be able to take advantage of at least some of these changes:[33]

> You may think of the earth like a caterpillar. All this time it's been growing, and for the last few thousand years it's almost like it's been in a cocoon, while all these souls have been playing out their roles on it. And now a butterfly is emerging. That is the best way to think of how the earth will be after the shift. This beautiful thing. And just like the caterpillar couldn't fly before and now it can, this energy will bring through new qualities, new things that can be done, new experiences, the earth will have another dimension to it. And the people on it will experience that dimension. There will be better communication. There will be better understanding. It will be a more gentle place to live. Duality will still remain but people will be more comfortable with the middle ground.

They also suggested that only a relatively small proportion of the human population will resist these changes in the long term, and one particularly charming member of the council emphasized just how wonderful it is to see how many people are 'waking up':[34]

> Be who you were born to be! There are so many wonderful souls here now who are in tune with themselves, and with us too. So shine that light! If you could look at all the souls now, as they really are with their light shining out, it's like fireflies at night. It's brilliant to watch from a distance as you look down and see all the people opening up! It's just so exciting, there's so many more people who are awake than you think! You can see them, I watch them at night, their night time, and it's my job to see where they still have some denseness and blockages. But these are getting less and less. It's wonderful, I can go through whole swathes of people and know that they can release what they need to on their own from now on.

Of course we all have different experiences, but it really does seem as if the rate of people waking up in this way is increasing exponentially – and spreading like a wonderfully benign virus. There are a great many signs of the old world order breaking down, in the West at least. Furthermore the council emphasized that, rather than our existing earth somehow being *replaced* by a new version, it is merely having what we might regard as another energetic dimension *added* to it. So, unlike many of the somewhat elitist messages about 2012, this is not a one-time-only opportunity whereby those who reach enlightenment in time will catch the train and those who do not will perish. Rather it is a gradual process, albeit one that is accelerating fast now we are nearing the peak; and according to the council those who do not wake up will simply feel increasingly uncomfortable in the new world, because they will perceive it with fear rather than love. But even then they emphasized, with one of their most brilliantly counter-intuitive messages, that we should not judge those who resist; and we should certainly *not* assume they are less experienced souls. They are merely acting out their planned roles.

This brings us to another counter-intuitive message, which is that absolutely everything is as it should be, even down to the way humanity generally has been ravaging the planet:[35]

> Everything that is being done to the earth at present that you tend to see as bad, for example taking its resources, will ultimately just enable it to fight back with a survival instinct similar to your own. It's calling on energy that it hasn't needed for quite some time to bring that back. There are people trying to help it now, and it's not that their efforts are futile, but the whole raising of consciousness will, in its own right, give the earth what it needs.

As more people become aware of the shift, without realizing it they are energetically helping the earth, they are putting their emotions and energy into it, which will help the process.

The way to understand this is that we as individual souls would grow very little if we stayed in the peace, harmony and unconditional love of the ethereal realms. In order to grow we need experiences, and according to many sources earth is one of the hardest proving grounds of them all because of its extreme duality of emotions – all of which can be categorized as either love-based or fear-based. So some of our experiences here will be harsh and difficult, and it is the way we face and overcome them that defines us as people, and influences our soul growth too. Moreover what is true of us as individual souls is also true of earth as a consciousness in its own right. How many of us on a spiritual path have felt that we are being blocked or having obstacles put in our way; and how many of us have recognized that as soon as we stop bemoaning this fact and see them as opportunities for growth, what seemed like insurmountable barriers become mere hurdles – the leaping of which massively raises our own energies. It is the same for earth herself.

Several times I have stressed that, although the messages from the council are hugely uplifting, they are grounded too; and it is when we come to some of these more practical aspects that we need to learn something hugely important for us all – and that is to adopt a soul rather than human perspective.[36] Although it has all been part of the plan that mother earth should have 'so many souls on her back like a parasite', it is clear that after the shift we will need to return to a more balanced position.[37] That means that significant upheavals, which will significantly reduce global population levels, will be required.

As much as this will be an understandably shocking statement for some, if we step back from any personal reaction for a moment, can any of us seriously argue that the hugely exponential population growth of the last century in particular is even remotely sustainable? But what hopefully makes all this somewhat more palatable is the council's further explanation that a significant proportion of the souls on earth at the moment are here deliberately so that they can move on to 'other places'.[38] It is not appropriate to go into this in detail here, but the idea is that they are using this energy shift to propel them to new dimensions they have never before been able to experience. Yes they will be leaving their physical bodies via the normal process – dying, in other words – and many will be doing so well before the end of their natural lifespan. But according to the council this is absolutely something they have been joyously planning on a soul level for many lifetimes.

On a more prosaic level the plan is that most of these souls will be leaving in large groups caught up in a variety of natural upheavals that will be happening in various parts of the globe over the coming years. We deliberately did not ask exactly where and when these upheavals would take place – indeed as we will see shortly all this may not be set in stone yet anyway – but the council did emphasize that the right people would feel drawn to these locations when the time was right.

Of course all this means there will almost certainly be some disruption over the coming years too, but they were keen to keep this in perspective: 'It's simply a time of adaption, there will not be too much hardship. It will mean people need to go back to basics though, for a time.'[39] The accompanying message was that, whether our life plan is to go to another place or to remain here to enjoy the wonderful new earth that is in the process of being created, we should go to *wherever* in the world we resonate with, and allow ourselves to be drawn to *whoever* we resonate with; and if that means moving out of big cities, or leaving relationships and friendships that no longer work for us, then so be it. On that note they did of course encourage the growth of smaller, self-sustaining communities, at least during the period of disruption.

Another aspect that the council were keen to stress was the major difference between the last shift and this one. Apparently the outcome of the last one was known at the 'higher levels':[40]

> Those above, for want of a better word, did know that this experiment of bringing in energy to a place of duality, and trying things that had worked in other places, would not work. They knew that we had much to learn about the soul, and how much it could remember while still functioning within the human form. But we needed to learn this... Subsequently there was a massive leap in evolution as a result of what was learned.

But this time their excitement at the fact there is 'all to play for' seems to be unbounded:[41]

> New experiences will be born out of it that even we haven't conceived yet. The spiritual awakening that is happening globally is like a baby opening its eyes for the first time. We decided this time to give a glimpse of eternity to people. This is one of the reasons why it's so exciting at this time. Never before have you had the chance to be in a body but also see eternity. How amazing that is! And we are watching to see how this will help you to grow and shift without people using it in a way that is wasn't meant for.

There is obviously a bigger picture here. It is clear that certain aspects of the current energy shift are part of the 'grand earth plan', such as the huge population buildup in the run-up followed by its reversal. But as discussed in chapter 2, aspects of the grand plan like this and any previous catastrophes should surely not be seen as things that are *imposed* on humanity, but rather as collective decisions that all of us souls who incarnate on and have an interest in earth reach *together*. It is also clear that many, perhaps the majority of us souls on earth at present, have individual soul plans that will either see us leaving for other places or staying to enjoy the new world. Not only that but the council reported there are huge numbers of guides and other light beings whose entire focus for some years has been on trying to make sure the souls on earth under their care take the right overall course. But we should always remember that *none* of this is set in stone. We *always, always* have free will, both individually and collectively. All the evidence suggests that if we were really determined to ignore all the pullings from our heart – all the intuitive feelings about where we are and what we are doing and who we are with – we could do so, and go off and have a completely different experience to the one we planned. What is more even if we do *end up* at the right point in our life plan, there are myriad ways of getting there; and we all know that the journey can be far more important than the destination.

The council themselves consistently demonstrated the lack of predetermination in all this; for example in the exact extent of population decrease, and in the number, location and timing of the upheavals. That is why it would be a huge mistake to concentrate on just one date such as 21 December 2012, as if everything is going to change, magically and suddenly, on that one day. *The changes have already been happening for a long time, and they will continue long after 2012.* Indeed the council regularly mentioned the flexibility they need to have in trying to keep things on broadly the right path:[42]

> We've had to adapt to a mindset in the West that we weren't used to. Our help might not be in the way we would have originally chosen, but it is working. For example, we are aware of the way people worship 'celebrities' in the West, often more than they do religious or political figures, and we have used that to bring about much knowledge and awakening. Many celebrities are waking up other souls in their own right, through mediums that the West will accept.

So the hugely important message from this is that what we do, both individually and collectively, can still make *all* the difference both to the outcome of this shift and to how we get there. A fascinating added dimension is that many of the souls who were on earth during the last shift have apparently returned to right perceived wrongs, and to make sure they do not squander the opportunity again:[43]

> So many of them are trying this experience of an energy shift for a second time now. And this time nothing is set in stone. That's the beauty of this experience, and why the whole galaxy is watching it. Never before has this been done, where the outcome is not certain.

Let us turn now, as we must, to the question of the reliability of these messages. The council rightly emphasized that we were just one amongst a great many individuals and groups channeling messages about 2012 at this time:[44]

> When you can see past what goes on immediately around you, the excitement for change is incredible! If you could feel what we feel! It is exciting for us to be able to be involved, and to be heard in your lives. This is a first. This we did not do the last time, and we're learning from it. And your group is just one of many. This is happening all over. And if we can instill anything in you it's the excitement of the culmination of this process, of why you have chosen to be here.

Of course we already know that not all channeled messages are entirely reliable, and that may be especially true of the current crop because of the potential lack of objectivity, given the huge focus on 2012 that already exists. Nor, of course, are the messages from the council itself in any sense infallible. Admittedly a question-and-answer setting such as ours was different from one whereby an individual channel engages in a lengthy, non-interactive monologue, and arguably this may have lessened the possibility of conscious interference by the channel. On the other hand in our setting there was the added problem of the questioner influencing the questions, and possibly even telepathically conveying some of their own conscious knowledge to the channel.

Having said that, as we have seen Janet knew very little about history, and I knew very little about 2012 and energetic cycles at the time. What is more, the one thing we all witnessed clearly was the violent shaking of her body throughout the whole of the first session, and the lesser but still evident shaking in the second. Its specific characteristics tended to change as different entities took over, but she was left extremely drained by the sessions – indeed quite ill for a time, which is why when she channels now she only does so via an intermediary between her and the council. These were powerful energies she was channeling, and the messages generally were indubitably not just the result of a vivid imagination.

In any case the only thing that really matters when we are dealing with channeled material is whether it resonates with us or not. So some aspects of the council's messages may resonate with you, while others may not, and that is absolutely fine. I have spent most of my time as a researcher coming entirely 'from the head', because that is historically my strength and why Rational Spirituality has a part to play. But in this departure into disseminating channeled material of our own I have had to come 'from the heart' instead; and that is what anyone who reads the council's messages should do too. Those who are meant to be drawn to them will be. Meanwhile there will be those who will only see the apparent negatives, perhaps because they are struggling to adopt anything but a purely human perspective; they may portray them as inhumane and even abhorrent as a result, but they will be just as entitled to their view.

The one dynamic underling the theme of 2012 and a global energy shift, which is arguably more important than any other, is the way it has created a focal point for the collective consciousness and indeed the collective unconscious. It really does not matter if everything in this chapter, and in all the plethora of other books, articles, lectures, films and other media that deal with the subject, is complete and utter nonsense. For those of us of a spiritual persuasion, indeed arguably for many others who simply do not much care for the kind of society we have evolved, the only thing that does matter is that we are creating a better world for ourselves just by imagining it and focusing on it.

The more we do that, and the more we help people to open up to the wonderful, simple, majestic fact they are *soul*, the greater will be the surge towards a new, more loving world... until it becomes an unstoppable force, sweeping away every obstacle in its path.

SOURCE REFERENCES

Wherever possible the most up-to-date and readily available English translations of ancient texts, as prepared by orthodox scholars, have been used. Biblical references are taken from the Authorized King James Bible unless otherwise stated.

Ellipses (...) in quotes occasionally indicate that something is missing from the incomplete original source text, but more often it indicates omitted elements that are considered inconsequential, irrelevant or repetitive. All italics and rounded brackets in quotes are original, whereas any explanatory comments are in square brackets.

Publication details for the books referenced below can be found in the bibliography. All website references were current when consulted late in 2010.

PREFACE

[1]   A multitude of ancient texts and traditions from nearly every continent on the globe record such an event, although we will not examine the detail of all of these in the current work because they have been well chronicled by others – and in any case we will meet with many of them in due course. For comprehensive descriptions and discussion see, for example, Oppenheimer, *Eden in the East*, chapters 8–10. A number of websites document flood myths; see, for example, http://en.wikipedia.org/wiki/Flood_myth.

[2]   Campbell, *Primitive Mythology*, introduction, p. 27.

[3]   Jung, *Psychology and Alchemy*, prefatory note to the English edition, p. v.

[4]   For an excellent discussion of ancient Egyptian myth and symbolism see West, *Serpent in the Sky*, pp. 127–34.

[5]   All these major changes are summarized chapter by chapter at www.ianlawton.com/hoschgs.htm.

CHAPTER 1: MYTHS IN THE MAKING

[1]   See Campbell, *Primitive Mythology*, prologue, pp. 14–15 and Eliade, *The Sacred and the Profane*, chronological survey, pp. 229–32.

[2]   For a full exposition see Campbell, *Primitive Mythology*, part 1.

[3]   For a full exposition see ibid., parts 2 and 3.

[4]   Ibid., chapter 3, pp. 146–7.

[5]   Ibid., chapter 10, pp. 403–4.

6   Ibid., conclusion, p. 462.

7   See http://en.wikipedia.org/wiki/Joseph_Campbell#Comparative_religion.

8   Campbell, *Primitive Mythology*, chapter 4, p. 164.

9   Campbell, *Occidental Mythology*, chapter 3, p. 95.

CHAPTER 2: DEBASEMENT AND DESTRUCTION

1   For a discussion of the various texts known to have formed the basis for the Torah see Campbell, *Occidental Mythology*, chapter 3, pp. 100–2.

2   See note 1 to the preface.

3   I have undertaken a detailed analysis of the contents of all these king lists from the original sources, because this information is rarely properly recorded. See Lawton, *Problems with King Lists* (2002, www.ianlawton.com/gul.htm).

4   Correspondence with me, 23 February 2001.

5   This verse, although not central to the current argument, has caused a great deal of confusion. A similar passage from the Dead Sea Scrolls, however, explains all: 'In the four hundred and eightieth year of Noah's life, he came to the end of them, and God said, "My spirit shall not dwell with man forever, their days shall be determined to be one hundred and twenty years until the waters of the flood come."' This fits in with Noah being 600 years old at the time of the flood, as reported in Genesis 7:6. See Wise et al., *The Dead Sea Scrolls,* part 2, section 44, p. 275, and also Saint Augustine, *The City of God* 15.24.

6   von Däniken, *Chariots of the Gods*, chapter 4, p. 61.

7   Ibid., plates section.

8   Although he has resurfaced in recent years and his popularity seems relatively intact.

9   I very much include myself in this group, because von Däniken captured my imagination as a teenager. Much later it was Sitchin's work that not only set me on the path of researching this work, but also forced me to recognize early on the generally poor standards of scholarship amongst revisionist historians – despite occasional appearances to the contrary. Indeed I laugh now that when I started out I did not even realize that Sitchin's complete lack of source references should have rung loud alarm bells.

10   Although there is insufficient space to provide detailed support for these strong allegations here, I do provide it in a number of papers published or referenced at www.ianlawton.com/mesindex.htm. It is worth pointing out that, as far as I am aware, Sitchin has never deigned to respond to any of his linguistic critics in any detail at all. What is worse, when he deliberately omits lines from the *middle* of text extracts that would provide enough original context to destroy his fanciful interpretations, one can only conclude he is doing it in the full

knowledge that he is deliberately misleading people. Note also that he uses the '120 years' in Genesis 6:3 to date the arrival of the Nephilim to 432,000 years before the flood, interpreting these years as 'sars' of 3600 years each; see *The Twelfth Planet*, chapter 8, pp. 227–9. See note 5 above for the proper interpretation that indicates Sitchin's version is a nonsense.

[11] The finest example of this is Sitchin's suggestion that Howard Vyse faked the infamous 'Khufu quarry marks' in the Great Pyramid. This appears to be largely a fabrication of his own that some other revisionists continue to perpetuate in attempting to justify an older date for it. We will discuss this more in Part 2.

[12] For a summary of Collins' chronology see *From the Ashes of Angels*, chart 3, pp. 345–6. Note that he was to some extent influenced by the research of Christian O'Brien who, in his 1985 work *The Genius Of The Few* and the follow-up *The Shining Ones*, devotes considerable time to reinterpreting the little-known Mesopotamian *Kharsag Epics* and various other better-known Mesopotamian and Judaic texts. From this he suggests that a well-educated group of fair-skinned Atlantean survivors settled in South Lebanon and began the postcatastrophe rebuilding process. While this analysis might suffer from similar chronological and contextual problems to Collins', O'Brien's attempts at retranslation do appear to be of a high scholastic standard. Also, while he tends towards a somewhat technological interpretation of their achievements, unusually he combines this with a high degree of respect for their spirituality. Preservation and continuation of his work is being undertaken by Edmund Marriage; for more information see www.goldenageproject.org.uk.

[13] Ancient History of the Jews 2; see Murray, *History of the Jews*, volume 1, pp. 26–7.

[14] The City of God 15.22; see www.ccel.org/ccel/schaff/npnf102.toc.html for a full translation.

[15] See Laurence's introductory notes to his 1883 translation of *The Book of Enoch*, pp. iv–vi.

[16] 1 Enoch 7; see ibid., pp. 5–7.

[17] 1 Enoch 8; see ibid., pp. 7–8.

[18] It is interesting that the original Hebrew word used for the angels can be translated as 'those who watch', and this correlates with the word used in the Greek versions of these texts that is now translated as 'Watchers'. However the other translation of the Hebrew word is 'those who are *awake*'. See Collins, *From the Ashes of Angels*, chapter 1, p. 3.

[19] 1 Enoch 10:1–5; see Laurence, *The Book of Enoch*, p. 10.

[20] 1 Enoch 10:6–29; see ibid., pp. 10–13.

[21] 1 Enoch 82:4–10 and 83:5–8; see ibid., pp. 118–19 and 120–1.

22   1 Enoch 90:6–7; see ibid., pp. 146–7.

23   The Ethiopian and Slavonic versions are normally referred to as '1 Enoch' and
      '2 Enoch' respectively. Note that there is another related but fragmentary text,
      the Enochian *Book of Giants*, that forms part of the Dead Sea Scrolls. But this
      appears to further distort any original message by accusing the fallen angels of
      bestiality and emphasizing the giant stature of their offspring; see Wise et al.,
      The Dead Sea Scrolls, part 2, section 33, pp. 246–50.

24   2 Enoch 35; see Morfill and Charles, *The Book of the Secrets of Enoch*, pp. 49–
      50.

25   1 Enoch 54:1–3; see Laurence, *The Book of Enoch*, p. 61.

26   Genesis 9:8–17.

27   1 Enoch 64:1–3 and 9; see Laurence, *The Book of Enoch*, pp. 78–9.

28   1 Enoch 79:3–7; see ibid., pp. 110–11.

29   These are described in Copenhaver, *Hermetica*, introduction, pp. xxxii–xl.

30   For more information on the various original compilations of source texts see
      ibid., introduction, pp. xl–xlv; and on the various commentaries that were then
      prepared by Arabian and European Hermeticists from the seventh century
      onward, see pp. xlv–lix. Cophenhaver's 1992 translation is the most recent
      available and as such incorporates all the scholarship of his multitude of
      predecessors. This is important given the problems of interpreting the many
      different versions of the original texts, and of ensuring that the translation is as
      faithful to these originals as possible. By contrast the popular translation by
      Walter Scott in the 1920s is regarded by most orthodox scholars as distorted
      and unreliable, even if his extensive commentaries are invaluable; see ibid.,
      introduction, p. liii. Having said that his is the only modern version that
      includes the philosophical Stobaeus manuscripts, to which we will refer on
      occasion.

31   Corpus Hermeticum 4:7; see Copenhaver, *Hermetica*, p. 16.

32   Asclepius 25; see ibid., p. 82. This passage is followed up in Asclepius 26 by
      the suggestion that the world will be cleansed by a catastrophe of flood and fire.
      It is impossible to interpret whether this is a confusion of something that
      happened long before the texts were prepared, even though the future tense is
      used; or merely a version of the Judaeo-Christian apocalypse; or a genuine
      suggestion that the same fate could befall us in the modern epoch if we fail to
      learn the lessons of the past.

33   For more information see Robinson, *The Nag Hammadi Library*, introduction,
      pp. 1–10. This is the most recent compilation of scholars' translations of the
      various tractates.

34   These are *The Discourse on the Eighth and Ninth, The Prayer of Thanksgiving,
      Scribal note* and *Asclepius* 21–9. Three of these were previously unknown but

can be identified because they are dialogues in which Hermes Trismegistus takes the lead role.

35 It is interesting to compare this with a passage in the Hermetic *Kore Kosmu*, which suggests that the first incarnations into human form were a karmic punishment for souls that had already erred by 'overstepping the bounds of their own divisions of the atmosphere' and claiming 'nobility equal to the gods in heaven'; the fact that this is so at odds with other Hermetic passages shows how self-contradictory these texts can become after centuries of editing and translation; see Stobaeus Excerpt 23 in Scott, *Hermetica*, p. 184. However for completeness we should also note the similarity between the Gnostic view of the initial fall and that of Islam, in which a 'lesser god' is condemned to incarnation on earth because he 'refused to bow before Adam'; he then pledges to act as a negative influence on humankind's development, which he achieves by making Adam partake of the 'forbidden tree'; see Koran 7:11–25.

36 The main Gnostic texts that contain this same basic message are the *Apocryphon of John*, the *Hypostatis of the Archons*, *On the Origin of the World* and the *Tripartite Tractate*. To a large extent they pick up on and elaborate the themes in Genesis.

37 For more on the potential pitfalls of the pursuit of apparent enlightenment see Lawton, *The Big Book of the Soul*, chapter 8, pp. 241–51.

38 Robinson, *The Nag Hammadi Library*, pp. 121–2. Although it adds nothing of interest, the only other Gnostic text to directly describe the fallen angels' perversion of humankind is *On the Origin of the World*; see ibid., p. 186.

39 Ibid., p. 121.

40 More details about the background to ancient Mesopotamia, the excavations, the decipherment of the various scripts and the pantheon of gods are available in a number of my papers at www.ianlawton.com/mesindex.htm. I have also prepared summaries of the various Sumerian and Akkadian literary texts, which are too numerous to list here. The main source for translations of the former is Thorkild Jacobsen's 1987 work *The Harps That Once... Sumerian Poetry in Translation,* and of the latter Stephanie Dalley's 1991 work *Myths from Mesopotamia.*

41 Dalley, *Myths from Mesopotamia*, p. 229.

42 Ibid., pp. 9–35; see especially pp. 18–24.

43 Jacobsen, *The Harps That Once...*, pp. 145–50.

44 See note 1 to the preface for global sources, and for a fuller discussion of this issue Lawton, *Problems with King Lists* (2002, www.ianlawton.com/gu1.htm).

45 Dalley, *Myths from Mesopotamia*, pp. 109–16.

46 Ibid., glossary (s.v. Seven Sages), p. 328.

[47] Erra and Ishum 1 and 2; see ibid., pp. 291 and 294.

[48] Ibid., glossary (s.v. Apsu), p. 318.

[49] Erra and Ishum 4; see ibid., p. 306.

[50] Erra and Ishum 3; see ibid., pp. 299 and 301.

[51] Erra and Ishum 1 and 5; see ibid., pp. 291 and 311.

[52] Erra and Ishum 1; see ibid., p. 290.

[53] The major breakthrough came when Jean François Champollion managed to decipher the multilingual Rosetta Stone in the early nineteenth century.

[54] Translations of all these are readily available. For the first two see Wallis Budge, *The Egyptian Heaven and Hell*, and for the remainder see the translations by Faulkner under the original titles.

[55] This can be found in a variety of forms in a variety of sources. The version quoted here comes from www.egyptianmyths.net/mythre.htm, but it is also summarized in the essay on Egypt by Baines and Pinch in Willis, *World Mythology*, p. 41; although the name of the source text is not provided here it is reported as being inscribed on one of the shrines in the tomb of Tutankhamun, and on the walls of later royal tombs.

[56] Campbell, *Primitive Mythology*, chapter 10, p. 435 and *Oriental Mythology*, chapter 4, p. 206.

[57] Campbell, *Oriental Mythology*, chapter 4, pp. 200–6.

[58] See Feuerstein et al., *In Search of the Cradle of Civilization*; chapter 9 deals with the Aryan invasion theory; chapter 2 emphasizes the importance and antiquity of the *Vedas* and contains a fine introduction to the various categories of Indian text; and chapter 7 discusses the Indus script.

[59] Prasad, *The Fountainhead of Religion*, conclusion, p. 171.

[60] Ibid., chapter 5, p. 87, footnote 1.

[61] See, for example, O'Flaherty, *The Rig Veda*, p. 37, note 11: 'The Asuras are the ancient dark divinities, at first the elder brothers and then the enemies of the gods (Devas);' also p. 212, note 9: 'Asura not in its later sense of "demon" but in its earlier sense of sky god;' and finally p. 29, note 9: 'The two opposed masses are armies, the polarized forces of gods and demons (Asuras).'

[62] Prasad, *The Fountainhead of Religion*, chapter 5, p. 87, footnote 1.

[63] Rig Veda 10.124; see O'Flaherty, *The Rig Veda*, pp. 110–2.

[64] Satapatha Brahmana 1:8:1:1–6; see Eggeling, *Satapatha Brahmana Part 1* in Müller, *The Sacred Books of the East*, volume 12, pp. 216–18.

[65] Campbell, *Oriental Mythology*, chapter 3, p. 107 and *Occidental Mythology*, chapter 3, pp. 106–9.

[66] I first developed this concept in *The Wisdom of the Soul* (see under question

2.1.3) then fleshed it out in *The Big Book of the Soul*, chapter 8, pp. 251–9.

[67] These ideas are discussed in, for example, Lawton, *The Wisdom of the Soul*, question 4.2.4.

[68] The problems with the concept of karma are discussed at some length in Lawton, *The Big Book of the Soul*, chapter 7, pp. 200–5.

CHAPTER 3: THE ARTS OF CIVILIZATION

[1] The various commentaries on Berossus' work were compiled by Cory in 1832 in *Ancient Fragments,* and are reproduced by Temple in the 1998 edition of *The Sirius Mystery*, appendix 3, pp. 548–63. See in particular the Polyhistor fragments on pp. 551–2.

[2] Temple, *The Sirius Mystery*, appendix 3, p. 562.

[3] Collins and others have suggested that Oannes is the Greek for Enki himself, via his Akkadian name Ea; see *Gods of Eden*, chapter 19, p. 293. But Dalley is quite clear that the name Oannes is the Greek form of Uan, another Akkadian name for Adapa, and that he is to be thought of as Enki's son; see *Myths from Mesopotamia*, glossary (s.v. Adapa and Oannes), pp. 317 and 326. On a different tack it is a moot point whether or not the fish symbolism associated with Jesus is esoteric and can be attributed to a Mesopotamian source.

[4] Dalley, *Myths from Mesopotamia*, pp. 182–8.

[5] Ibid., p. 2.

[6] Erra and Ishum 2; see ibid., p. 292.

[7] Kramer, *The Sumerians*, chapter 4, p. 116. He provides a full list of the translated *me's*.

[8] Campbell, *Primitive Mythology*, chapter 10, pp. 454–5.

[9] This is discussed in ibid., chapter 10, p. 457.

[10] Berossus fragments recorded by Polyhistor; see Temple, *The Sirius Mystery*, appendix 3, p. 554.

[11] Ancient History of the Jews 2; see Murray, *History of the Jews*, volume 1, p. 29.

[12] Ibid., volume 1, 'Autobiography of Flavius Josephus', p. 1.

[13] Robinson, *The Nag Hammadi Library*, pp. 396–401.

[14] 2 Enoch 40; see Morfill and Charles, *The Book of the Secrets of Enoch*, pp. 53–5.

[15] Hall, *The Secret Teachings of All Ages*, 'Freemasonic Symbolism', p. 173. I am at a loss to establish the original source of Hall's detailed information, either from his own work or from anyone else's. See also Collins, *From the Ashes of Angels*, endnote 10 to chapter 2, pp. 384–5 in which he discusses the

background to Enochian traditions in Masonry. In addition Blavatsky has much to say on the topic of Enoch and the knowledge he preserved in *The Secret Doctrine*, volume 2, part 2, chapter 21, pp. 529–35.

[16] This is described at the beginning of the *Kore Kosmu*; see Scott, *Hermetica*, Stobaeus Excerpt 23, pp. 179–80 and also p. 191.

[17] Reymond, *The Mythical Origin of the Egyptian Temple*, chapter 1, p. 9. She also references Boylan, *Thoth: the Hermes of Egypt*, pp. 92–7. The *Edfu Documents* are inscribed on the walls of a Late Period Ptolemaic temple located midway between Luxor and Aswan in Upper Egypt.

[18] Lawton and Ogilvie-Herald, *Giza: The Truth*, chapter 1, pp. 16–7.

[19] Ibid., chapter 5, pp. 223–37.

[20] The whole topic of 'legends of the hall' is covered in detail in ibid., chapter 5.

[21] I have personally been into the intrusive, Late Period tombs dug into the Sphinx's rump; and into the modern, manmade chamber located between its paws behind the Thutmose IV stele; and, for that matter, into the passage to the side of the lowest relieving chamber above the King's Chamber in the Great Pyramid, excavated by Caviglia in the early 1800s. There is nothing untoward or exciting in any of them. This evidence is scattered throughout *Giza: The Truth*, including in the plates section.

[22] For more on the akashic records see Lawton, *The Big Book of the* Soul, chapter 6, p. 169 and chapter 7, pp. 221–2.

CHAPTER 4: THE GOLDEN AGE

[1] Genesis 1:28–30.

[2] Enoch 31:2; see Morfill and Charles, *The Book of the Secrets of Enoch*, p. 44.

[3] Ancient History of the Jews 2; see Murray, *History of the Jews*, volume 1, p. 28.

[4] Jacobsen, *The Harps That Once...*, pp. 181–204 and especially pp. 185–6.

[5] Rundle Clark, *Myth and Symbol in Ancient Egypt*, chapter 8, pp. 263–4. In Bauval and Hancock's *Keeper of Genesis* the Egyptian phrase is rendered as *zep tepi* instead of *tep zepi,* presumably in error.

[6] Reymond, *The Mythical Origin of the Egyptian Temple*, chapter 1, pp. 6–11. These original texts apparently include the *Specification of the Mounds of the Early Primeval Age* and the *Sacred Book of the Early Primeval Age*.

[7] Campbell, *Oriental Mythology*, chapter 6, p. 327.

[8] Ramayana 1; see Dutt, *The Ramayana and The Mahabharata*, pp. 1–3.

[9] See Legge, *Sacred Books of China*, 'Confucian Texts', parts 1–4 in Müller, *The Sacred Books of the East*, volumes 3, 16, 27 and 28; and ibid., 'Taoist Texts',

parts 1–2 in ibid., volumes 39 and 40.

[10] Kwang Tze 12; see ibid., volume 39, pp. 325–6.

[11] Kwang Tze 9; see ibid., volume 39, p. 278.

[12] Morgan, *Essays from Huai Nan Tzu*, pp. 35–6.

[13] Ibid., pp. 80–2.

[14] Works and Days 108–122; see West, *Hesiod: Theogony and Works and Days*, p. 40.

[15] Metamorphosis 1:88–111; see Melville, *Ovid: Metamorphosis*, pp. 3–4.

[16] See, for example, Metamorphosis 1:310–449 in ibid., pp. 10–14.

[17] Edda 1; see Young, *The Prose Edda*, pp. 37 and 40.

[18] It is interesting to note, however, that the prologue to Snorri's *Edda* seems to have been written as a sop to Christianity, which is in complete contrast to the convoluted and more indigenous tradition of multiple world ages contained in the main body of the work. It includes references to how the second race 'left off paying homage to God', 'lost the very name of God' and 'had not been given spiritual understanding' that are hardly unrelated to the idea of spiritual debasement. See ibid., pp. 23–4.

[19] Critias 5; see Lee, *Plato: Timaeus and Critias*, p. 145.

CHAPTER 5: WORLD AGES AND UNIVERSAL CYCLES

[1] Works and Days 123–201; see West, *Hesiod: Theogony and Works and Days*, pp. 40–2.

[2] Metamorphosis 1:112–162; see Melville, *Ovid: Metamorphosis*, pp. 4–6.

[3] A related tradition of multiple world ages is found in the *Sibylline Oracles*, a proliferation of texts from the fourth century BCE onwards that originated variously in Egypt, the Near East and Europe, and even held a degree of authority for the early Christian Church. Book 1 of these oracles describes five 'generations' before the flood and several thereafter. See Collins, 'The Sibylline Oracles' in Charlesworth, *The Old Testament Pseudepigrapha*, volume 1, pp. 335–42.

[4] Timaeus 2; see Lee, *Plato: Timaeus and Critias*, pp. 35–6.

[5] See http://en.wikipedia.org/wiki/Axial_precession_(astronomy).

[6] Plato's precessional 'Great Year' is not the same as although often confused with the so-called 'Platonic Year' or 'Perfect Year', which he refers to elsewhere in the *Timaeus*, and which describes the far shorter time it takes for all the planets to return to the same position relative to earth; see http://en.wikipedia.org/wiki/Great_year.

[7] Critias 2; see Lee, *Plato: Timaeus and Critias*, pp. 131–2.

[8] Mackenzie, *Myths of China and Japan*, chapter 15, p. 276.

[9] Tao Teh King 18; see Legge, *Sacred Books of China*, 'Taoist Texts', part 1 in Müller, *The Sacred Books of the East*, volume 39, pp. 60–1.

[10] These extracts are taken from the lengthy description provided in Waters, *Book of the Hopi*, part 1, pp. 11–21.

[11] Leyenda de los Soles 75:1–77:32; see Bierhorst, *History and Mythology of the Aztecs*, pp. 142–7. See also Thompson, *Maya History and Religion*, chapter 9, pp. 331–3. The narrative contains clear influences from across the Atlantic in that a god tells the flood survivors to hide inside a hollowed-out cypress tree, and when they emerge and cook a fish the gods are angry; this idea of the gods smelling the food that the survivors first cook is found in virtually every Near Eastern flood tradition.

[12] Anales de Cuauhtitlan 2:24–49; see Bierhorst, *History and Mythology of the Aztecs*, p. 26.

[13] Thompson, *Maya Hieroglyphic Writing*, chapter 1, p. 10.

[14] See, for example, Severin, Gregory, 'The Paris Codex: Decoding an Astronomical Ephemeris', chapter 5, pp. 68–9 in *Transactions of the American Philosophical Society* 71:5 (1981). Among other problems he makes the mistake of assuming that each age lasts 2028 years, whereas this is the stated duration of *all four* previous ages.

[15] No English translation of this text is readily available, so my source is an Italian version published in 1900; see *Il Manoscritto Messicano Vaticano 3738, Detto Il Codice Rios*, folios 4–7, pp. 24–5. Note that there appears to be some confusion about these numbers: in *Maya Hieroglyphic Writing*, chapter 1, p. 10 Thompson quotes a total of 18,028 years, while in *The Mayan Prophecies*, chapter 4, pp. 71–2 Gilbert and Cotterell quote 4081 and 5026 years for the last two ages.

[16] Ibid., folio 4, p. 24.

[17] Alexander, 'Latin American Mythology', chapter 7, p. 240 in Gray, *The Mythology of All Races*, volume 11. The sources quoted are: de Molina, 'An Account of the Fables and Rights of the Yncas' translated in Markham, *Rites and Laws of the Yncas* (London, 1873); Cieza de Leon, 'Segunda parte de la cronica del Peru' (Seville, 1553), translated in Markham, *The Second part of the Chronicle of Peru* (London, 1883), chapter 5, pp. 5–10; Sarmiento, *History of the Incas,* translated in Markham, *History of the Incas* (Cambridge, 1907), pp. 27–39; and Pietschmann, 'Some Account of the Illustrated Chronicle by the Peruvian Indian, D. Felipe Huaman Poma de Ayala', *Comptes rendus du Congres des Americanistes* 18 (London, 1913), pp. 511–2.

[18] Thompson provides a useful summary of these in *Maya Hieroglyphic Writing*, chapter 1, pp. 23–6.

[19] See http://en.wikipedia.org/wiki/Mesoamerican_Long_Count_calendar.

[20] Mahabharata 3.187; see Ray, *The Mahabharata*, volume 2, pp. 557–8.

[21] Ibid., volume 2, pp. 558–60.

[22] Mahabharata 12.231; see ibid., volume 7, pp. 235–7.

[23] Vishnu Purana 1.3 and 6.3; see Dutt, *Vishnu Purana*, pp. 12–3 and 434–7. See also Dimmitt and van Buitenen, *Classical Hindu Mythology*, chapter 1, pp. 19–24 and 36–43 and Wilkins, *Hindu Mythology*, chapter 10, pp. 353–60.

[24] Mahabharata 3.187; see Ray, *The Mahabharata*, volume 2, pp. 560–2.

[25] Keith, 'Indian Mythology', chapter 8, p. 221 in Gray, *The Mythology of All Races*, volume 6.

[26] For more details on the Jain cycle see Campbell, *Oriental Mythology*, chapter 4, pp. 219–23. He suggests that this concept may originally date back to the time of the early Indus civilization.

[27] Baines and Pinch in Willis, *World Mythology*, p. 41. Note that this cycle is connected with the traditions surrounding the death and rebirth of the legendary phoenix; for more information see R. Van Den Broek, *The Myth of the Phoenix* (E. J. Brill, 1972).

[28] At the very least this would have occurred while the Jewish people were held in captivity in Babylon in the sixth century BCE. For more information see Collins, *From the Ashes of Angels*, chapter 7.

[29] Translated by Darmesteter in Müller, *The Sacred Books of the East*, volume 4.

[30] For more detailed discussions of all of this see Lawton, *The Big Book of the Soul*, chapter 8, pp. 240 and 259–61.

[31] For more on the Qabalistic tree of life see www.ianlawton.com/gu3.htm, and on Dion Fortune's channeled material on these matters see www.ianlawton.com/gu4.htm.

CHAPTER 6: TAKING ON THE EXPERTS

[1] Campbell, *Oriental Mythology*, chapter 7, p. 395.

[2] Ibid., chapter 3, pp. 127–8. For some reason his figure of 432,000 years is merely the duration of a kali yuga rather than an entire maha yuga; see Figure 3.

[3] See ibid., chapter 3, pp. 116, 120 and 129 in which he refers to an analysis by Oppert in his paper *The Dates of Genesis*. Integral to his analysis are the numbers used in various versions of the Mesopotamian king lists; see Lawton, *Problems with King Lists* (2002, www.ianlawton.com/gu1.htm) for more details.

[4] Eliade, *Myth and Reality*, chapter 4, p. 55. In pp. 60–8 he goes on to discuss the

various world age theories, and then the Judaeo-Christian apocalyptic traditions, but nowhere do we receive any additional explanation for these themes. His only other relevant comment is on p. 69 when, discussing the golden age, he suggests the Communist and Nazi movements of the twentieth century were attempts to recreate it; and that this is a powerful and natural human trait. For more information see also his earlier work *The Myth of the Eternal Return*.

[5]   Eliade, *The Sacred and the Profane*, chapter 3, pp. 130–1.

CHAPTER 7: THE CREATION OF MAN

[1]   See, for example, Lawton, *The Wisdom of the Soul*, question 2.2 and *The Big Book of the Soul*, note 3 to chapter 7, p. 293.

[2]   This comes from the descriptions of Enoch's visionary trip to, in particular, the second and fifth 'heavens' in 2 Enoch 7 and 18, and even more from the footnoted commentary that accompanies them; see Morfill and Charles, *The Book of the Secrets of Enoch*, especially pp. 20–2.

[3]   Corpus Hermeticum 1:14; see Copenhaver, *Hermetica*, p. 3.

[4]   Robinson, *The Nag Hammadi Library*, pp. 182–3.

[5]   Jacobsen, *The Harps That Once...*, pp. 151–66; see especially pp. 154 and 157.

[6]   Almost certainly this does not have a symbolic or hidden meaning, but is a prosaic interweaving of the idea that the gods created the world they inhabited with their localized experience that was dominated by the massive effort involved in the annual 'corvée'.

[7]   Atrahasis 1; see Dalley, *Myths from Mesopotamia*, pp. 15–16.

[8]   Epic of Creation 6; see ibid., p. 261.

[9]   Berossus fragments recorded by Polyhistor; see Temple, *The Sirius Mystery*, appendix 3, pp. 553–4.

[10]   Genesis 1:26–27. Note there is some confusion in the biblical account that derives from combining the original Elohist and Yahwist texts. The first, Elohist-derived chapter simply says 'male and female created he them'; that is men and women were created together. But the second, Yahwist-derived chapter contradicts this by stating that Adam was created first 'of the dust of the ground', followed by Eve who was fashioned from one of his ribs to act as his 'help-meet' or companion; see Genesis 2:7 and 2:20–2.

[11]   It is interesting to note that this is followed by a recommendation about the rituals that should be performed 'wherever a woman gives birth' that are remarkably similar to those followed by the Hopi of North America; see Waters, *Book of the Hopi*, part 1, pp. 8–9.

[12]   Epic of Gilgamesh 1; see Dalley, *Myths from Mesopotamia*, pp. 52–3.

[13] There are also a number of similar if less detailed accounts of multiple creations or world ages in Mayan tradition; see Thompson, *Maya History and Religion*, chapter 9, pp. 336–73.

[14] Popol Vuh 1 and 4; see Tedlock, *Popol Vuh*, pp. 66–73 and 145–8.

[15] Waters, *Book of the Hopi*, part 1, pp. 5–9.

[16] Dixon, 'Oceanic Mythology', part 3, chapter 1, pp. 174–6 in Gray, *The Mythology of All Races*, volume 9.

[17] Also referred to as Stobaeus Excerpt 23; see Scott, *Hermetica*, p. 179

[18] Ibid., p. 186. See also Corpus Hermeticum 10:15 in Copenhaver, *Hermetica*, p. 33.

[19] Popol Vuh 4; see Tedlock, *Popol Vuh*, p. 148.

[20] Genesis 3:22.

[21] Robinson, *The Nag Hammadi Library*, p. 116. Yet with typical inconsistency the Gnostics seem to display far greater spiritual awareness when they report in the same text that Adam himself was taught about his 'descent' into manifestation, and about the 'way of ascent' back into the ethereal realm.

[22] For Campbell's commentary on the *Birth of Man* see *Oriental Mythology*, chapter 3, pp. 108–11; on the *Epic of Creation* see *Occidental Mythology*, chapter 2, pp. 84–5; and on the *Epic of Gilgamesh* see *Occidental Mythology*, chapter 2, pp. 87–90.

[23] Campbell, *Occidental Mythology*, chapter 2, pp. 85–6.

[24] Campbell, *Oriental Mythology*, chapter 3, p. 103.

[25] Newton, *Journey of Souls*, chapter 11, p. 171. Note that when I first came up with this idea in the first draft of *Genesis Unveiled* I had never even heard of Newton's work, which is why this corroboration was so exciting for me. It is also worth pointing out that in *The Wisdom of the Soul* our subjects gave a degree of confirmation of it; see question 3.1.1.

CHAPTER 8: THE ORIGINS OF THE WORLD

[1] This collation of origin traditions took a great deal of time and effort in the British Library in the days before the internet made research far simpler. It is sincerely to be hoped that this spiritual reinterpretation thereof may yet receive some recognition in more academic circles, because arguably it is one of the most important contributions made by this work.

[2] Corpus Hermeticum 3:1; see Copenhaver, *Hermetica*, p. 13.

[3] Corpus Hermeticum 4:10, 5:10 and 12:20–2; see ibid., pp. 17, 20 and 47–8.

[4] Robinson, *The Nag Hammadi Library*, pp. 171–3.

[5] Ibid, pp. 61 and 64. Further descriptions of the ultimate deity can be found, for

example, in the *Apocryphon of John*; see ibid, pp. 106–7.

[6] Dalley, *Myths from Mesopotamia*, p. 233. Note that the opening to the earlier Sumerian text the *Eridu Genesis* would probably have contained something relevant, but unfortunately it is missing.

[7] Orthodox scholars suggest that they regarded the earth (Ki) as a flat disc that was separated from heaven (An) by the atmosphere (Lil), with the whole ensemble immersed like a gigantic bubble in the primeval waters of Tiamat; see, for example, Kramer, *The Sumerians*, chapter 4, pp. 112–13 and Roux, *Ancient Iraq*, chapter 6, p. 93. Not only does this tend to ignore the esoteric significance of the primeval waters, which may or may not be a fair reflection of the Mesopotamians' own understanding, but it may also be somewhat at odds with the astronomical knowledge they possessed.

[8] Taken from www.egyptianmyths.net/mythre.htm.

[9] Baines and Pinch in Willis, *World Mythology*, p. 38.

[10] Ibid., p. 128. See also West, *Hesiod: Theogony and Works and Days*, explanatory note to Theogony 116, p. 64.

[11] Müller, 'Egyptian Mythology', chapter 4, pp. 68–9 in Gray, *The Mythology of All Races*, volume 12. This text is described as a 'papyrus copy written in the reign of Alexander II (310 BCE), but which seems to go back to originals that are considerably earlier'.

[12] Rig Veda 10.129; see O'Flaherty, *The Rig Veda*, pp. 25–6.

[13] Morgan, *Essays from Huai Nan Tzu*, 'Beginning and Reality', pp. 31–3.

[14] Ibid., 'Life and Soul', p. 58.

[15] Nihongi 1; see Aston, *Nihongi*, pp. 1–3.

[16] Metamorphosis 1:6–31; see Melville, *Ovid: Metamorphosis*, pp. 1–2.

[17] Dixon, 'Oceanic Mythology', part 1, chapter 1, p. 5 in Gray, *The Mythology of All Races*, volume 9.

[18] Ibid., part 1, chapter 1, p. 13.

[19] Ibid., part 1, chapter 1, pp. 7–8. The source is Taylor, *New Zealand and Its Inhabitants* (London, 1870), p. 109.

[20] Ibid., part 1, chapter 1, p. 11.

[21] Waters, *Book of the Hopi*, part 1, p. 3.

[22] Popol Vuh 1; see Tedlock, *Popol Vuh*, pp. 64–5.

[23] Willis, *World Mythology*, p.266.

[24] Ibid., p. 267.

[25] For example the *World Mythology* compendium and the *Larousse Encyclopaedia of Mythology* are both littered with an emphasis on the more prosaic aspects of cosmogony traditions. In making a distinction between

'creation myths' that involve a supreme creator and those that describe the powers in the void in more metaphysical terms they also ignore the consistent fundamental message in all these traditions, irrespective of the extent to which they anthropomorphize. See, for example, the description of Oceanic cosmogony in the *Larousse Encyclopaedia of Mythology*, p. 465.

26 Campbell, *Primitive Mythology*, chapter 2, pp. 84–8.

27 Ibid., chapter 6, pp. 232–8.

28 Indian and Chinese mythology are discussed in Campbell, *Oriental Mythology*, parts 2 and 3. Concerning the latter he even asserts that there are 'no stories of creation, either in these early myths of the Chou period, or in the later Confucian classics'; see chapter 7, p. 380. But surely this is more likely to be due to them not surviving the 'burning of the books' than due to original absence; and in any case it does not justify his failure to discuss later Taoist cosmogony.

29 Ibid., chapter 2, pp. 83–9.

30 Eliade, *Myth and Reality*, chapter 2.

31 I may be missing a crucial symbolic point, but I have never been able to square the idea that the physical body should be preserved by mummification and that food and drink should be provided for the afterlife, for example, with a worldview of any real metaphysical sophistication.

CHAPTER 9: ARCHAEOLOGY

1 This view links with the theory of a 'finely-tuned universe' that we discussed in the conclusion to chapter 5. The term 'intelligent design' is a far simpler way to describe the divine guidance of the evolution process, but it was hijacked in the late 1980s by Christian creationists in their attempt to overturn a legal ruling that creationism could not be taught in US classrooms because it was not scientific.

2 Newton, *Destiny of Souls*, chapter 8, pp. 334–44.

3 See www.ianlawton.com/bosextr4.htm.

4 For refutations of their theories see www.ianlawton.com/gu2.htm.

5 The main source of this data is Richard Klein's 1999 work *The Human Career*, although the earlier dates are rounded to the nearest 5 million years and the start of the Pleistocene has recently been moved back.

6 Leakey, *The Origin of Humankind*, chapter 2, pp. 29–30. Most of this and the next two sections are summaries of chapters 1–5. There have been refinements to the various dates, species and so on since this book was published but for our nonspecialist purposes most of its general thrust remains valid.

7 See http://en.wikipedia.org/wiki/Mirror_test.

[8]   See http://en.wikipedia.org/wiki/Origin_of_language.

[9]   See http://en.wikipedia.org/wiki/Omo_remains.

[10] Oefner et al. in the *Proceedings of the National Academy of Sciences*, June 2000.

[11] Ambrose, 'Late Pleistocene human population bottlenecks, volcanic winter, and differentiation of modern humans', *Journal of Human Evolution* 35 (1998), pp. 115–8.

[12] See http://en.wikipedia.org/wiki/Early_human_migrations.

[13] Leakey, *The Origin of Humankind*, chapter 5, p. 114.

[14] The work of Lawrence Barham is described by Elizabeth J Himelfarb in 'Prehistoric Body Paint', *Archaeology* 53:4 (2000).

[15] See http://en.wikipedia.org/wiki/Qafzeh. It is regularly reported that Neanderthals were ritually burying their dead from around 75,000 years ago, but in fact the evidence for this is sparse and inconclusive. The most cited example is that of the Shanidar Cave. However there are no grave goods, merely unusual pollen remains suggesting flowers were placed in the grave, but some researchers suggest these could easily have been intrusively introduced by small rodents; see http://en.wikipedia.org/wiki/Shanidar.

[16] See http://en.wikipedia.org/wiki/Blombos_Cave.

[17] Marshack, Alexander, 'A Middle Paleolithic Symbolic Composition from the Golan Heights: The Earliest Known Depictive Image', *Current Anthropology* 37:2 (1996), pp. 357–65.

[18] Bahn, Paul, 'Excavation of a Paleolithic Plank from Japan', *Nature* 32:9 (1987), p. 110. Finds on some northern Japanese sites are now known to have been faked by the amateur archaeologist Fujimura Shinichi, but he was not involved here; see http://en.wikipedia.org/wiki/Japanese_paleolithic_hoax.

[19] See http://en.wikipedia.org/wiki/Behavioral_modernity.

[20] For general background see http://en.wikipedia.org/wiki/Upper_Paleolithic.

[21] Kuhn et al., 'Ornaments of the Earliest Upper Paleolithic: New Insights from the Levant', *Proceedings of the National Academy of Sciences*, 5 June 2001.

[22] The earliest examples so far found come from a site in Moravia; see http://en.wikipedia.org/wiki/Venus_of_Dolni_Vestonice.

[23] See http://en.wikipedia.org/wiki/Yuchanyan_Cave.

[24] See http://en.wikipedia.org/wiki/Cave_art.

[25] For more information on the changes indicated by late Paleolithic cave art see Leakey, *The Origin of Humankind*, chapter 6 and Campbell, *Primitive Mythology*, chapter 8. For information on the last glacial maximum see http://en.wikipedia.org/wiki/Last_Glacial_Maximum.

[26] Experiments conducted by Iegor Reznikoff and Michel Dauvois in the mid-1980s have shown that the acoustics tend to be enhanced in these caves; see Leakey, *The Origin of Humankind*, chapter 6, pp. 139–40.

[27] See Leakey, *The Origin of Humankind*, chapter 6, p. 143 and Campbell, *Primitive Mythology*, chapter 3, p. 141, chapter 8, p. 328 and chapter 9, p. 376. See also http://en.wikipedia.org/wiki/Rock_art.

[28] See http://en.wikipedia.org/wiki/Megalithic_art. Pictures of some of these marks are reproduced in Michael Balfour's beautifully illustrated *Megalithic Mysteries*.

[29] For a fine study see Jean Clottes and David Lewis-Williams' 1998 work *The Shamans of Prehistory: Trance and Magic in Painted Caves*. See also Richard Rudgley's *Lost Civilizations of the Stone Age*, published a year later.

[30] See http://en.wikipedia.org/wiki/History_of_agriculture.

[31] See http://en.wikipedia.org/wiki/Natufian.

[32] See, for example, http://en.wikipedia.org/wiki/Qadan_Culture; Wendorf, Fred and Schild, Romauld, 'The Earliest Food Producers', *Archaeology* 34:5 (1981); and Unger-Hamilton, Romana, 'Microscopic striations on flint sickle-blades as an indication of plant cultivation: Preliminary results', *World Archaeology* 17:1 (1985), pp. 121–6.

[33] See www.mnsu.edu/emuseum/archaeology/sites/middle_east/jericho.html.

[34] The best sources for further information on and pictures of all these Turkish sites are Wikipedia and www.ancient-wisdom.co.uk/turkey.htm.

[35] Arnaud, Bernadette, 'First Farmers', *Archaeology* 53:6 (2000). See also www.cnrs.fr/Cnrspresse/Archeo2000/html/archeo11.htm.

[36] For more information on the excavations at Tell Hamoukar see http://oi.uchicago.edu/research/projects/ham.

[37] Bednarik, *Beads and the Origins of Symbolism* (2000, www.semioticon.com/frontline/bednarik.htm). The remainder of the information about his work in this section is taken from this paper, unless otherwise stated.

[38] These controversial finds were made by the same team that in 2003 discovered the remains of *Homo floresiensis*, nicknamed the 'hobbit' because of its short stature. This gained widespread exposure while the potentially much more fascinating earlier tool finds went largely unreported. See http://en.wikipedia.org/wiki/Homo_floresiensis.

[39] Bednarik, 'Seafaring in the Pleistocene', *Cambridge Archaeological Journal* 13:1 (2003), pp. 41–66. As someone not scared to put his theories into practice he made several experimental sea crossings in the area using bamboo rafts; see http://mc2.vicnet.net.au/home/mariners/web/mariners.html.

[40] Belitsky, S, Goren-Inbar, N and Werker, E, 'A Middle Pleistocene Wooden Plank with Man-Made Polish', *Journal of Human Evolution* 20 (1991), pp. 349–53.

[41] See http://en.wikipedia.org/wiki/Venus_of_Berekhat_Ram. The evidence for deliberate human working of this figurine is analyzed in detail by Alexander Marshack in *Antiquity* 71:272 (1997), pp. 327–38 (reproduced at www.utexas.edu/courses/classicalarch/readings/Berekhat_Ram.pdf).

[42] For analysis see www.ianlawton.com/gu8.htm and www.badarchaeology.net; the latter includes some pictures.

[43] Rudgley also ascribes a great many other firsts to the Upper Paleolithic, for example arguing that a rudimentary symbolic script was used throughout, and that protowriting existed in a variety of forms in the early Neolithic; see *Lost Civilizations of the Stone Age*, chapters 4 and 5. Although it is fair to say that as a television presenter his work is often aimed at a populist audience, in the latter he may be supported by examples of an 8000-year-old pictographic script that have been found at Damaidi in China; see http://en.wikipedia.org/wiki/Damaidi.

[44] Some scholars look at it the other way round and argue that farming developed *as a result* of hunter-gatherers deliberately deciding to adopt a more settled lifestyle, even though they had known *how* to farm for a long time. For an excellent rebuttal of this argument see Forrester, Rochelle, *The Discovery of Agriculture* (2002, http://homepages.paradise.net.nz/rochelle.f/The-Discovery-of-Agriculture.html).

[45] See, for example, www.flintknapperman.com.

CHAPTER 10: GEOLOGY

[1] See http://en.wikipedia.org/wiki/Pleistocene, and also the entries for 'last glacial period' and 'last glacial maximum'.

[2] See http://en.wikipedia.org/wiki/Sea_level_rise.

[3] Taken from Blyth and de Freitas, *A Geology for Engineers*, figure 2.1.9, p. 29 (after E. Antevs).

[4] See http://en.wikipedia.org/wiki/Milankovitch_cycles.

[5] The paper was Alvarez et al, 'Extraterrestrial cause for the Cretaceous-Tertiary Extinction', *Science* 208:4448 (1980), pp. 1095–1107; see also http://en.wikipedia.org/wiki/Impact_event#Mass_extinctions_and_impacts.

[6] See the bibliography for details of their work.

[7] See, for example, Martin and Klein's 1984 work *Quaternary Extinctions*, pp. 358–61 and also http://en.wikipedia.org/wiki/Quaternary_extinction_event.

[8] Velikovsky, *Earth in Upheaval*, chapter 1; his main source is Whitley, D G,

'The Ivory Islands in the Arctic Ocean', *Journal of the Philosophical Society of Great Britain* 12 (1910).

9   Hapgood, *The Path of the Pole*, chapter 10, pp. 259–64 and 272–5; unfortunately he does not provide a source for the dating information.

10 For a fine summary see Bishop, Sue, *Woolly Mammoth Remains: Catastrophic Origins?* (undated, www.talkorigins.org/faqs/mammoths.html).

11 Velikovsky, *Earth in Upheaval*, chapter 1; his main sources are Rainey, F, 'Archaeological Investigation in Central Alaska', *American Antiquity* 5 (1940) and Hibben, F C, 'Evidence of Early Man in Alaska', *American Antiquity* 8 (1943).

12 Hapgood, *The Path of the Pole*, chapter 10, pp. 275–7; the original source is Hibben's 1946 work *The Lost Americans*, pp. 90–2 and 176–8; only a small part of the original quote has been reproduced.

13 I am indebted to geologist Paul Heinrich for pointing me in the direction of this more recent research (correspondence with me, 13 June 2001). A selection of the references he cites regarding the Alaskan muck are as follows: Guthrie, Dale and Guthrie, M Lee, 'Death on the Steppe: The Case of the Frozen Bison', *New Scientist* 127:1727 (1990), pp. 47–51; Westgate, J A, Stemper, B A and Pewe, T L, 'A 3 m.y. Record of Pliocene-Pleistocene Loess in Interior Alaska', *Geology* 18:9 (1990), pp. 858–61; and Preece et al., 'Tephrochronology of Late Cenozoic Loess at Fairbanks, Alaska', *Geological Society of America Bulletin* 111:1 (1999), pp. 71–90.

14 Velikovsky, *Earth in Upheaval*, chapter 2; his main source is Buckland's *Reliquiae Diluvianae*. The caves themselves were at Kirkdale, Brentford, Cefn and Bleadon in Britain, and at Breugue and Arcy in France.

15 Ibid., chapter 5; his source for much of the European material is Joseph Prestwich's 1895 work *On Certain Phenomena Belonging to the Close of the Last Geological Period*; Prestwich was a professor of geology at Oxford who investigated many of the sites himself. The British sites were in Plymouth and Pembrokeshire; the European sites were Kesserloch in Switzerland, Neukoln in Germany, and in central and southern France, Gibraltar, Corsica, Sardinia and Sicily; the US sites were Cumberland Cavern in Maryland, La Brea Asphalt Pit near Los Angeles, Agate Spring Quarry in Nebraska, Big Bone Lick in Kentucky, San Pedro Valley in California, John Day Basin in Oregon and Lake Florissant in Colorado; the Asian sites were Choukoutien in northern China, the Siwalik foothills in India and the gorges of the Irrawady River in central Burma.

16 See http://en.wikipedia.org/wiki/William_Buckland.

17 For example no one now seriously considers the La Brea Tar Pit to be anything other than a trap for unsuspecting animals that have strayed into it at their peril for tens of thousands of years. There is no mention of evidence of a catastrophe

at http://en.wikipedia.org/wiki/La_Brea_Tar_Pits.

[18] Velikovsky, *Earth in Upheaval*, chapter 4, pp. 46–7.

[19] One of the few places they are discussed on the internet is at, for example, www.sentex.net/~tcc/michwls.html.

[20] See www.lakemichiganwhales.com. Velikovsky reports similar remains in more southerly states such as Alabama, Georgia and Florida in *Earth in Upheaval*, chapter 4, pp. 48–9, but I can find no corroboration of this.

[21] Ibid., chapter 16, p. 264.

[22] Paine, Michael and Peiser, Benny, *The Frequency and Consequences of Cosmic Impacts Since the Demise of the Dinosaurs* (2002, http://homepage.mac.com/mpaineau/filechute/bioastr2002.pdf).

[23] Napier, 'Cometary Catastrophes, Cosmic Dust and Ecological Disasters in Historical Times: The Astronomical Framework' in Peiser et al., *Natural Catastrophes During Bronze Age Civilizations*, pp. 21–32.

[24] Allan and Delair, *When the Earth Nearly Died*, part 4, chapters 15–17. The *Epic of Creation* continues on from the extract in chapter 8 to describe how Tiamat is cut into pieces to form heaven and earth. The folly of anyone interpreting this as an account of the destruction wrought on earth by a stray planet winding its way through our solar system is demonstrated by the context of the other traditions in which a god's body is broken up for similar purposes; for example P'an Gu and Ymir in Chinese and Scandinavian traditions respectively; see Dalley, *Myths from Mesopotamia*, p. 19.

[25] Some of their diagrams and figures are almost identical to those in Sitchin's *The Twelfth Planet*.

[26] Geological engineer Colin Reader points out that the features of relict glaciation that litter northern Europe and North America are directly comparable to those found in modern ice fields; while there are features that usually accompany rock striations, for example roches moutonnées and drumlins, that are exclusively formed by ice flows and cannot be replicated by water flows (correspondence with me, 4 March 2001).

[27] Velikovsky, *Earth in Upheaval*, chapter 7, pp. 98–9.

[28] See http://en.wikipedia.org/wiki/Carolina_Bay.

[29] Melton and Shriever, 'The Carolina Bays: Are They Meteorite Scars?' *Journal of Geology* 41 (1933), pp. 52–66. This and all the following material about the bays is taken from Andrew Collins' compilation of reports in *Gateway to Atlantis*, chapters 21–2.

[30] Prouty, 'Carolina Bays and their Origin', *Bulletin of the Geological Society of America* 63 (1952), pp. 167–222.

[31] See Carson and Hussey, 'The Oriented Lakes of Arctic Alaska', *Journal of*

Geology 70 (1962), pp. 417–39; Kelly, 'The Origin of the Carolina Bays and the Oriented Lakes of Alaska', *Popular Astronomy* 59 (1951), p. 204; and Plafker, 'Oriented Lakes and Lineaments in Northern Bolivia', *Bulletin of the Geological Society of America* 75 (1964), pp. 503–22.

[32] Ingram, Robinson and Odum, 'Clay Mineralogy of some Carolina Bay Sediments', *Southeastern Geology* 1 (1959), pp. 1–10.

[33] See http://en.wikipedia.org/wiki/Carolina_Bay; see also, for example, Heinrich, Paul, *An Evaluation of the Geological Evidence Presented by Gateway to Atlantis for Terminal Pleistocene Catastrophe* (2007, www.hallofmaat.com/modules.php?name=Articles&file=article&sid=86).

[34] Again see http://en.wikipedia.org/wiki/Carolina_Bay. For further details of the former see various papers by Ivester et al in the *Geological Society of America Abstracts with Programs*, specifically 34:6 (2002), p. 273; 35:6 (2003), p. 169; 36:5 (2004), p. 69; and 39:2 (2007), p. 5. For the latter see May, James and Warne, Andrew, 'Hydrogeologic and geochemical factors required for the development of Carolina Bays', *Environmental and Engineering Geoscience* 5:3 (1999), pp. 261–70.

[35] See http://en.wikipedia.org/wiki/Clovis_culture.

[36] See http://en.wikipedia.org/wiki/Folsom_tradition.

[37] See http://en.wikipedia.org/wiki/Younger_Dryas.

[38] Firestone et al, *The Cycle of Cosmic Catastrophes*, chapter 1.

[39] Ibid., chapters 2–7, 9, 34 and appendix D.

[40] Ibid., chapter 10, pp. 125–8.

[41] Ibid., chapter 8.

[42] See http://en.wikipedia.org/wiki/Drumlin.

[43] Firestone et al, *The Cycle of Cosmic Catastrophes*, chapters 10, 17–20 and 27. One of his arguments is that no Clovis era finds are noted in the literature about the bays, even though if they existed at that time they should have been used as water sources; but they would surely have contained stagnant rather than fresh, flowing water, so this argument may be suspect.

[44] Surovell et al, 'An independent evaluation of the Younger Dryas extraterrestrial impact hypothesis', *Proceedings of the National Academy of Sciences* 106:43 (2009), pp. 18155–8 (reproduced at www.pnas.org/content/106/43/18155.full).

[45] Firestone et al, *The Cycle of Cosmic Catastrophes*, chapter 9, p. 109.

[46] For further general references, discussion and analysis see http://en.wikipedia.org/wiki/Younger_Dryas_event; for new supportive research see, for example, the presentation by Mustafa Fayek and Sharon Hull to the Pecos Archaeological Conference in Arizona in 2008 (YouTube video, *Pecos Archeological Conference evidence of the Clovis Comet extinction*).

47   Velikovsky, *Earth in Upheaval*, chapter 8, p. 117.

48   Ibid., chapter 4, pp. 40–4.

49   Ibid., chapter 4, pp. 44–6.

50   The former in *When the Sky Fell* and the latter in *Fingerprints of the Gods*, both published in 1995.

51   Velikovsky, *Earth in Upheaval,* chapter 9.

52   Barbiero, 'On the Possibility of Very Rapid Shifts of the Poles', *Aeon* 4:6 (1997). This paper contains complex mathematics, at least for a nonspecialist, but it certainly appears to be the most in-depth and scholarly study of this subject undertaken to date.

53   See Heinrich's *Wild Side of Geoarchaeology* webpage, especially the links under the headings 'Fingerprints of the Gods' and 'Alleged Evidence of Earth Crustal Displacement' (http://members.cox.net/pyrophyllite/wildside.shtml).

54   For further general references, discussion and analysis see http://en.wikipedia.org/wiki/Cataclysmic_pole_shift_hypothesis.

55   See http://en.wikipedia.org/wiki/Geomagnetic_reversal.

56   See http://en.wikipedia.org/wiki/Earth's_magnetic_field.

57   See http://en.wikipedia.org/wiki/Coronal_mass_ejection.

58   Allan and Delair provide a comprehensive review of these traditions; see *When the Earth Nearly Died*, part 3 and in particular table 3B, pp. 162–4. Firestone et al also provide details of a number of especially Amerindian myths throughout part 3 of *The Cycle of Cosmic Catastrophes*. However they are all curiously labeled as 'retold from' their source and close examination of, for example, their 'retelling' of the Indian flood myth of Manu, and of Plato's supposed account of the flood, shows a great deal of poetic license has been taken – especially with modern-style references to 'fires falling from the sun', 'planets whirling through the sky' and 'shaking lose bodies from space' (see chapter 25, p. 263 and chapter 33, p. 328). This is somewhat disappointing given the far more reliable nature of their physical evidence.

59   See, for example, Jacobsen's introduction to the 'Cylinders of Gudea' in *The Harps That Once...*, p. 387.

60   Dalley, *Myths from Mesopotamia*, glossary (s.v. *abubu* and *kasusu*), pp. 317 and 324.

61   Jacobsen, *The Harps That Once...*, footnotes 7 and 8, p. 237. However we might note that the entire third part of this composite text is comprised of a somewhat enigmatic description of Ninurta passing judgment on the various rocks and minerals found on the earth.

62   Ninurta 80–96; see ibid., pp. 240–1.

63   Ninurta 167–8; see ibid., p. 244.

[64] Ninurta 174–81; see ibid., p. 245.

[65] Ninurta 334–44; see ibid., pp. 251–2. This second part of the text then goes on to describes how Ninurta set up irrigation systems, but that seems to shed little in the way of useful contextual light on the extract under review.

[66] Of course the Mesopotamian *Epic of Creation* has some similarities with this, and I have rejected literal interpretations of it by Sitchin and Allan and Delair. Lest I be accused of double standards this is because it is clearly an origin myth that shares much in common with those from other cultures, whereas the *Ninurta Myth* is clearly not and is arguably more comparable to other catastrophe traditions. As for suggestions that this latter describes an aeronautical or even nuclear conflict, we will return to the issue of supposed advanced technology in chapter 12.

[67] Theogony 682–707 and 820–68; see West, *Hesiod: Theogony and Works and Days*, pp. 23–4 and 27–8.

[68] Edda 1; see Young, *The Prose Edda*, pp. 86–92.

[69] Picture adapted from www.planetaryvisions.com.

[70] See http://en.wikipedia.org/wiki/Sea_level.

[71] See http://en.wikipedia.org/wiki/Sunda_Shelf.

[72] See http://en.wikipedia.org/wiki/Last_Glacial_Maximum.

[73] Although note that he argues there were three main flood events due to glacial melt, at around 14,000, 11,500 and 8400 years ago; see *Eden in the East*, chapter 1, pp. 29–38. Also his detailed review and interpretation of global origin and creation traditions is largely prosaic and connected to the flood events; see ibid., chapters 11–13.

CHAPTER 11: LOST CONTINENTS

[1] An excellent listing of various researchers' favored locations from Plato's time through to 1954 is provided by Sprague de Camp in *Lost Continents*, appendix C; most of these can be cross-referenced with his extensive bibliography.

[2] The location is described in Timaeus 2, and the layout and other aspects in Critias 4; see Lee, *Plato: Timaeus and Critias*, pp. 37–8 and 136–42.

[3] Although Plato suggests this metal is 'now unknown' it was actually well known to all ancient Greeks, and to the Romans who referred to it as 'aurichalcum'; it is what we now refer to as brass; see http://en.wikipedia.org/wiki/Brass.

[4] The Thera hypothesis is supported by, for example, Luce in *The End of Atlantis* and Mavor in *Voyage to Atlantis*, both published in 1969.

[5] This is based on the enigmatic *Oera Linda Book*, which is alleged to be a

thirteenth-century Frisian text from Denmark; see Scrutton's 1979 work *Secrets of Lost Atland.*

6   See the Flem-Ath's 1995 work *When the Sky Fell.* We will why theirs and Hapgood's use of the Piri Re'is map to support this theory is suspect in the next chapter.

7   See, for example, Collins' 2000 work *Gateway to Atlantis*; note that his proposed date for this submergence is rather later then Plato's.

8   Proponents of the Atlantic continent idea are, for example, Donnelly in *Atlantis: The Antediluvian World* and Muck in his 1979 work *The Secret of Atlantis.*

9   See http://en.wikipedia.org/wiki/Mu_(lost_continent)#Geological_arguments. However, while the theory of continental drift relies primarily on *horizontal* plate movement, at least one critic suggests that sediment cores taken from various parts of the Atlantic Ocean bed and other anomalies indicate that significant and rapid *vertical* movements of the crust have occurred; see Pratt, David, 'Plate Tectonics: A Paradigm Under Threat', *Journal of Scientific Exploration* 14:3 (2000), pp. 307–52 (reproduced at http://davidpratt.info/tecto.htm).

10 See http://en.wikipedia.org/wiki/Sunken_continent, and in particular the links to the two continents mentioned.

11 Unfortunately I discovered this work very late so was unable to obtain a copy before my own publication deadline. However from the details at www.atlan.org/faq it appears some aspects of Santos' work may be somewhat speculative to say the least, and certainly he credits the Atlanteans with a more advanced level of technology than I would; see, for example, question 19.

12 Sprague de Camp, *Lost Continents*, chapter 1; he also provides an excellent compilation of extracts from these original works in appendix A.

13 Ibid., chapter 2, pp. 28–35; for more on the translation issue see http://en.wikipedia.org/wiki/Diego_de_Landa.

14 Ibid., chapter 2, pp. 35–6.

15 Ibid., chapter 3, pp. 52–4.

16 Ibid., chapter 2, pp. 43–5.

17 See ibid., chapter 2, pp. 39–43, in which Sprague de Camp provides a sensible critique of a number of aspects of Donnelly's work.

18 For more background see http://en.wikipedia.org/wiki/Helena_Blavatsky.

19 For more on the book see http://en.wikipedia.org/wiki/Book_of_Dzyan; and on Reigle's work see Lawton, *The Theosophical Perspective* (2003, www.ianlawton.com/gu4.htm).

20 All the quoted stanzas from the *Book of Dzyan* can be found in Blavatsky, *The*

Secret Doctrine, volume 2, part 1, pp. 17–21. Stanzas 1 to 4 have been omitted here, and apparently there are others that she has herself omitted.

21   Although Blavatsky suggests in her commentary that the second race were 'the most heterogeneous gigantic semi-human monsters – the first attempts of material nature at building human bodies'; see ibid., volume 2, part 1, p. 138.

22   Blavatsky herself may or may not have been a racist but her undoubted emphasis on the Aryan race was terribly distorted by some of her successors, particularly the occult-inspired Nazi regime in Germany. She does however emphasize that this particular expression 'black with sin' is merely a 'figure of speech' in the stanzas. See ibid., volume 2, part 1, p. 408, footnote. See also note 27 below.

23   Ibid., volume 2, 'Preliminary Notes', pp. 6–9.

24   Ibid., volume 2, part 1, pp. 429 and 432.

25   Ibid., volume 2, part 1, pp. 317 and 430.

26   Ibid., volume 2, part 1, p. 426.

27   The details of the nature of the subraces within each root race, particularly the third and fourth, are sprinkled liberally and somewhat confusingly all over the second volume of *The Secret Doctrine*. But basically Blavatsky describes a bewildering array of seven subraces within each root race, and seven further branches or families within each subrace. Their natures appear to derive from different levels of advancement in the incarnating 'monads' or souls; see ibid., volume 2, part 1, pp. 249 and 434–5. It is the way she ties some of these into some modern nationalities, tribes and cultures that led to her being branded racist; see http://en.wikipedia.org/wiki/Helena_Blavatsky#Controversies.

28   The two volumes of *The Secret Doctrine* are entitled 'Cosmogenesis' and 'Anthropogenesis'; the material we have been considering only comes from the latter.

29   See, for example, his *Histoire des Vierges* (Paris, 1879). Many of the references to these works can be easily traced using the index appended to later publications of *The Secret Doctrine*; although, at least with respect to these two authors, it is by no means exhaustive and a number of references are omitted.

30   Blavatsky, *The Secret Doctrine*, volume 1, 'Introductory', p. xviii.

31   Scott-Elliot, *The Story of Atlantis and The Lost Lemuria*, p. 34; one wonders if he had come across Arabian tales of King Saurid in the course of his research (refer back to chapter 3).

32   Ibid., pp. 46–9. In mentioning 'personal *vril*' as the early power source he appears to be following Blavatsky's discussions of John Worrell Keely's experiments with 'sympathetic vibratory apparatus' in Philadelphia in the late nineteenth century; see *The Secret Doctrine*, volume 1, part 3, p. 563 and also Lawton and Ogilvie-Herald, *Giza: The Truth*, chapter 4, p. 206.

33   Scott-Elliot, *The Lost Lemuria*, p. 13.

34   The Lemurian maps are reproduced at www.sacred-texts.com/atl/tll/tll01.htm, and the Atlantean at www.sacred-texts.com/atl/soa/soamap.htm.

35   See http://en.wikipedia.org/wiki/William_Scott-Elliot.

36   Scott-Elliot, *The Lost Lemuria*, pp. 19–21.

37   For further discussion of this idea see www.ianlawton.com/bosextr4.htm#3.

38   Steiner, *Atlantis and Lemuria*, introduction, p. 8.

39   Ibid., chapter 1, pp. 13–14 and chapter 3, pp. 51–3.

40   These dates are discussed in Churchward, *The Lost Continent of Mu*, chapter 7; see also chapter 2 for the nature of its inhabitants and history, and chapter 3, p. 36 for a map showing its supposed size and location. Note that Scott-Elliot's maps show Lemuria as occupying not just the Indian Ocean but also considerable portions of the Pacific.

41   Ibid., chapter 1. A page of the 'vignettes' on the Naacal tablets is reproduced on p. 7, revealing many esoteric symbols that are commonly known but with somewhat strange embellishments.

42   Ibid., addendum, preface and following pages. Note that the 1994 edition from which our quotes come contains the original 1926 edition, and the 1931 updates to it in the addendum.

43   Ibid., chapter 4, pp. 51–9.

44   Spence's map of these landmasses can be found in *History of Atlantis*, opposite p. 62. Note that his emphasis on the western island being in the area of the Sargasso Sea is a clear forerunner of the theory that Atlantis lay in the vicinity of the Caribbean.

45   Ibid., chapters 6–7.

46   Spence's map of these landmasses can be found in *The Problem of Lemuria*, opposite p. 160.

47   Spence, *The Occult Sciences in Atlantis*, chapter 1, pp. 7–10.

48   Ibid., chapter 3, pp. 27–31.

49   Background information from Randall-Stevens himself can be found in *From Atlantis to the Latter Days*, foreword and part 1, chapters 1–3.

50   Ibid., part 1, chapters 4–5 and part 2, between pp. 108 and 109.

51   Ibid., part 1, chapter 6, p. 52.

52   Ibid., part 1, chapter 7, including plates 5–7. For arguments against these specific assertions see Lawton and Ogilvie-Herald, *Giza: The Truth*, chapter 5, pp. 250–1 and figures 19–20. More generally see also note 21 to chapter 3.

53   Almost identical drawings appear in Harvey Spencer Lewis' 1936 work *The Symbolic Prophecy of the Great Pyramid*; see Lawton and Ogilvie-Herald,

Giza: The Truth, chapter 5, pp. 236–7 and http://towers-online.co.uk/pages/shafted4.htm.

54   From the cover copy.

55   See, for example, Johnson, *Edgar Cayce in Context*, chapter 1, p. 35.

56   Johnson provides a thorough comparison of Cayce's 'Christian theosophy' with Blavatsky's 'esoteric theosophy' in ibid., chapter 2, pp. 43–8.

57   A number of readings consistently mention the often touted date of 10,500 BCE; see *Edgar Cayce on Atlantis*, chapter 5, pp. 142–3.

58   Johnson, *Edgar Cayce in Context*, introduction, p. 6.

59   Sugrue, *The Story of Edgar Cayce*, chapter 15, p. 200.

60   Johnson, *Edgar Cayce in Context*, introduction, p. 7.

61   See www.ianlawton.com/bosextr4.htm.

62   This was one of the impressions that came through from our subjects in *The Wisdom of the Soul*, even if we do not regard the lost civilizations section as one of the most independent elements of our research; see question 3.2.

63   Williamson, R W, *Religious and Cosmic Beliefs of Central Polynesia* (Cambridge, 1933), volume 1, p. 8; cited in Allan and Delair, *When the Earth Nearly Died*, part 3, chapter 5, p. 155.

64   Ellis, W, *Polynesian Researches* (London, 1829), volume 2, p. 57; cited in ibid., part 3, chapter 5, pp. 155–6.

65   Churchward, *The Lost Continent of Mu*, chapter 4, pp. 63–79.

66   See the bibliography for details of his works on Pacific Islands.

CHAPTER 12: LET'S GET REAL

1   Two excellent resources for articles debunking many of the non-mysteries covered in this chapter, as well as many others, are www.hallofmaat.com (see articles section) and www.badarchaeology.net.

2   Dalley, *Myths from Mesopotamia*, pp. 203–27; once again this text involves the warmongering Ninurta and an array of weapons.

3   These include, for example, the 'fiery whirlwind' that took Ezekiel away (Ezekiel 1:4–28 and 3:12–4), although to anyone familiar with the Qabalah this passage is replete with esoteric symbolism; and the Lord taking Elijah up to heaven in a 'chariot of fire' (2 Kings 2:11).

4   For detailed discussions of this model, first 'identified' in 1969 by maverick Egyptologist Khalil Messiha, see www.catchpenny.org/model.html and www.badarchaeology.net/data/ooparts/aeroplanes.php.

5   See www.badarchaeology.net/data/ooparts/aeroplanes_2.php.

[6] This was first brought to the public's attention by a certain Ruth *Hover* in 1989. For undoctored pictures of the panel, and an explanation of how recarving gave it its current look, see http://members.tripod.com/a_u_r_a/abydos.html. See also http://en.wikipedia.org/wiki/Abydos,_Egypt.

[7] See James and Thorpe's essay on the subject in *Ancient Mysteries*, and also http://en.wikipedia.org/wiki/Dogon_people#Dogon_and_Sirius.

[8] Temple, *The Sirius Mystery*, chapter 1, p. 32.

[9] The most obvious objection is the fact that the enclosure effectively has only three sides due to the slope of the plateau, so there is no retaining wall at the front (east) end on which the Sphinx Temple stands. It is also beyond question that the latter structure is contemporary with the Sphinx, having been erected using blocks from the quarrying of the enclosure. Temple does not explain how water can be retained in a container that only has three sides.

[10] For further information see, for example, Welfare and Fairley, *Arthur C Clarke's Mysterious World*, chapter 3, pp. 64–7; De Solla Price, *Gears from the Greeks* (American Philosophical Society, 1974); and www.badarchaeology.net/data/ooparts/antikythera.php.

[11] See Welfare and Fairley, *Arthur C Clarke's Mysterious World*, chapter 3, pp. 62–4 and www.badarchaeology.net/data/ooparts/batteries.php.

[12] See Heinrich, Paul and Stromberg, Pierre, *The Coso Artifact* (2000, www.hallofmaat.com/modules.php?name=Articles&file=article&sid=77).

[13] For reproductions of these two maps see Hapgood, *Maps of the Ancient Sea Kings*, frontispiece and figure 49.

[14] Schoch, *Voices of the Rocks*, chapter 4, pp. 101–6.

[15] For example on the Oronteus Finaeus map the continent is marked as 'Terra Australis Re'.

[16] West, *Serpent in the Sky*, introduction, pp. 1–2.

[17] Lawton and Ogilvie-Herald, *Giza: The Truth*, chapter 2, pp. 60–4.

[18] For full details see ibid., chapters 7 and 16 and also the papers and correspondence under the heading 'The Age of the Sphinx' at www.ianlawton.com/gttindex.htm.

[19] For the 10,500 BCE date see ibid., chapter 9, pp. 349–51 and chapter 16, pp. 475–6.

[20] This earlier date is used by West in, for example, his 2006 documentary *Magical Egypt*.

[21] To appreciate the extent to which Sitchin distorted the evidence for this assertion see Lawton and Ogilvie-Herald, *Giza: The Truth*, chapter 2, pp. 94–111. His original arguments were presented in *The Stairway to Heaven*, chapter 13, pp. 253–82.

[22] The basic premise of the so-called Orion correlation was the subject of Bauval and Gilbert's 1994 work *The Orion Mystery*. This was subsequently expanded by Bauval and Hancock in *Keeper of Genesis*, particularly with respect to the 10,500 BCE dating, but the basic premise is almost certainly questionable irrespective of its supposed date. For more information on this see Lawton and Ogilvie-Herald, *Giza: The Truth*, chapter 9 and also the papers and correspondence under the heading 'The Orion Correlation' at www.ianlawton.com/gttindex.htm.

[23] Bauval and Hancock, *Keeper of Genesis*, chapter 6, pp. 106–9.

[24] Ibid., chapter 3, pp. 27–33.

[25] Lawton and Ogilvie-Herald, *Giza: The Truth*, chapter 4.

[26] See Doernenburg, Frank, *Baalbek, The Romans Really Did Build It!* (1996, www.ramtops.co.uk/baalbek.html).

[27] See the papers and correspondence under the heading 'Giza Pyramid and Temple Construction' at www.ianlawton.com/gttindex.htm.

[28] A detailed report and photographs are available at www.pbs.org/wgbh/nova/lostempires/obelisk/cutting.html. For more on Stock's research generally see, for example, 'Sticks and Stones of Egyptian Technology', *Popular Archaeology* 7:3 (1986), pp. 24–9; 'Tools of the Ancient Craftsman', *Popular Archaeology* 7:6 (1986), pp. 25–9; and 'Stone Sarcophagus Manufacture in Ancient Egypt', *Antiquity* 73:282 (1999), pp. 918–22. For more on the ultrasonics theory see Lawton and Ogilvie-Herald, *Giza: The Truth*, chapter 4, pp. 211–20 and chapter 16, pp. 477–8, and also my correspondence with Dunn under the heading 'Ancient Egyptian Machining' at www.ianlawton.com/gttindex.htm.

[29] The purpose and context of the Great Pyramid is discussed in detail in Lawton and Ogilvie-Herald, *Giza: The Truth*, chapter 3 and appendices 2 and 3. For more on the power plant theory see my correspondence with Dunn under the heading 'The Giza Power Plant' at www.ianlawton.com/gttindex.htm.

[30] See, for example, his article in *UFO Reality* 3, August–September 1996.

[31] See http://en.wikipedia.org/wiki/Chinese_pyramids.

[32] See http://en.wikipedia.org/wiki/Bosnian_pyramids.

[33] See www.andrewcollins.com/page/interactive/bahamas.htm for the best account of the circumstances of its discovery.

[34] See http://en.wikipedia.org/wiki/Bimini_Road.

[35] Schoch, *Voices of the Rocks*, chapter 4, pp. 106–13; see also his plates section.

[36] http://en.wikipedia.org/wiki/Marine_archaeology_in_the_Gulf_of_Cambay.

[37] See www.hinduonnet.com/fline/fl1905/19050670.htm.

[38] Fleming, *Review of Flooded Kingdoms of the Ice Age* (undated,

www.hallofmaat.com/modules.php?name=Articles&file=article&sid=36).

39 Tompkins, *Secrets of the Great Pyramid*, chapter 13, pp. 159–69.

40 See http://en.wikipedia.org/wiki/Angkor_Wat. Alford, for example, stresses the extent to which Hancock has to be selective with the temples at Angkor and the stars in the Draco constellation to obtain his correlation; see his comments at www.eridu.co.uk/Author/News_and_Views/archive.html#hancock.

41 Although rather more debatable is their assertion that the template for this 'calendar machine' was part of the wisdom imparted to Enoch by the angel Uriel, which allowed him to anticipate a cometary impact that occurred in 3150 BCE.

42 See http://en.wikipedia.org/wiki/History_of_Australia.

43 See http://en.wikipedia.org/wiki/Solutrean_hypothesis.

44 See http://en.wikipedia.org/wiki/Crystal_skull. Two skulls that were tested by the British Museum and thought to be recent fakes were one bought from Tiffany's auction house in 1898, which resides in the British Museum itself, and another that was sent to the Smithsonian Institute by an anonymous donor. Two further skulls on which the museum apparently refused to comment are 'Max', owned by JoAnn Parks 'Sha Na Ra' found by Nick Nocerino. See Morton and Thomas, *The Mystery of the Crystal Skulls*, chapter 16 and plates 8–11; and our own Plates 18 and 19.

45 Ibid., chapter 5. Two separate reconstructions of the face by forensic experts suggested that the original subject was an indigenous American woman; see ibid., chapter 17, pp. 259–60.

46 This is confirmed in the original report that appeared in Hewlett-Packard's in-house magazine *Measure*, February 1971, pp. 8–10 (reproduced at www.hparchive.com/measure_magazine/HP-Measure-1971-02.pdf).

47 They only consist of attempts to smear the reputations of Mitchell-Hedges and his stepdaughter and suggestions of other owners in the mid-twentieth century; see www.badarchaeology.net/data/ooparts/crystal.php. By contrast the Bad Archaeology website's rebuttals of other anomalous artifacts are mostly well founded (for examples see also www.ianlawton.com/gu8.htm).

48 Watkins, 'How Did the Incas Create such Beautiful Stone Masonry', *Rocks and Minerals* 65 (1990, reproduced at www.ianlawton.com/am10.htm).

EPILOGUE: IMPLICATIONS FOR TODAY

1 The original sessions mainly involved myself, Janet, co-director of the Academy Hazel Newton and another assistant trainer Tracey Robins; see Lawton et al, *The Future of the Soul*, pp. 1–10.

2 Ibid., pp. 46–7. Any ellipses used in the quotes from the council indicate that a

question from me has been omitted, or occasionally that a section is not especially relevant to this work.

[3] This session was conducted at Gaunts House with just Janet and myself on 22 July 2010.

[4] See http://en.wikipedia.org/wiki/Laws_of_Manu.

[5] Laws of Manu 1:68–72; see Bühler, *The Laws of Manu* in Müller, *The Sacred Books of the East*, volume 25, p. 2. Note that in this translation the words *of the gods* have been inserted in brackets after the word *years* in verse 69, but presumably this is not original and an assumption on the part of the translator, which is not helpful in the current context.

[6] See http://en.wikipedia.org/wiki/Yuga.

[7] Ibid., chapter 3, pp. 39–40.

[8] See, for example, Stray, *Beyond 2012*, chapter 1, p. 23. In fact the number 26,000 is frequently used even though this is clearly not the product of 5 times 5125.

[9] See http://alignment2012.com/whatisga.htm.

[10] See http://en.wikipedia.org/wiki/2012_phenomenon.

[11] See, for example, Stray, *Beyond 2012*, chapter 7, pp 89–90.

[12] Collins, *The Cygnus Mystery*, chapters 21–2.

[13] Although he says the Meinel Institute have attempted a correlation using a 23,000 year precessional cycle; see ibid., chapter 22, p. 267.

[14] As a check using any internet-based planetary model will show; see, for example, www.fourmilab.ch/cgi-bin/Solar.

[15] This is mentioned in the context of souls moving on to other places, which we will come to shortly.

[16] Lawton et al, *The Future of the Soul*, pp. 43–4.

[17] Ibid., p. 44.

[18] Ibid., p. 21.

[19] Ibid., pp. 23–5.

[20] Ibid., pp. 25–6.

[21] Ibid., pp. 27–8.

[22] Ibid., p. 29.

[23] See http://en.wikipedia.org/wiki/Supervolcano#Known_super_eruptions. These are the only VEI 8 scale eruptions in that period, defined as producing more than 1000 km^2 of ejected material.

[24] See www.wonderfulbali.com/centralbali/batur.htm.

[25] See www.saudiaramcoworld.com/issue/197304/santorini.htm.

26 See http://archives.cnn.com/2000/world/americas/12/19/popo.timeline.

27 Lawton et al, *The Future of the Soul*, p. 29.

28 Ibid., pp. 33–4. Note that in my questions I used the date from *Genesis Unveiled* of 11,500 years ago rather than the new estimate for the Younger-Dryas Event of 13,000 years ago. Ethereal beings tend not to get too excited about exact dates.

29 Ibid., pp. 40 and 43.

30 Ibid., p. 42.

31 Ibid., p. 26.

32 The whole topic of the current shift and the buildup to it is covered in ibid., pp. 15–16 and 74–93.

33 Ibid., pp. 112–13.

34 Ibid., p. 102.

35 Ibid., pp. 106–7.

36 For more on this see Lawton, *Your Holographic Soul*, pp. 110–18.

37 Lawton et al, *The Future of the Soul*, p. 105.

38 The whole topic of souls moving to other places is covered in ibid., pp. 49–72.

39 Ibid., p. 79.

40 Ibid., p. 31.

41 Ibid., p. 111.

42 Ibid., pp. 17–18 and 108.

43 Ibid., p. 20.

44 Ibid., p. 112.

BIBLIOGRAPHY

By the Author

Lawton, Ian and Ogilvie-Herald, Chris, *Giza: The Truth*, Virgin, 2000 (paperback edition; hardback edition first published in 1999).
Lawton, Ian, *Genesis Unveiled*, Virgin, 2003.
Lawton, Ian, *The Wisdom of the Soul*, Rational Spirituality Press, 2007.
Lawton, Ian, *The Little Book of the Soul*, Rational Spirituality Press, 2007.
Lawton, Ian, *The Big Book of the Soul*, Rational Spirituality Press, 2008.
Lawton, Ian, *Your Holographic Soul*, Rational Spirituality Press, 2010.
Lawton, Ian et al, *The Future of the Soul*, Rational Spirituality Press, 2010.

Ancient Texts, Traditions and Mythology

Aston, W G (trans.), *Nihongi*, Kegan Paul, 1896.
Augustine, Saint, *The City of God* (7 volumes), Heinemann Young, 1958–98.
Baines, John and Malek, Jaromir, *Atlas of Ancient Egypt*, Oxford, 1980.
Best, Robert M, *Noah's Ark and the Ziusudra Epic: Sumerian Origins of the Flood Myth*, Enlil Press, 1999.
Bierhorst, John (trans.), *History and Mythology of the Aztecs: The Codex Chimalpopoca*, University of Arizona Press, 1992.
Budge, E A Wallis (trans.), *The Egyptian Heaven and Hell* (3 volumes in 1), Dover, 1996.
Budge, E A Wallis, *Osiris and the Egyptian Resurrection* (2 volumes), Philip Lee Warner, 1911.
Campbell, Joseph, *The Masks of God* (4 volumes: *Primitive Mythology*, *Oriental Mythology*, *Occidental Mythology* and *Creative Mythology*), Arkana, 1991 (first published 1959–68).
Campbell, Joseph and Musès, Charles, *In All Her Names*, Harper, 1991.
Charlesworth, James H (ed.), *The Old Testament Pseudepigrapha* (2 volumes), Darton, Longman and Todd, 1983.
Coomaraswamy, Ananda K and Sister Nivedita, *Myths of the Hindus and Buddhists*, Dover Publications, 1967 (first published 1916).
Copenhaver, Brian (trans.), *Hermetica: The Greek Corpus Hermeticum and the Latin Asclepius*, Cambridge University Press, 1998.
Cory, I C, *Ancient Fragments*, Wizards Bookshelf, 1975 (first published 1832).
Cotterell, Arthur (ed.), *The Penguin Encyclopaedia of Ancient Civilizations*, Penguin, 1988.
Dalley, Stephanie (trans.), *Myths from Mesopotamia: Creation, The Flood, Gilgamesh and Others*, Oxford World's Classics, 1991.

Dimmitt, Cornelia and van Buitenen, J A B, *Classical Hindu Mythology: A Reader in the Sanskrit Puranas*, Temple University Press, 1978.

Dutt, Manmatha Nath (trans.), *Vishnu Purana*, Calcutta, 1894.

Dutt, Romesh C (trans.), [Extracts from] *The Ramayana and The Mahabharata*, Everyman, 1944 (first published 1910).

Eisenman, Robert and Wise, Michael (trans.), *The Dead Sea Scrolls Uncovered*, Penguin, 1993.

Eliade, Mircea, *The Myth of the Eternal Return*, New York, 1954.

Eliade, Mircea, *The Sacred and the Profane: The Nature of Religion*, Harcourt, 1959.

Eliade, Mircea, *Myth and Reality*, Waveland Press, 1998 (first published 1963).

Eliade, Mircea, *Shamanism: Archaic Techniques of Ecstasy*, Arkana, 1989 (first published 1964).

Faulkner, Raymond (trans.), *The Ancient Egyptian Pyramid Texts*, Oxford University Press, 1969.

Faulkner, Raymond (trans.), *The Ancient Egyptian Coffin Texts*, Aris and Phillips, 1978.

Faulkner, Raymond (trans.), *The Ancient Egyptian Book of the Dead*, British Museum Press, 1996.

Feuerstein, Georg, Kak, Subhash and Frawley, David, *In Search of the Cradle of Civilization*, Quest, 1995.

Fowden, Garth, *The Egyptian Hermes*, Cambridge University Press, 1986.

Frazer, James George, *The Golden Bough: A Study in Magic and Religion*, Penguin, 1996 (12 volumes, first published 1890–1915).

Graves, Robert, *The White Goddess*, Faber and Faber, 1999 (first published 1948).

Gray, Louis Herbert (ed.), *The Mythology of All Races* (13 volumes), Marshall Jones Co., Boston, 1916–64.

Guirand, Felix (ed.), *The Larousse Encyclopaedia of Mythology*, Paul Hamlyn, 1965.

Hall, Manley P, *The Secret Teachings of All Ages: An Encyclopedic Outline of Masonic, Hermetic, Qabalistic and Rosicrucian Symbolic Philosophy*, Philosophical Research Society, 1988 (first published 1928).

Heidel, Alexander, *The Gilgamesh Epic and Old Testament Parallels*, University of Chicago Press, 1949.

Heidel, Alexander (trans.), *The Babylonian Genesis*, University of Chicago Press, 1951.

Hodge, Stephen, *The Dead Sea Scrolls*, Piatkus, 2001.

Il Manoscritto Messicano Vaticano 3738, Detto Il Codice Rios, Rome, 1900.

Jacobsen, Thorkild, *The Sumerian King List*, Chicago, 1939.

Jacobsen, Thorkild (trans.), *The Harps That Once... Sumerian Poetry in Translation*, Yale University Press, 1987.

Jung, Carl, *Psychology and Alchemy*, Routledge, 1993 (first published 1953).

Kramer, Samuel N, *Sumerian Mythology*, Harper and Bros., 1961.

Kramer, Samuel N, *Mythologies of the Ancient World*, Anchor, 1961.

Kramer, Samuel N, *The Sumerians, Their History, Culture and Character*, University of Chicago Press, 1971 (first published 1963).

Laurence, Richard (trans.), *The Book of Enoch the Prophet*, Wizards Bookshelf, 1995 (first published 1883).

Lee, Desmond (trans.), *Plato: Timaeus and Critias*, Penguin Classics, 1977.

Lenormant, François and Chevallier, E, *The Ancient History of the East* (3 volumes), Asher and Co, 1870.

Levi-Strauss, Claude, *Myth and Meaning*, Routledge, 1978.

Lewy, Hans, *Chaldaean Oracles and Theurgy*, Études Augustiniennes, 1978.

Mackenzie, Donald A, *Myths of China and Japan*, Gresham, 1923.

Melville, A D (trans.), *Ovid: Metamorphosis*, Oxford World Classics, 1998.

Meyer, Eduard, *Chronologie Egyptienne* (trans. from German by Alexandre Moret in *Annales du Musée Guimet*, Bibliotheque D'Études, 24), Paris, 1912.

Milik, J T, *The Books of Enoch – Aramaic Fragments of Qumran Cave 4*, Oxford University Press, 1976.

Morfill, W R (trans.) and Charles, R H, *The Book of the Secrets of Enoch*, Oxford, 1896.

Morgan, Evan, Tao, *The Great Luminant: Essays from Huai Nan Tzu*, Kegan Paul, 1933.

Müller, Max (ed.), *The Sacred Books of the East* (50 volumes), Oxford, 1879–91 (see also www.sacred-texts.com/sbe/index.htm).

Murray, Alex (ed.), *History of the Jews* (2 volumes), London, 1874.

O'Flaherty, Wendy Doniger (trans.), *The Rig Veda*, Penguin Classics, 1981.

Philippi, Donald L (trans.), *Kojiki*, Princetown University Press, 1969.

Prasad, Ganga, *The Fountainhead of Religion*, Book Tree, 2000 (first published 1927).

Rackham, H, Jones, W H S and Eichholz, D E, *Pliny: Natural History* (10 volumes), William Heinemann, 1938–57.

Ray, Pratapa Chandra (trans.), *The Mahabharata* (9 volumes), Calcutta, 1884–94.

Reymond, Eve, *The Mythical Origin of the Egyptian Temple*, Barnes and Noble, 1969.

Robinson, James M, *The Nag Hammadi Library*, HarperCollins, 1990.

Roux, Georges, *Ancient Iraq*, Penguin, 1992 (first published 1964).

Rundle Clark, R T, *Myth and Symbol in Ancient Egypt*, Thames and Hudson, 1959.

Scott, Walter, *Hermetica*, Solos Press, 1992 (first published in 4 volumes 1924–36).

Smith, George, *The Chaldean Account of Genesis*, London, 1876.

Taylor, Thomas (trans.), *The Hymns of Orpheus*, Philosophical Research Society, 1981 (first published 1792).

Tedlock, Dennis (trans.), *Popol Vuh: The Mayan Book of the Dawn of Life*, Touchstone, 1996.

Thompson, J Eric S, *Maya Hieroglyphic Writing*, University of Oklahoma, 1960.

Thompson, J Eric S, *Maya History and Religion*, University of Oklahoma Press, 1970.

Thompson, J Eric S, 'The Dresden Codex: A Maya Hieroglyphic Book', *Memoirs of the American Philosophical Society* 93 (1972).

Vermes, Geza, *The Dead Sea Scrolls in English*, Penguin, 1962.

Waddell, W G (trans.), *Manetho*, Harvard University Press, 1997 (first published 1940).

Wallis, R T, *Neoplatonism*, Duckworth, 1972.

Waterfield, Robin (trans.), *Herodotus: The Histories*, Oxford World Classics, 1998.

Waters, Frank, *Book of the Hopi*, Penguin, 1977.

Werner, Edward T C, *Myths and Legends of China*, Sinclair Browne, 1984 (first published 1922).

Werner, Edward T C, *A Dictionary of Chinese Mythology*, Kelly and Walsh, 1932.

West, M L (trans.), *Hesiod: Theogony and Works and Days*, Oxford World Classics, 1999.

West, M L, *The Orphic Poems*, Oxford University Press, 1983.

Westcott, W Wynn, *Collectanea Hermetica* (6 volumes), Theosophical Publishing Society, 1895.

Willis, Roy (ed.), *World Mythology*, Duncan Baird, 1993.

Wilkins, W J, *Hindu Mythology*, Curzon Press, 1900.

Wise, Michael, Abegg, Martin and Cook, Edward, *The Dead Sea Scrolls: A New Translation*, HarperCollins, 1996.

Woolley, Leonard, *The Sumerians*, Oxford, 1929.

Young, Jean I (trans.), *Snorri Sturluson: The Prose Edda*, University of California Press, 1964.

Yukteswar, Sri, *The Holy Science*, Self-Realization Fellowship, 1986 (first published 1894).

ARCHAEOLOGY AND EVOLUTION

Balfour, Michael, *Megalithic Mysteries*, Parkgate Books, 1997.

Behe, Michael, *Darwin's Black Box: The Biochemical Challenge to Evolution*, Free Press, 1996.

Brass, Michael, *The Antiquity of Man: Artifactual, Fossil and Gene Records Explored*, PublishAmerica, 2002.

Breuil, Abbe H, *Four Hundred Centuries of Cave Art*, Centre d'Études et de Documentation Prehistorique, undated.

Chomsky, Noam, *Language and Mind*, Harcourt Brace Jovanovich, 1972.

Chomsky, Noam, *Language and Problems of Knowledge*, MIT Press, 1988.

Clottes, Jean and Lewis-Williams, David, *The Shamans of Prehistory: Trance and Magic in Painted Caves*, Harry N, Abrams, 1998.

Crick, Francis H C, *Life Itself: Its Origin and Nature*, Simon and Schuster, 1981.

Darwin, Charles, *On the Origin of Species*, Penguin, 1985 (first published 1859).
Darwin, Charles, *The Descent of Man*, John Murray, 1871.
Dawkins, Richard, *The Selfish Gene*, Oxford University Press, 1989 (first published 1976).
Dawkins, Richard, *The Blind Watchmaker*, Longmans, 1986.
Dawkins, Richard, *River Out of Eden*, Phoenix, 1996.
Deacon, Hillary, *Human Beginnings in South Africa: Uncovering the Secrets of the Stone Age*, David Philip, 1999.
Dennett, Daniel, *Consciousness Explained*, Little Brown, 1991.
Dennett, Daniel, *Darwin's Dangerous Idea*, Penguin, 1995.
Feder, Kenneth L, *Frauds, Myths and Mysteries: Science and Pseudoscience in Archaeology*, Mayfield, 1999.
Gould, Stephen Jay, *The Panda's Thumb*, Norton, 1980.
Gould, Stephen Jay, *The Flamingo's Smile*, Norton, 1985.
Gould, Stephen Jay, *Bully for Brontosaurus*, Norton, 1991.
Gould, Stephen Jay, *The Book of Life*, Norton, 1993.
Klein, Richard, *The Human Career*, University of Chicago Press, 1999.
Leakey, Richard, *The Making of Humankind*, E P Dutton, 1981.
Leakey, Richard, *The Origin of Humankind*, Phoenix, 1995.
Leakey, Richard and Lewin, Roger, *Origins Reconsidered*, Doubleday, 1992.
Lewin, Roger, *Complexity: Life at the Edge of Chaos*, Macmillan, 1992.
Lewin, Roger, *The Origin of Modern Humans*, W H Freeman, 1993.
Morell, Virginia, *Ancestral Passions: The Leakey Family and the Quest for Humankind's Beginnings*, Touchstone, 1996.
Pinker, Steven, *The Language Instinct: The New Science of Language and Mind*, William Morrow, 1994.
Popper, Karl and Eccles, John, *The Self and its Brain*, Springer-Verlag, 1977.
Rudgley, Richard, *Lost Civilizations of the Stone Age*, Arrow, 1999.
Rudgley, Richard, *Secrets of the Stone Age*, Century, 2000.
Tudge, Colin, *Neanderthals, Bandits and Farmers: How Agriculture Really Began*, Yale University Press, 1999.
Wesson, Robert, *Beyond Natural Selection*, MIT Press, 1991.

GEOLOGY AND CATASTROPHE

Allan, Derek and Delair, Bernard, *When the Earth Nearly Died*, Gateway, 1995 (republished in the US under the title *Cataclysm*).
Clube, Victor and Napier, Bill, *The Cosmic Winter*, Basil Blackwell, 1990.
Firestone, Richard, West, Allen and Warwick-Smith, Simon, *The Cycle of Cosmic Catastrophes*, Bear and Co, 2006.
Flem-Ath, Rand and Rose, *When the Sky Fell*, Wiedenfeld and Nicolson, 1995.
Hapgood, Charles, *The Path of the Pole*, Souvenir, 2001 (first published 1958 under the title *Earth's Shifting Crust*).

Hibben, Frank C, *The Lost Americans*, Thomas Y Crowell, 1946.

Hugget, Richard, *Cataclysms and Earth History: The Development of Diluvialism*, Clarendon Press, 1989.

Martin, Paul S and Klein, Richard (eds.), *Quaternary Extinctions: A Prehistoric Revolution*, University of Arizona Press, 1984.

Oppenheimer, Stephen, *Eden in the East: The Drowned Continent of Southeast Asia*, Phoenix, 1999.

Palmer, Trevor, *Perilous Planet Earth: Catastrophes and Catastrophism through the Ages*, Cambridge University Press, 1999.

Peiser, Benny, Palmer, Trevor and Bailey, Mark (eds.), *Natural Catastrophes During Bronze Age Civilizations*, Archaeopress, 1998.

Schoch, Robert M, *Voices of the Rocks*, Harmony, 1999.

Spedicato, Emilio, *Apollo Objects, Atlantis and the Deluge: A Catastrophist Scenario for the End of the Last Glaciation*, Instituto Universitario di Bergamo, 1990.

Velikovsky, Immanuel, *Worlds in Collision*, Abacus, 1972 (first published 1950).

Velikovsky, Immanuel, *Earth in Upheaval*, Buccaneer, 1955.

White, John, *Pole Shift*, A.R.E. Press, 1997 (first published 1980).

LOST CONTINENTS AND THEOSOPHY

Bailey, Alice A, *Initiation, Human and Solar*, Lucis Publishing, 1922.

Bailey, Alice A, *A Treatise on Cosmic Fire*, Lucis Publishing, 1973 (first published 1925).

Bailey, Alice A, *A Treatise on the Seven Rays* (5 volumes), Lucis Publishing, 1936.

Blavatsky, Helena, *Isis Unveiled* (2 volumes), Theosophical Publishing House, 1972 (first published 1877).

Blavatsky, Helena, *The Secret Doctrine* (2 volumes), Theosophical University Press, 1988 (first published 1888).

Blavatsky, Helena, *The Voice of the Silence*, Quest Books, 1996 (first published 1889).

Blavatsky, Helena, *Collected Writings* (15 volumes), Quest Books, 1960–80.

Cayce, Edgar Evans, *Edgar Cayce on Atlantis*, Howard Baker, 1969.

Childress, David Hatcher, *Ancient Tonga and the Lost City of Mu'a*, Adventures Unlimited Press, 1996.

Childress, David Hatcher, *Ancient Micronesia and the Lost City of Nan Madol*, Adventures Unlimited Press, 1997.

Childress, David Hatcher, *Lost Cities of Ancient Lemuria and the Pacific*, Adventures Unlimited Press, 1998.

Churchward, James, *The Lost Continent of Mu*, BE Books, 1994 (first published 1926).

Churchward, James, *The Sacred Symbols of Mu*, BE Books, 1988 (first published 1933).

Collins, Andrew, *Gateway to Atlantis*, Headline, 2000.

Cranston, Sylvia, *HPB: The Extraordinary Life and Influence of Helena Blavatsky*, Putnam, 1993.

Donnelly, Ignatius, *Atlantis, the Antediluvian World*, Sampson Low and Co, 1882.

Donnelly, Ignatius, *Ragnarok, the Age of Fire and Gravel*, Sampson Low and Co, 1883.

Johnson, K Paul, *The Masters Revealed: Madame Blavatsky and the Myth of the Great White Lodge*, State University of New York Press, 1994.

Johnson, K Paul, *Edgar Cayce in Context*, State University of New York Press, 1998.

Leslie, J Ben, *Submerged Atlantis Restored* (2 volumes), Kessinger Publishing Co, 2003 (first published 1911).

Luce, J V, *The End of Atlantis*, Thames and Hudson, 1969.

Mavor, James W, *Voyage to Atlantis*, Souvenir Press, 1969.

Muck, Otto, *The Secret of Atlantis*, Fontana, 1979.

Randall-Stevens, H C, *From Atlantis to the Latter Days*, Knights Templars, 1981 (first published 1954).

Reigle, David, *The Books of Kiu-te*, Wizards Bookshelf, 1983.

Reigle, David and Nancy, *Blavatsky's Secret Books*, Wizards Bookshelf, 1999.

Santos, Arysio, *Atlantis: The Lost Continent Finally Found*, Atlantis Publications, 2005.

Scott-Elliot, W, *The Story of Atlantis and The Lost Lemuria*, Theosophical Publishing House, 1968 (first published 1925).

Scrutton, Robert, *Secrets of Lost Atland*, Sphere Books, 1979.

Sinnett, Alfred Percy, *Esoteric Buddhism*, Houghton Mifflin, 1884.

Smith, A Robert, *The Lost Memoirs of Edgar Cayce*, A.R.E. Press, 1997.

Spence, Lewis, *History of Atlantis*, Senate, 1995 (first published 1926).

Spence, Lewis, *The Problem of Lemuria, the Sunken Continent of the Pacific*, Rider and Co, 1932.

Spence, Lewis, *The Occult Sciences in Atlantis*, Aquarian Press, 1978 (first published 1943).

Sprague de Camp, Lyon, *Lost Continents: The Atlantis Theme in History, Science and Literature*, Dover, 1970 (first published 1954).

Steiner, Rudolf, *Atlantis and Lemuria*, Anthroposophical Publishing Company, 1923 (first published 1911).

Sugrue, Thomas, *The Story of Edgar Cayce: There Is a River*, A.R.E. Press, 1997 (first published 1942).

Tomas, Andrew, *Shambhala: Oasis of Light*, Sphere, 1972.

Tomas, Andrew, *Atlantis: From Legend to Discovery*, Sphere, 1973.

MODERN REVISIONISM AND 2012

Alford, Alan, *Gods of the New Millennium*, Hodder and Stoughton, 1997.

Arguelles, José, *The Mayan Factor*, Bear and Co, 1987.

Baigent, Michael, *Ancient Traces*, Penguin, 1999.

Bauval, Robert and Gilbert, Adrian, *The Orion Mystery*, Mandarin, 1995.

Bauval, Robert and Hancock, Graham, *Keeper of Genesis*, Mandarin, 1997 (republished in the US under the title *The Message of the Sphinx*).

Childress, David Hatcher, *Vimana Aircraft of Ancient India and Atlantis*, Adventures Unlimited Press, 1991.

Collins, Andrew, *From the Ashes of Angels*, Signet, 1997.

Collins, Andrew, *Gods of Eden*, Headline, 1998.

Collins, Andrew, *The Cygnus Mystery*, Watkins Publishing, 2008.

Corliss, William R, *Ancient Man: A Handbook of Puzzling Artifacts*, Sourcebook Project, 1978.

Cremo, Michael A and Thompson, Richard L, *Forbidden Archaeology*, Bhaktivedanta Institute, 1993.

Cremo, Michael A and Thompson, Richard L, *The Hidden History of the Human Race*, Govardhan Hill, 1994 (condensed version of above).

Cremo, Michael, *Forbidden Archaeology's Impact*, Bhaktivedanta Book Publishing, 1998.

Drake, W Raymond, *Gods and Spacemen in the Ancient East*, Sphere, 1973 (first published 1968).

Dunn, Christopher, *The Giza Power Plant*, Bear and Co, 1998.

Elkington, David and Ellson, Paul Howard, *In the Name of the Gods: The Mystery of Resonance and the Prehistoric Messiah*, Green Man Press, 2001.

Flem-Ath, Rand and Wilson, Colin, *The Atlantis Blueprint*, Little Brown, 2000.

Gardner, Laurence, *Genesis of the Grail Kings*, Bantam, 2000.

Gilbert, Adrian, *Signs in the Sky*, Bantam, 2000.

Gilbert, Adrian and Cotterell, Maurice, *The Mayan Prophecies*, Element, 1995.

Gooch, Stan, *Cities of Dreams: When Women Ruled the World*, Aulis Books, 1995.

Hancock, Graham, *Fingerprints of the Gods*, Mandarin, 1996.

Hancock, Graham and Faiia, Santha, *Heaven's Mirror*, Michael Joseph, 1998.

Hapgood, Charles, *Maps of the Ancient Sea Kings*, Adventures Unlimited Press, 1996 (first published 1966).

James, Peter and Thorpe, Nick, *Ancient Inventions*, Ballantine, 1994.

Jenkins, John Major, *Maya Cosmogenesis 2012*, Bear and Co, 1998.

Jenkins, John Major, *Galactic Alignment*, Bear and Co, 2002.

Knight, Christopher and Lomas, Robert, *Uriel's Machine*, Century, 1999.

Kolosimo, Peter, *Not of this World*, Sphere, 1971.

Kolosimo, Peter, *Timeless Earth*, Sphere, 1974.

LaViolette, Paul, *Earth Under Fire*, Starlane Publications, 1997.

Lockyer, Norman, *The Dawn of Astronomy*, Macmillan, 1894.

Miller, Crichton, *The Golden Thread of Time*, Pendulum Publishing, 2001.

Morton, Chris and Thomas, Ceri Louise, *The Mystery of the Crystal Skulls*, Thorsons, 1998.

O'Brien, Christian and O'Brien, Joy, *The Genius of the Few*, Dianthus Publishing, 1999 (first published 1985).

O'Brien, Christian and O'Brien, Joy, *The Shining Ones*, Dianthus Publishing, 1997.

de Santillana, Giorgio and von Dechend, Hertha, *Hamlet's Mill*, Godine, 1977 (first published 1969).

Schwaller de Lubicz, René, *Sacred Science*, Inner Traditions, 1988 (first published 1961).

Sitchin, Zecharia, *The Twelfth Planet*, Bear and Co, 1991 (first published 1976).

Steiger, Brad, *Worlds Before Our Own*, Berkley, 1979.

Stray, Geoff, *Beyond 2012*, Vital Signs Publishing, 2006.

Temple, Robert, *The Sirius Mystery*, Arrow, 1999 (first published 1976).

Temple, Robert, *The Crystal Sun*, Century, 2000.

Tomas, Andrew, *We Are Not the First*, Souvenir, 1971.

Tomas, Andrew, *On the Shores of Ancient Worlds*, Souvenir, 1974.

Tompkins, Peter, *Secrets of the Great Pyramid*, Galahad, 1997 (first published 1971).

von Däniken, Erich, *Chariots of the Gods*, Souvenir Press, 1969.

von Däniken, Erich, *In Search of Ancient Gods*, Souvenir Press, 1975.

Welfare, Simon and Fairley, John, *Arthur C Clarke's Mysterious World*, Collins, 1980.

West, John Anthony, *Serpent in the Sky*, Quest, 1993 (first published 1979).

Wilkins, Harold T, *Mysteries of Ancient South America*, Rider and Co, 1946.

Wilkins, Harold T, *Secret Cities of Old South America: Atlantis Unveiled*, Rider and Co, 1950.

Wilson, Colin, *From Atlantis to the Sphinx*, Virgin, 1997.

INDEX

Plate 1 One of the deliberate burials in the Qafzeh cave in Israel, dated to 95,000 years ago. Here we see a woman with a child at her feet. (wikepedia.org)

Plate 2 Ochre block found in the Blombos cave in South Africa and dated to 100-70,000 years ago. Surely these abstract markings suggest a sophisticated level of thought? (wikepedia.org)

Plate 3 The 'Quneitra artifact' found in Israel and dated to 54,000 years ago. Again its patterns of nested semicircles and vertical lines appear to be symbolic and to indicate sophisticated abstract thought. (Alexander Marshack)

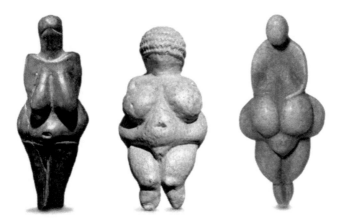

Plate 4 A variety of 'Venus figurines'. These European examples are as much as 40,000 years old and, although stylized, are carefully sculpted. (Ancient Art and Architecture Collection)

Plate 5 The 'Venus of Brassempouy'. This beautifully sculpted ivory figurine from France is 25,000 years old. Were such fine artists merely subsisting in cold, damp caves? (Agence Photographique de la Réunion des Musées Nationaux)

Plate 6 One of the 'Sungir skeletons'. This adult was buried in Russia 28,000 years ago with full regalia, including clothing adorned with hundreds of drilled ivory beads. Would purely nomadic tribes struggling for survival have time for such luxuries? (Science Photo Library)

Plate 7 Decorated spear thrower. This beautiful 16,000 year-old example from Le Mas d'Azil in France is carved from bone and shows two fighting bison. (Ancient Art and Architecture Collection)

Plate 8 Bison painting. This is a reproduction of a fine example of Upper Paleolithic art from the Altamira Caves in Spain that dates to around 15,000 years ago. Is it not the equal of anything produced in the modern era? (StockphotoPro)

Plate 9 Jerf el-Ahmar. This sizeable settlement in Syria is more than 11,000 years old. Does the fact that it has no precursors prove that it was built by the survivors of a global catastrophe? (Danielle Stordeur/CNRS)

Plate 10 Aerial view of one of the round communal buildings at Jerf el-Ahmar, surrounded by individual houses. Stone has been used throughout for construction, and there are clear signs of early agriculture. Were our antediluvian ancestors engaging in settled agriculture long beforehand? (Danielle Stordeur/CNRS)

Plate 11 The site of Jerf el-Ahmar about to be flooded by a newly-constructed dam in 1999. It is now buried under 15 meters of water. How much evidence of our coastal-dwelling forgotten race was lost when sea levels rose by as much as 120 meters at the end of the Pleistocene? (Danielle Stordeur/CNRS)

Plate 12 Close up of one of the communal buildings at Jerf el-Ahmar. (Danielle Stordeur/CNRS)

Plate 13 Etched terracotta plaquette from Jerf el-Ahmar. Are the symbols mnemonics of some sort? (Danielle Stordeur/CNRS)

Plate 14 Drawings of more etched plaquettes from Jerf el-Ahmar, showing a variety of symbolism. (Danielle Stordeur/CNRS)

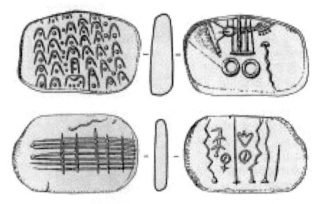

Plate 15 Example of late Sumerian pictographic script, which first emerged some 5000 years ago. Is this merely a development of the etchings from Jerf el-Ahmar many millennia before? (Ancient Art and Architecture Collection)

Matrice suivie de son empreinte:

Inscrite en écriture inversée et destinée à multiplier un texte à l'infini sur les briques en cours de séchage.
Rédigée à la première personne, la dédicace qu'elle porte commémore la construction d'un temple au dieu-Soleil par un roi de Larsa.

Plate 16 Hand-held model of the 'Celtic cross'. Note how the bob-weighted dial revolves and is read through holes in the upright. Were our antediluvian ancestors using such a simple but effective device to navigate the oceans? (Crichton Miller)

Plate 17 Full-sized model of the 'Celtic cross' being used by its 'reinventor' to measure the angle of the sun. (Crichton Miller)

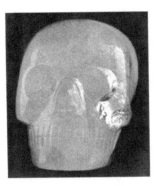

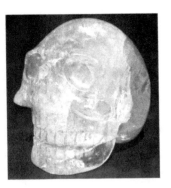

Plate 18 The crystal skull owned by JoAnn Parks, known as 'Max'. It is less sophisticated than the Mitchell-Hedges skull. (www.crystalskulls.com)

Plate 19 The crystal skull found by Nick Nocerino, known as 'Sha Na Ra'. It is far less lifelike than the Mitchell-Hedges skull. (www.crystalskulls.com)

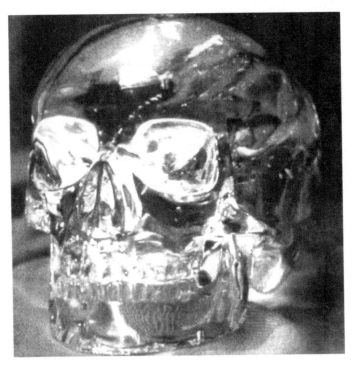

Plate 20 The Mitchell-Hedges crystal skull. It is anatomically detailed, life-sized and has a detachable jaw fashioned from the same block of totally pure quartz crystal. Experts from Hewlett-Packard's Santa Clara laboratories confirmed it was sculpted without the use of machine tools. (Galde Press/Frank Dorland)

THE WISDOM OF THE SOUL
profound insights from the life between lives

by Ian Lawton *with* Andy Tomlinson

Rational Spirituality Press, 2007
www.rspress.org

'This fine book provides much-needed information about everything from trapped spirits to demonic beings; from the purpose of incarnation to extraterrestrial realms; and from legends of Atlantis to global warming and humanity's future. I cannot recommend it highly enough.' Edith Fiore, pioneering regression therapist and author of *You Have Been Here Before*

'The research in this book poses questions that have rarely, if ever, been asked before.' Hans TenDam, pioneering regression therapist and author of *Exploring Reincarnation*

For thousands of years our view of the afterlife has been handed down to us by a variety of prophets and gurus
But in the last few decades thousands of ordinary people have been taken back into their 'life between lives' in the light realms
Their consistent reports form one of the most profound sources of spiritual wisdom ever available to humanity
And now two researchers have decided to push this source to its limits...

It is important enough that we should understand what happens to us between lives in the light realms: how we receive energy healing to lighten our vibrations; how we review our lives without judgment from higher beings; and how we choose and plan our next lives along with close soul mates, in order to face the lessons and experiences that will most allow us to grow.

But what if we could use the interlife experience to answer a host of more universal questions of spiritual, historical and philosophical importance? About everything from unusual soul behavior and soul development, through humanity's past and future, to the true nature of reality and time? What if multiple regression subjects came up with consistent answers? And what if they displayed wisdom so profound as to be way beyond any normal human capacity?

THE BIG BOOK OF THE SOUL
Rational Spirituality for the twenty-first century

by Ian Lawton

Rational Spirituality Press, 2008
www.rspress.org

'I predict that the author's proposal of a holographic model of the soul will be one of the most important concepts of our time.' Hans TenDam, pioneering regression therapist and author of *Exploring Reincarnation*

'This book is filled with thorough reviews of research and thoughtful analysis of its implications. It makes a significant contribution to the field. I recommend it highly.' Jim Tucker, University of Virginia Division of Perceptual Studies and author of *Life Before Life*

'This fine book is masterly and scholarly.' Edith Fiore, pioneering regression therapist and author of *You Have Been Here Before*

Rational spirituality... surely this is a contradiction in terms?
How can spirituality be rational, when it relies on faith and revelation?
The simple answer is it does not have to any more...

There is persuasive evidence from near-death and out-of-body experiences that the physical brain is merely the instrument through which our soul consciousness expresses itself in the physical world. There is equally persuasive evidence from children who remember past lives, and from past-life and interlife regression, that we are individual souls who reincarnate to experience and grow.

A careful analysis of skeptics' arguments in each of these areas of research proves in most cases just how reductionist, and in fact illogical, they are. Nevertheless not all the evidence put forward by believers stands up, and careful discrimination is required. Such a balanced and in-depth critique of both sides of the argument is rare if not unique. Equally unique is the accompanying collation and comparison of the interlife regression research of a number of pioneering psychologists.

But what of the idea that 'we are all One', which is the universal message of all transcendental experiences? Can it be squared with the idea of the individual, reincarnating soul, or is this merely an 'illusion' in itself? Perhaps the answer lies in a theory of total elegance and simplicity... that of the holographic soul.

THE LITTLE BOOK OF THE SOUL
true stories that could change your life

by Ian Lawton

Rational Spirituality Press, 2007
www.rspress.org

'This is a wonderful collection of stories, which I very much enjoyed. I will keep a copy for myself and happily pass the others on.' Peter Fenwick, fellow of the Royal College of Psychiatrists and author of *The Truth in the Light*

'This is a very nice collection of intriguing cases. I hope it gets a lot of attention.' Jim Tucker, University of Virginia Division of Perceptual Studies and author of *Life Before Life*

'I like this little book a lot. It's a perfect hand-out for past-life clients, or especially skeptical friends.' Thelma Freedman, Secretary of the International Board for Regression Therapy

How did a Russian scientist left for dead in a mortuary for three days make contact with his neighbor's sick baby... and wake up with a cure that all the doctors had missed?

What about the Indian girl with memories of a past life... who astonished her former husband by reminding him how he had borrowed money from her just before she died?

Or the Australian woman who recalled past-life details of a carving on the stone floor of a small cottage... and was able to locate it under decades of chicken droppings when brought to England for the first time?

These amazing reports are not new age mumbo jumbo. They have been properly investigated by professionals. And they will make you think long and hard about who you are and what you are doing here.

[This is a short, simple pocket book, written in a storybook style. It contains a selection of the most interesting near-death and past-life cases that support Rational Spirituality, interspersed with simple summaries and analysis.]

YOUR HOLOGRAPHIC SOUL
and how to make it work for you

by Ian Lawton

Rational Spirituality Press, 2010
www.rspress.org

'I predict that the author's proposal of a holographic model of the soul will be one of the most important concepts of our time.' Hans TenDam, pioneering regression therapist and author of *Exploring Reincarnation*

'The idea of the holographic soul brilliantly solves many spiritual conundrums.' Judy Hall, pioneering regression therapist and renowned spiritual author

If you're a newcomer to spirituality, would you like to know about the evidence that your soul consciousness will survive without your physical body, and that you have many lives? Would you like to understand why you reincarnate, and what that means for how to approach your everyday life? And would you like to learn about your true relationship to God?

Or if you're a more experienced spiritual seeker, would you like to unravel the enigma of being part of All That Is and yet also an individual soul? And would you like to understand the oft-misunderstood interplay between experience and illusion, and between conscious creation and active surrender?

It's only now that we can finally answer all these questions and more using a spiritual framework that is logical, coherent and philosophically elegant. One that unites a modern scientific discovery with ageless spiritual wisdom in a simple yet revolutionary new concept... that of the holographic soul.

[This is a short, simple pocket book, written in a question-and-answer style. It tackles seven key questions to build a Rational Spiritual framework, and then offers ten suggestions for how we can use it to get the most out of our day-to-day lives.]

THE FUTURE OF THE SOUL
2012 & the global shift in consciousness

by Ian Lawton *with* Janet Treloar, Hazel Newton & Tracey Robins

Rational Spirituality Press, 2010
www.rspress.org

DON'T WAIT FOR 2012... THE SHIFT IS HAPPENING ALREADY!!

So much has been written about 2012 and the global shift in consciousness. From catastrophic doom and gloom to sugar-coated messages that avoid the stark realities of what might lie ahead. But what if we were to be given channeled messages that are incredibly positive and exciting, yet also grounded? Well now we have.

These messages come from a diverse group of souls who refer to themselves as 'the council'. They provide information rarely if ever encountered elsewhere, including:

- Everything is just as planned, even including over-population and the exploitation of earth's resources.
- A similar shift occurred 26,000 years ago, but this time the conditions are deliberately very different.
- So many souls are on earth now to take advantage of an incredible opportunity that has been known about, planned for and eagerly awaited for thousands of years.

The attention of the entire universe is excitedly trained on our planet. If you want to know why each and every one of us has a crucial role to play in this amazing transformation, as we blossom into our full spiritual potential, read on...

[This is a short, simple pocket book. It contains crucial channeled messages about 2012 and the global shift in consciousness.]

The Little Book of the Soul, Your Holographic Soul and *The Future of the Soul* are also available in a large format compilation entitled *An Introduction to the Soul.*

IAN LAWTON was born in 1959. In his mid-thirties he became a writer-researcher specializing in ancient history, esoterica and spiritual  philosophy. His first two books, *Giza: The Truth* (1999) and *Genesis Unveiled* (2003), have sold over 30,000 copies worldwide.

In *The Book of the Soul* (2004) he developed the idea of Rational Spirituality, also establishing himself as one of the world's leading authorities on the interlife. And in *The Wisdom of the Soul* (2007) he first introduced the idea of the holographic soul. His other books include *The Little Book of the Soul* (2007), *The Big Book of the Soul* (2008, a complete rewrite of the 2004 book), *Your Holographic Soul* (2010), *The Future of the Soul* (2010) and *The History of the Soul* (2010, a revision of the 2003 book).

He is also a practicing current, past and between life regression therapist. For further information see *www.ianlawton.com.*

Lightning Source UK Ltd.
Milton Keynes UK
11 January 2011

165501UK00001BB/51/P